CW00730202

DICTIONARY
THEME–BASED

ENGLISH-
UKRAINIAN

The most useful words
To expand your lexicon and sharpen
your language skills

9000 words

Theme-based dictionary British English-Ukrainian - 9000 words

By Andrey Taranov

T&P Books vocabularies are intended for helping you learn, memorize and review foreign words. The dictionary is divided into themes, covering all major spheres of everyday activities, business, science, culture, etc.

The process of learning words using T&P Books' theme-based dictionaries gives you the following advantages:

- Correctly grouped source information predetermines success at subsequent stages of word memorization
- Availability of words derived from the same root allowing memorization of word units (rather than separate words)
- Small units of words facilitate the process of establishing associative links needed for consolidation of vocabulary
- Level of language knowledge can be estimated by the number of learned words

T&P Books Publishing
www.tpbooks.com

This book is also available in E-book formats.
Please visit www.tpbooks.com or the major online bookstores.

UKRAINIAN THEME-BASED DICTIONARY
British English collection

T&P Books vocabularies are intended to help you learn, memorize, and review foreign words. The vocabulary contains over 9000 commonly used words arranged thematically.

- Vocabulary contains the most commonly used words
- Recommended as an addition to any language course
- Meets the needs of beginners and advanced learners of foreign languages
- Convenient for daily use, revision sessions, and self-testing activities
- Allows you to assess your vocabulary

Special features of the vocabulary

- Words are organized according to their meaning, not alphabetically
- Words are presented in three columns to facilitate the reviewing and self-testing processes
- Words in groups are divided into small blocks to facilitate the learning process
- The vocabulary offers a convenient and simple transcription of each foreign word

The vocabulary has 256 topics including:

Basic Concepts, Numbers, Colors, Months, Seasons, Units of Measurement, Clothing & Accessories, Food & Nutrition, Restaurant, Family Members, Relatives, Character, Feelings, Emotions, Diseases, City, Town, Sightseeing, Shopping, Money, House, Home, Office, Working in the Office, Import & Export, Marketing, Job Search, Sports, Education, Computer, Internet, Tools, Nature, Countries, Nationalities and more …

TABLE OF CONTENTS

PRONUNCIATION GUIDE

Letter	Ukrainian example	T&P phonetic alphabet	English example

Vowels

Letter	Ukrainian example	T&P phonetic alphabet	English example
А а	акт	[a]	shorter than in 'ask'
Е е	берет	[e], [ɛ]	absent, pet
Є є	модельєр	[ɛ]	man, bad
И и	ритм	[k]	clock, kiss
I i	компанія	[i]	shorter than in 'feet'
Ї ї	поїзд	[ji]	playing, spying
О о	око	[ɔ]	bottle, doctor
У у	буря	[u]	book
Ю ю	костюм	[ʲu]	cued, cute
Я я	маяк	[ja], [ʲa]	royal

Consonants

Letter	Ukrainian example	T&P phonetic alphabet	English example
Б б	бездна	[b]	baby, book
В в	вікно	[w]	vase, winter
Г г	готель	[h]	between [g] and [h]
Ґ ґ	ґудзик	[g]	game, gold
Д д	дефіс	[d]	day, doctor
Ж ж	жанр	[ʒ]	forge, pleasure
З з	зброя	[z]	zebra, please
Й й	йти	[j]	yes, New York
К к	крок	[k]	clock, kiss
Л л	лев	[l]	lace, people
М м	мати	[m]	magic, milk
Н н	назва	[n]	name, normal
П п	приз	[p]	pencil, private
Р р	радість	[r]	rice, radio
С с	сон	[s]	city, boss
Т т	тир	[t]	tourist, trip
Ф ф	фарба	[f]	face, food
Х х	холод	[h]	home, have
Ц ц	церква	[ʦ]	cats, tsetse fly
Ч ч	час	[ʧ]	church, French
Ш ш	шуба	[ʃ]	machine, shark
Щ щ	щука	[ɕ]	sheep, shop
ь	камінь	[ʲ]	soft sign - no sound
ъ	ім'я	[']	hard sign, no sound

ABBREVIATIONS
used in the dictionary

English abbreviations

ab.	-	about
adj	-	adjective
adv	-	adverb
anim.	-	animate
as adj	-	attributive noun used as adjective
e.g.	-	for example
etc.	-	et cetera
fam.	-	familiar
fem.	-	feminine
form.	-	formal
inanim.	-	inanimate
masc.	-	masculine
math	-	mathematics
mil.	-	military
n	-	noun
pl	-	plural
pron.	-	pronoun
sb	-	somebody
sing.	-	singular
sth	-	something
v aux	-	auxiliary verb
vi	-	intransitive verb
vi, vt	-	intransitive, transitive verb
vt	-	transitive verb

Ukrainian abbreviations

ж	-	feminine noun
мн	-	plural
с	-	neuter
ч	-	masculine noun

BASIC CONCEPTS

Basic concepts. Part 1

1. Pronouns

I, me	я	[ja]
you	ти	[ti]
he	він	[win]
she	вона	[wo'na]
we	ми	[mi]
you (to a group)	ви	[wi]
they	вони	[wo'ni]

2. Greetings. Salutations. Farewells

Hello! (fam.)	Здрастуй!	['zdrastuj]
Hello! (form.)	Здрастуйте!	['zdrastujtɛ]
Good morning!	Доброго ранку!	['dɔbroɦo 'ranku]
Good afternoon!	Добрий день!	['dɔbrij dɛnʲ]
Good evening!	Добрий вечір!	['dɔbrij 'wɛʧir]
to say hello	вітатися	[wi'tatisʲa]
Hi! (hello)	Привіт!	[pri'wit]
greeting (n)	вітання (c)	[wi'tanʲa]
to greet (vt)	вітати	[wi'tati]
How are you?	Як справи?	[jak 'sprawi]
What's new?	Що нового?	[ɕo no'wɔɦo]
Bye-Bye! Goodbye!	До побачення!	[do po'baʧɛnʲa]
See you soon!	До швидкої зустрічі!	[do ʃwid'kɔji 'zustriʧi]
Farewell! (to a friend)	Прощавай!	[proɕa'waj]
Farewell! (form.)	Прощавайте!	[proɕa'wajtɛ]
to say goodbye	прощатися	[pro'ɕatisʲa]
Cheers!	Бувай!	[bu'waj]
Thank you! Cheers!	Дякую!	['dʲakuʲu]
Thank you very much!	Щиро дякую!	['ɕiro 'dʲakuʲu]
My pleasure!	Будь ласка.	[budʲ 'laska]
Don't mention it!	Не варто подяки	[nɛ 'warto po'dʲaki]
It was nothing	Нема за що.	[nɛ'ma za ɕo]
Excuse me! (fam.)	Вибач!	['wibaʧ]
Excuse me! (form.)	Вибачте!	['wibaʧtɛ]
to excuse (forgive)	вибачати	[wiba'ʧati]

to apologize (vi)	вибачатися	[wiba'tʃatisʲa]
My apologies	Моє вибачення.	[mo'ɛ 'wibatʃɛnʲa]
I'm sorry!	Вибачте!	['wibatʃtɛ]
to forgive (vt)	пробачати	[proba'tʃati]
please (adv)	будь ласка	[budʲ 'laska]

Don't forget!	Не забудьте!	[nɛ za'budʲtɛ]
Certainly!	Звичайно!	[zwi'tʃajno]
Of course not!	Звичайно ні!	[zwi'tʃajno ni]
Okay! (I agree)	Згоден!	['zɦɔdɛn]
That's enough!	Досить!	['dɔsitʲ]

3. How to address

mister, sir	Пан	[pan]
madam	Пані	['pani]
miss	Дівчино	['diwtʃino]
young man	Хлопче	['hlɔptʃɛ]
young man (little boy)	Хлопчику	['hlɔptʃiku]
miss (little girl)	Дівчинко	['diwtʃinko]

4. Cardinal numbers. Part 1

0 zero	нуль	[nulʲ]
1 one	один	[o'din]
2 two	два	[dwa]
3 three	три	[tri]
4 four	чотири	[tʃo'tiri]

5 five	п'ять	[pʲatʲ]
6 six	шість	[ʃistʲ]
7 seven	сім	[sim]
8 eight	вісім	['wisim]
9 nine	дев'ять	['dɛwʲatʲ]

10 ten	десять	['dɛsʲatʲ]
11 eleven	одинадцять	[odi'nadtsʲatʲ]
12 twelve	дванадцять	[dwa'nadtsʲatʲ]
13 thirteen	тринадцять	[tri'nadtsʲatʲ]
14 fourteen	чотирнадцять	[tʃotir'nadtsʲatʲ]

15 fifteen	п'ятнадцять	[pʲat'nadtsʲatʲ]
16 sixteen	шістнадцять	[ʃist'nadtsʲatʲ]
17 seventeen	сімнадцять	[sim'nadtsʲatʲ]
18 eighteen	вісімнадцять	[wisim'nadtsʲatʲ]
19 nineteen	дев'ятнадцять	[dɛwʲat'nadtsʲatʲ]

20 twenty	двадцять	['dwadtsʲatʲ]
21 twenty-one	двадцять один	['dwadtsʲatʲ o'din]
22 twenty-two	двадцять два	['dwadtsʲatʲ dwa]
23 twenty-three	двадцять три	['dwadtsʲatʲ tri]
30 thirty	тридцять	['tridtsʲatʲ]

31 thirty-one	тридцять один	['tridtsʲatʲ o'din]
32 thirty-two	тридцять два	['tridtsʲatʲ dwa]
33 thirty-three	тридцять три	['tridtsʲatʲ tri]

40 forty	сорок	['sɔrok]
41 forty-one	сорок один	['sɔrok o'din]
42 forty-two	сорок два	['sɔrok dwa]
43 forty-three	сорок три	['sɔrok tri]

50 fifty	п'ятдесят	[pʲʲatdɛ'sʲat]
51 fifty-one	п'ятдесят один	[pʲʲatdɛ'sʲat o'din]
52 fifty-two	п'ятдесят два	[pʲʲatdɛ'sʲat dwa]
53 fifty-three	п'ятдесят три	[pʲʲatdɛ'sʲat tri]

60 sixty	шістдесят	[ʃizdɛ'sʲat]
61 sixty-one	шістдесят один	[ʃizdɛ'sʲat o'din]
62 sixty-two	шістдесят два	[ʃizdɛ'sʲat dwa]
63 sixty-three	шістдесят три	[ʃizdɛ'sʲat tri]

70 seventy	сімдесят	[simdɛ'sʲat]
71 seventy-one	сімдесят один	[simdɛ'sʲat odin]
72 seventy-two	сімдесят два	[simdɛ'sʲat dwa]
73 seventy-three	сімдесят три	[simdɛ'sʲat tri]

80 eighty	вісімдесят	[wisimdɛ'sʲat]
81 eighty-one	вісімдесят один	[wisimdɛ'sʲat o'din]
82 eighty-two	вісімдесят два	[wisimdɛ'sʲat dwa]
83 eighty-three	вісімдесят три	[wisimdɛ'sʲat tri]

90 ninety	дев'яносто	[dɛwʲʲa'nɔsto]
91 ninety-one	дев'яносто один	[dɛwʲʲa'nɔsto o'din]
92 ninety-two	дев'яносто два	[dɛwʲʲa'nɔsto dwa]
93 ninety-three	дев'яносто три	[dɛwʲʲa'nɔsto tri]

5. Cardinal numbers. Part 2

100 one hundred	сто	[sto]
200 two hundred	двісті	['dwisti]
300 three hundred	триста	['trista]
400 four hundred	чотириста	[tʃo'tirista]
500 five hundred	п'ятсот	[pʲʲa'tsɔt]

600 six hundred	шістсот	[ʃist'sɔt]
700 seven hundred	сімсот	[sim'sɔt]
800 eight hundred	вісімсот	[wisim'sɔt]
900 nine hundred	дев'ятсот	[dɛwʲʲa'tsɔt]

1000 one thousand	тисяча	['tisʲatʃa]
2000 two thousand	дві тисячі	[dwi 'tisʲatʃi]
3000 three thousand	три тисячі	[tri 'tisʲatʃi]
10000 ten thousand	десять тисяч	['dɛsʲatʲ 'tisʲatʃ]
one hundred thousand	сто тисяч	[sto 'tisʲatʃ]
million	мільйон (ч)	[milʲʲjon]
billion	мільярд (ч)	[mi'ljard]

6. Ordinal numbers

first (adj)	перший	['pɛrʃij]
second (adj)	другий	['druɦij]
third (adj)	третій	['trɛtij]
fourth (adj)	четвертий	[ʧɛt'wɛrtij]
fifth (adj)	п'ятий	['pʲatij]
sixth (adj)	шостий	['ʃɔstij]
seventh (adj)	сьомий	['sʲɔmij]
eighth (adj)	восьмий	['wɔsʲmij]
ninth (adj)	дев'ятий	[dɛ'wʲatij]
tenth (adj)	десятий	[dɛ'sʲatij]

7. Numbers. Fractions

fraction	дріб (ч)	[drib]
one half	одна друга	[od'na 'druɦa]
one third	одна третя	[od'na 'trɛtʲa]
one quarter	одна четверта	[od'na ʧɛt'wɛrta]
one eighth	одна восьма	[od'na 'wɔsʲma]
one tenth	одна десята	[od'na dɛ'sʲata]
two thirds	дві третіх	[dwi 'trɛtih]
three quarters	три четвертих	[tri ʧɛt'wɛrtih]

8. Numbers. Basic operations

subtraction	віднімання (с)	[widni'manʲa]
to subtract (vi, vt)	відняти	[wid'nʲati]
division	ділення (с)	['dilɛnʲa]
to divide (vt)	ділити	[di'liti]
addition	додавання (с)	[doda'wanʲa]
to add up (vt)	додати	[do'dati]
to add (vi)	додавати	[doda'wati]
multiplication	множення (с)	['mnɔʒɛnʲa]
to multiply (vt)	множити	['mnɔʒiti]

9. Numbers. Miscellaneous

digit, figure	цифра (ж)	['ʦifra]
number	число (с)	[ʧis'lɔ]
numeral	числівник (ч)	[ʧis'liwnik]
minus sign	мінус (ч)	['minus]
plus sign	плюс (ч)	[plʲus]
formula	формула (ж)	['fɔrmula]
calculation	розрахунок (ч)	[rozra'hunok]
to count (vi, vt)	рахувати	[rahu'wati]

| to count up | підраховувати | [pidra'hɔwuwati] |
| to compare (vt) | зрівнювати | ['zriwnʲuwati] |

How much?	Скільки?	['skilʲki]
sum, total	сума (ж)	['suma]
result	результат (ч)	[rɛzulʲ'tat]
remainder	залишок (ч)	['zaliʃok]

a few (e.g., ~ years ago)	декілька	['dɛkilʲka]
little (I had ~ time)	небагато …	[nɛba'ɦato]
the rest	решта (ж)	['rɛʃta]
one and a half	півтора	[piwtoʹra]
dozen	дюжина (ж)	['dʲuʒina]

in half (adv)	навпіл	['nawpil]
equally (evenly)	порівну	['pɔriwnu]
half	половина (ж)	[polo'wina]
time (three ~s)	раз (ч)	[raz]

10. The most important verbs. Part 1

to advise (vt)	радити	['raditi]
to agree (say yes)	погоджуватися	[po'ɦɔdʒuwatisʲa]
to answer (vi, vt)	відповідати	[widpowi'dati]
to apologize (vi)	вибачатися	[wiba'tʃatisʲa]
to arrive (vi)	приїжджати	[priji'ʒati]

to ask (~ oneself)	запитувати	[za'pituwati]
to ask (~ sb to do sth)	просити	[pro'siti]
to be (vi)	бути	['buti]

to be afraid	боятися	[boʹʲatisʲa]
to be hungry	хотіти їсти	[ho'titi 'jisti]
to be interested in …	цікавитися	[tsi'kawitisʲa]
to be needed	бути потрібним	['buti po'tribnim]
to be surprised	дивуватись	[diwu'watisʲ]

to be thirsty	хотіти пити	[ho'titi 'piti]
to begin (vt)	починати	[potʃi'nati]
to belong to …	належати	[na'lɛʒati]
to boast (vi)	хвастатися	['hwastatisʲa]
to break (split into pieces)	ламати	[la'mati]
to call (~ for help)	кликати	['klikati]

can (v aux)	могти	[moɦ'ti]
to catch (vt)	ловити	[lo'witi]
to change (vt)	поміняти	[pomi'nʲati]
to choose (select)	вибирати	[wibi'rati]
to come down (the stairs)	спускатися	[spus'katisʲa]

to compare (vt)	зрівнювати	['zriwnʲuwati]
to complain (vi, vt)	скаржитися	['skarʒitisʲa]
to confuse (mix up)	помилятися	[pomi'lʲatisʲa]
to continue (vt)	продовжувати	[pro'dɔwʒuwati]

to control (vt)	контролювати	[kontrol^ju'wati]
to cook (dinner)	готувати	[ɦotu'wati]
to cost (vt)	коштувати	['koʃtuwati]
to count (add up)	лічити	[li'tʃiti]
to count on …	розраховувати на …	[rozraɦowuwati na]
to create (vt)	створити	[stwo'riti]
to cry (weep)	плакати	['plakati]

11. The most important verbs. Part 2

to deceive (vi, vt)	обманювати	[ob'man^juwati]
to decorate (tree, street)	прикрашати	[prikra'ʃati]
to defend (a country, etc.)	захищати	[zahi'ɕati]
to demand (request firmly)	вимагати	[wima'ɦati]
to dig (vt)	рити	['riti]
to discuss (vt)	обговорювати	[obɦo'wor^juwati]
to do (vt)	робити	[ro'biti]
to doubt (have doubts)	сумніватися	[sumni'watis^ja]
to drop (let fall)	упускати	[upus'kati]
to enter (room, house, etc.)	входити	['wɦoditi]
to exist (vi)	існувати	[isnu'wati]
to expect (foresee)	передбачити	[pɛrɛd'batʃiti]
to explain (vt)	пояснювати	[po^j'asn^juwati]
to fall (vi)	падати	['padati]
to fancy (vt)	подобатися	[po'dobatis^ja]
to find (vt)	знаходити	[zna'ɦoditi]
to finish (vt)	закінчувати	[za'kintʃuwati]
to fly (vi)	летіти	[lɛ'titi]
to follow … (come after)	іти слідом	[i'ti 'slidom]
to forget (vi, vt)	забувати	[zabu'wati]
to forgive (vt)	прощати	[pro'ɕati]
to give (vt)	давати	[da'wati]
to give a hint	натякати	[nat^ja'kati]
to go (on foot)	йти	[jti]
to go for a swim	купатися	[ku'patis^ja]
to go out (for dinner, etc.)	виходити	[wi'ɦoditi]
to guess (the answer)	відгадати	[widɦa'dati]
to have (vt)	мати	['mati]
to have breakfast	снідати	['snidati]
to have dinner	вечеряти	[wɛ'tʃɛr^jati]
to have lunch	обідати	[o'bidati]
to hear (vt)	чути	['tʃuti]
to help (vt)	допомагати	[dopoma'ɦati]
to hide (vt)	ховати	[ɦo'wati]
to hope (vi, vt)	сподіватися	[spodi'watis^ja]
to hunt (vi, vt)	полювати	[pol^ju'wati]
to hurry (vi)	поспішати	[pospi'ʃati]

12. The most important verbs. Part 3

to inform (vt)	інформувати	[informu'wati]
to insist (vi, vt)	наполягати	[napolʲaʲɦati]
to insult (vt)	ображати	[obra'ʒati]
to invite (vt)	запрошувати	[za'proʃuwati]
to joke (vi)	жартувати	[ʒartu'wati]
to keep (vt)	зберігати	[zbɛri'ɦati]
to keep silent, to hush	мовчати	[mow'tʃati]
to kill (vt)	убивати	[ubi'wati]
to know (sb)	знати	['znati]
to know (sth)	знати	['znati]
to laugh (vi)	сміятися	[smiʲʲatisʲa]
to liberate (city, etc.)	звільняти	[zwilʲ'nʲati]
to look for … (search)	шукати	[ʃu'kati]
to love (sb)	кохати	[ko'hati]
to make a mistake	помилятися	[pomiʲlʲatisʲa]
to manage, to run	керувати	[kɛru'wati]
to mean (signify)	означати	[ozna'tʃati]
to mention (talk about)	згадувати	['zɦaduwati]
to miss (school, etc.)	пропускати	[propus'kati]
to notice (see)	помічати	[pomi'tʃati]
to object (vi, vt)	заперечувати	[zapɛ'rɛtʃuwati]
to observe (see)	спостерігати	[spostɛri'ɦati]
to open (vt)	відчинити	[widtʃi'niti]
to order (meal, etc.)	замовляти	[zamow'lʲati]
to order (mil.)	наказувати	[na'kazuwati]
to own (possess)	володіти	[wolo'diti]
to participate (vi)	брати участь	['brati 'utʃastʲ]
to pay (vi, vt)	платити	[pla'titi]
to permit (vt)	дозволяти	[dozwo'lʲati]
to plan (vt)	планувати	[planu'wati]
to play (children)	грати	['ɦrati]
to pray (vi, vt)	молитися	[mo'litisʲa]
to prefer (vt)	воліти	[wo'liti]
to promise (vt)	обіцяти	[obi'tsʲati]
to pronounce (vt)	вимовляти	[wimow'lʲati]
to propose (vt)	пропонувати	[proponu'wati]
to punish (vt)	покарати	[poka'rati]

13. The most important verbs. Part 4

to read (vi, vt)	читати	[tʃi'tati]
to recommend (vt)	рекомендувати	[rɛkomɛndu'wati]
to refuse (vi, vt)	відмовлятися	[widmow'lʲatisʲa]
to regret (be sorry)	жалкувати	[ʒalku'wati]
to rent (sth from sb)	наймати	[naj'mati]

to repeat (say again)	повторювати	[pow'tɔr'uwati]
to reserve, to book	резервувати	[rɛzɛrwu'wati]
to run (vi)	бігти	[ˈbiɦti]
to save (rescue)	рятувати	[rʲatuˈwati]

to say (~ thank you)	сказати	[skaˈzati]
to scold (vt)	лаяти	[ˈlaʲati]
to see (vt)	бачити	[ˈbatʃiti]
to sell (vt)	продавати	[prodaˈwati]

to send (vt)	відправляти	[widprawˈlʲati]
to shoot (vi)	стріляти	[striˈlʲati]
to shout (vi)	кричати	[kriˈtʃati]
to show (vt)	показувати	[poˈkazuwati]
to sign (document)	підписувати	[pidˈpisuwati]

to sit down (vi)	сідати	[siˈdati]
to smile (vi)	посміхатися	[posmiˈhatisʲa]
to speak (vi, vt)	розмовляти	[rozmowˈlʲati]
to steal (money, etc.)	красти	[ˈkrasti]
to stop (for pause, etc.)	зупинятися	[zupiˈnʲatisʲa]

to stop (please ~ calling me)	припиняти	[pripiˈnʲati]
to study (vt)	вивчати	[wiwˈtʃati]
to swim (vi)	плавати	[ˈplawati]
to take (vt)	брати	[ˈbrati]
to think (vi, vt)	думати	[ˈdumati]

to threaten (vt)	погрожувати	[poɦˈrɔʒuwati]
to touch (with hands)	торкати	[torˈkati]
to translate (vt)	перекладати	[pɛrɛklaˈdati]
to trust (vt)	довіряти	[dowiˈrʲati]
to try (attempt)	пробувати	[ˈprɔbuwati]

to turn (e.g., ~ left)	повертати	[powɛrˈtati]
to underestimate (vt)	недооцінювати	[nɛdooˈtsinʲuwati]
to understand (vt)	розуміти	[rozuˈmiti]
to unite (vt)	об'єднувати	[oˈbʲɛdnuwati]
to wait (vt)	чекати	[tʃɛˈkati]

to want (wish, desire)	хотіти	[hoˈtiti]
to warn (vt)	попереджувати	[popɛˈrɛdʒuwati]
to work (vi)	працювати	[pratsʲuˈwati]
to write (vt)	писати	[piˈsati]
to write down	записувати	[zaˈpisuwati]

14. Colours

colour	колір (ч)	[ˈkɔlir]
shade (tint)	відтінок (ч)	[widˈtinok]
hue	тон (ч)	[ton]
rainbow	веселка (ж)	[wɛˈsɛlka]
white (adj)	білий	[ˈbilij]
black (adj)	чорний	[ˈtʃɔrnij]

grey (adj)	сірий	['sirij]
green (adj)	зелений	[zɛ'lɛnij]
yellow (adj)	жовтий	['ʒɔwtij]
red (adj)	червоний	[ʧɛr'wɔnij]

blue (adj)	синій	['sinij]
light blue (adj)	блакитний	[bla'kitnij]
pink (adj)	рожевий	[ro'ʒɛwij]
orange (adj)	помаранчевий	[poma'ranʧɛwij]
violet (adj)	фіолетовий	[fio'lɛtowij]
brown (adj)	коричневий	[ko'riʧnɛwij]

| golden (adj) | золотий | [zolo'tij] |
| silvery (adj) | сріблястий | [srib'lʲastij] |

beige (adj)	бежевий	['bɛʒɛwij]
cream (adj)	кремовий	['krɛmowij]
turquoise (adj)	бірюзовий	[birʲu'zɔwij]
cherry red (adj)	вишневий	[wiʃ'nɛwij]
lilac (adj)	бузковий	[buz'kɔwij]
crimson (adj)	малиновий	[ma'linowij]

light (adj)	світлий	['switlij]
dark (adj)	темний	['tɛmnij]
bright, vivid (adj)	яскравий	[jas'krawij]

coloured (pencils)	кольоровий	[kolʲo'rɔwij]
colour (e.g. ~ film)	кольоровий	[kolʲo'rɔwij]
black-and-white (adj)	чорно-білий	['ʧɔrno 'bilij]
plain (one-coloured)	однобарвний	[odno'barwnij]
multicoloured (adj)	різнобарвний	[rizno'barwnij]

15. Questions

Who?	Хто?	[hto]
What?	Що?	[ɕo]
Where? (at, in)	Де?	[dɛ]
Where (to)?	Куди?	[ku'di]
From where?	Звідки?	['zwidki]
When?	Коли?	[ko'li]
Why? (What for?)	Навіщо?	[na'wiɕo]
Why? (~ are you crying?)	Чому?	[ʧo'mu]

What for?	Для чого?	[dlʲa 'ʧoho]
How? (in what way)	Як?	[jak]
What? (What kind of ...?)	Який?	[ja'kij]
Which?	Котрий?	[kot'rij]

To whom?	Кому?	[ko'mu]
About whom?	Про кого?	[pro 'koho]
About what?	Про що?	[pro ɕo]
With whom?	З ким?	[z kim]
How many? How much?	Скільки?	['skilʲki]
Whose?	Чий?	[ʧij]

16. Prepositions

with (accompanied by)	з	[z]
without	без	[bɛz]
to (indicating direction)	в	[w]
about (talking ~ …)	про	[pro]
before (in time)	перед	['pɛrɛd]
in front of …	перед	['pɛrɛd]
under (beneath, below)	під	[pid]
above (over)	над	[nad]
on (atop)	над	[nad]
from (off, out of)	з	[z]
of (made from)	з	[z]
in (e.g. ~ ten minutes)	за	[za]
over (across the top of)	через	['ʧɛrɛz]

17. Function words. Adverbs. Part 1

Where? (at, in)	Де?	[dɛ]
here (adv)	тут	[tut]
there (adv)	там	[tam]
somewhere (to be)	десь	[dɛsʲ]
nowhere (not in any place)	ніде	[ni'dɛ]
by (near, beside)	біля	['bilʲa]
by the window	біля вікна	['bilʲa wik'na]
Where (to)?	Куди?	[ku'di]
here (e.g. come ~!)	сюди	[sʲu'di]
there (e.g. to go ~)	туди	[tu'di]
from here (adv)	звідси	['zwidsi]
from there (adv)	звідти	['zwidti]
close (adv)	близько	['blizʲko]
far (adv)	далеко	[da'lɛko]
near (e.g. ~ Paris)	біля	['bilʲa]
nearby (adv)	поряд	['pɔrʲad]
not far (adv)	недалеко	[nɛda'lɛko]
left (adj)	лівий	['liwij]
on the left	зліва	['zliwa]
to the left	ліворуч	[li'wɔruʧ]
right (adj)	правий	['prawij]
on the right	справа	['sprawa]
to the right	праворуч	[pra'wɔruʧ]
in front (adv)	спереду	['spɛrɛdu]
front (as adj)	передній	[pɛ'rɛdnij]

ahead (the kids ran ~)	уперед	[upɛˈrɛd]
behind (adv)	позаду	[poˈzadu]
from behind	ззаду	[ˈzzadu]
back (towards the rear)	назад	[naˈzad]
middle	середина (ж)	[sɛˈrɛdina]
in the middle	посередині	[posɛˈrɛdini]
at the side	збоку	[ˈzbɔku]
everywhere (adv)	скрізь	[skrizʲ]
around (in all directions)	навколо	[nawˈkɔlo]
from inside	зсередини	[zsɛˈrɛdini]
somewhere (to go)	кудись	[kuˈdisʲ]
straight (directly)	напрямки	[naprʲamˈki]
back (e.g. come ~)	назад	[naˈzad]
from anywhere	звідки-небудь	[ˈzwidki ˈnɛbudʲ]
from somewhere	звідкись	[ˈzwidkisʲ]
firstly (adv)	по-перше	[po ˈpɛrʃɛ]
secondly (adv)	по-друге	[po ˈdruɦɛ]
thirdly (adv)	по-третє	[po tˈrɛtɛ]
suddenly (adv)	раптом	[ˈraptom]
at first (in the beginning)	спочатку	[spoˈtʃatku]
for the first time	уперше	[uˈpɛrʃɛ]
long before …	задовго до …	[zaˈdɔwɦo do]
anew (over again)	заново	[ˈzanowo]
for good (adv)	назовсім	[naˈzɔwsim]
never (adv)	ніколи	[niˈkɔli]
again (adv)	знову	[ˈznɔwu]
now (at present)	тепер	[tɛˈpɛr]
often (adv)	часто	[ˈtʃasto]
then (adv)	тоді	[toˈdi]
urgently (quickly)	терміново	[tɛrmiˈnɔwo]
usually (adv)	звичайно	[zwiˈtʃajno]
by the way, …	до речі	[do ˈrɛtʃi]
possibly	можливо	[moʒˈliwo]
probably (adv)	мабуть	[maˈbutʲ]
maybe (adv)	може бути	[ˈmɔʒɛ ˈbuti]
besides …	крім того, …	[krim ˈtɔɦo]
that's why …	тому	[toˈmu]
in spite of …	незважаючи на …	[nɛzwaˈʒajutʃi na]
thanks to …	завдяки …	[zawdʲaˈki]
what (pron.)	що	[ɕo]
that (conj.)	що	[ɕo]
something	щось	[ɕosʲ]
anything (something)	що-небудь	[ɕo ˈnɛbudʲ]
nothing	нічого	[niˈtʃoɦo]
who (pron.)	хто	[hto]
someone	хтось	[htosʲ]

somebody	хто-небудь	[hto 'nɛbudʲ]
nobody	ніхто	[nih'tɔ]
nowhere (a voyage to ~)	нікуди	['nikudi]
nobody's	нічий	[ni'tʃij]
somebody's	чий-небудь	[tʃij 'nɛbudʲ]

so (I'm ~ glad)	так	[tak]
also (as well)	також	[ta'kɔʒ]
too (as well)	також	[ta'kɔʒ]

18. Function words. Adverbs. Part 2

Why?	Чому?	[tʃo'mu]
for some reason	чомусь	[tʃo'musʲ]
because …	тому, що …	[to'mu, ɕo …]
for some purpose	навіщось	[na'wiɕosʲ]

and	і	[i]
or	або	[a'bɔ]
but	але	[a'lɛ]
for (e.g. ~ me)	для	[dlʲa]

too (excessively)	занадто	[za'nadto]
only (exclusively)	тільки	['tilʲki]
exactly (adv)	точно	['tɔtʃno]
about (more or less)	приблизно	[prib'lizno]

approximately (adv)	приблизно	[prib'lizno]
approximate (adj)	приблизний	[prib'liznij]
almost (adv)	майже	['majʒɛ]
the rest	решта (ж)	['rɛʃta]

each (adj)	кожен	['kɔʒɛn]
any (no matter which)	будь-який	[budʲ ja'kij]
many, much (a lot of)	багато	[ba'ɦato]
many people	багато хто	[ba'ɦato hto]
all (everyone)	всі	[wsi]

| in return for … | в обмін на … | [w 'ɔbmin na] |
| in exchange (adv) | натомість | [na'tɔmistʲ] |

| by hand (made) | вручну | [wrutʃ'nu] |
| hardly (negative opinion) | навряд чи | [naw'rʲad tʃi] |

probably (adv)	мабуть	[ma'butʲ]
on purpose (intentionally)	навмисно	[naw'misno]
by accident (adv)	випадково	[wipad'kɔwo]

very (adv)	дуже	['duʒɛ]
for example (adv)	наприклад	[na'priklad]
between	між	[miʒ]
among	серед	['sɛrɛd]
so much (such a lot)	стільки	['stilʲki]
especially (adv)	особливо	[osob'liwo]

Basic concepts. Part 2

19. Opposites

rich (adj)	багатий	[ba'ɦatij]
poor (adj)	бідний	['bidnij]
ill, sick (adj)	хворий	['hwɔrij]
well (not sick)	здоровий	[zdo'rɔwij]
big (adj)	великий	[wɛ'likij]
small (adj)	маленький	[ma'lɛnʲkij]
quickly (adv)	швидко	['ʃwidko]
slowly (adv)	повільно	[po'wilʲno]
fast (adj)	швидкий	[ʃwid'kij]
slow (adj)	повільний	[po'wilʲnij]
glad (adj)	веселий	[wɛ'sɛlij]
sad (adj)	сумний	[sum'nij]
together (adv)	разом	['razom]
separately (adv)	окремо	[ok'rɛmo]
aloud (to read)	вголос	['wɦɔlos]
silently (to oneself)	про себе	[pro 'sɛbɛ]
tall (adj)	високий	[wi'sɔkij]
low (adj)	низький	[nizʲ'kij]
deep (adj)	глибокий	[ɦli'bɔkij]
shallow (adj)	мілкий	[mil'kij]
yes	так	[tak]
no	ні	[ni]
distant (in space)	далекий	[da'lɛkij]
nearby (adj)	близький	[blizʲ'kij]
far (adv)	далеко	[da'lɛko]
nearby (adv)	поруч	['pɔrutʃ]
long (adj)	довгий	['dɔwɦij]
short (adj)	короткий	[ko'rɔtkij]
good (kindhearted)	добрий	['dɔbrij]
evil (adj)	злий	['zlij]

| married (adj) | одружений | [od'ruʒɛnij] |
| single (adj) | холостий | [holos'tij] |

| to forbid (vt) | заборонити | [zaboro'niti] |
| to permit (vt) | дозволити | [doz'wɔliti] |

| end | кінець (ч) | [ki'nɛʧ] |
| beginning | початок (ч) | [po'ʧatok] |

| left (adj) | лівий | ['liwij] |
| right (adj) | правий | ['prawij] |

| first (adj) | перший | ['pɛrʃij] |
| last (adj) | останній | [os'tanij] |

| crime | злочин (ч) | ['zlɔʧin] |
| punishment | кара (ж) | ['kara] |

| to order (vt) | наказати | [naka'zati] |
| to obey (vi, vt) | підкоритися | [pidko'ritisʲa] |

| straight (adj) | прямий | [prʲa'mij] |
| curved (adj) | кривий | [kri'wij] |

| paradise | рай (ч) | [raj] |
| hell | пекло (с) | ['pɛklo] |

| to be born | народитися | [naro'ditisʲa] |
| to die (vi) | померти | [po'mɛrti] |

| strong (adj) | сильний | ['silʲnij] |
| weak (adj) | слабкий | [slab'kij] |

| old (adj) | старий | [sta'rij] |
| young (adj) | молодий | [molo'dij] |

| old (adj) | старий | [sta'rij] |
| new (adj) | новий | [no'wij] |

| hard (adj) | твердий | [twɛr'dij] |
| soft (adj) | м'який | [mʲʲa'kij] |

| warm (tepid) | теплий | ['tɛplij] |
| cold (adj) | холодний | [ho'lɔdnij] |

| fat (adj) | товстий | [tows'tij] |
| thin (adj) | худий | [hu'dij] |

| narrow (adj) | вузький | [wuzʲ'kij] |
| wide (adj) | широкий | [ʃi'rɔkij] |

| good (adj) | добрий | ['dɔbrij] |
| bad (adj) | поганий | [po'ɦanij] |

| brave (adj) | хоробрий | [ho'rɔbrij] |
| cowardly (adj) | боягузливий | [boja'ɦuzliwij] |

20. Weekdays

Monday	понеділок (ч)	[ponɛ'dilok]
Tuesday	вівторок (ч)	[wiw'tɔrok]
Wednesday	середа (ж)	[sɛrɛ'da]
Thursday	четвер (ч)	[tʃɛt'wɛr]
Friday	п'ятниця (ж)	['pʲatnitsʲa]
Saturday	субота (ж)	[su'bɔta]
Sunday	неділя (ж)	[nɛ'dilʲa]

today (adv)	сьогодні	[sʲo'ɦɔdni]
tomorrow (adv)	завтра	['zawtra]
the day after tomorrow	післязавтра	[pislʲa'zawtra]
yesterday (adv)	вчора	['wtʃora]
the day before yesterday	позавчора	[pozaw'tʃora]

day	день (ч)	[dɛnʲ]
working day	робочий день (ч)	[ro'bɔtʃij dɛnʲ]
public holiday	святковий день (ч)	[swʲat'kɔwij dɛnʲ]
day off	вихідний день (ч)	[wihid'nij dɛnʲ]
weekend	вихідні (мн)	[wihid'ni]

all day long	весь день	[wɛsʲ dɛnʲ]
the next day (adv)	на наступний день	[na na'stupnij dɛnʲ]
two days ago	2 дні тому	[dwa dni 'tomu]
the day before	напередодні	[napɛrɛ'dɔdni]
daily (adj)	щоденний	[ɕo'dɛnij]
every day (adv)	щодня	[ɕod'nʲa]

week	тиждень (ч)	['tiʒdɛnʲ]
last week (adv)	на минулому тижні	[na mi'nulomu 'tiʒni]
next week (adv)	на наступному тижні	[na na'stupnomu 'tiʒni]
weekly (adj)	щотижневий	[ɕotiʒ'nɛwij]
every week (adv)	щотижня	[ɕo'tiʒnʲa]
twice a week	два рази на тиждень	[dwa 'razi na 'tiʒdɛnʲ]
every Tuesday	кожен вівторок	['kɔʒɛn wiw'tɔrok]

21. Hours. Day and night

morning	ранок (ч)	['ranok]
in the morning	вранці	['wrantsi]
noon, midday	полудень (ч)	['pɔludɛnʲ]
in the afternoon	після обіду	['pislʲa o'bidu]

evening	вечір (ч)	['wɛtʃir]
in the evening	увечері	[u'wɛtʃɛri]
night	ніч (ж)	[nitʃ]
at night	уночі	[uno'tʃi]
midnight	північ (ж)	['piwnitʃ]

second	секунда (ж)	[sɛ'kunda]
minute	хвилина (ж)	[hwi'lina]
hour	година (ж)	[ɦo'dina]

half an hour	**півгодини** (мн)	[piwɦo'dini]
a quarter-hour	**чверть** (ж) **години**	[ʧwɛrtʲ ɦo'dini]
fifteen minutes	**15 хвилин**	[pʲat'nadtsʲatʲ hwi'lin]
24 hours	**доба** (ж)	[do'ba]

sunrise	**схід** (ч) **сонця**	[shid 'sɔntsʲa]
dawn	**світанок** (ч)	[swi'tanok]
early morning	**ранній ранок** (ч)	['ranij 'ranok]
sunset	**захід** (ч)	['zahid]

early in the morning	**рано вранці**	['rano 'wrantsi]
this morning	**сьогодні вранці**	[sʲo'ɦodni 'wrantsi]
tomorrow morning	**завтра вранці**	['zawtra 'wrantsi]

this afternoon	**сьогодні вдень**	[sʲo'ɦodni wdɛnʲ]
in the afternoon	**після обіду**	['pislʲa o'bidu]
tomorrow afternoon	**завтра після обіду** (ч)	['zawtra 'pislʲa o'bidu]

| tonight (this evening) | **сьогодні увечері** | [sʲo'ɦodni u'wɛʧɛri] |
| tomorrow night | **завтра увечері** | ['zawtra u'wɛʧɛri] |

at 3 o'clock sharp	**рівно о третій годині**	['riwno o t'rɛtij ɦo'dini]
about 4 o'clock	**біля четвертої години**	['bilʲa ʧɛt'wɛrtoji ɦo'dini]
by 12 o'clock	**до дванадцятої години**	[do dwa'nadtsʲatoji ɦo'dini]

in 20 minutes	**за двадцять хвилин**	[za 'dwadtsʲatʲ hwi'lin]
in an hour	**за годину**	[za ɦo'dinu]
on time (adv)	**вчасно**	['wʧasno]

a quarter to …	**без чверті**	[bɛz 'ʧwɛrti]
within an hour	**на протязі години**	[na 'protʲazi ɦo'dini]
every 15 minutes	**що п'ятнадцять хвилин**	[ɕo pʲat'nadtsʲatʲ hwi'lin]
round the clock	**цілодобово**	[tsilodo'bowo]

22. Months. Seasons

January	**січень** (ч)	['siʧɛnʲ]
February	**лютий** (ч)	['lʲutij]
March	**березень** (ч)	['bɛrɛzenʲ]
April	**квітень** (ч)	['kwitɛnʲ]
May	**травень** (ч)	['trawɛnʲ]
June	**червень** (ч)	['ʧɛrwɛnʲ]

July	**липень** (ч)	['lipɛnʲ]
August	**серпень** (ч)	['sɛrpɛnʲ]
September	**вересень** (ч)	['wɛrɛsɛnʲ]
October	**жовтень** (ч)	['ʒowtɛnʲ]
November	**листопад** (ч)	[listo'pad]
December	**грудень** (ч)	['ɦrudɛnʲ]

spring	**весна** (ж)	[wɛs'na]
in spring	**навесні**	[nawɛs'ni]
spring (as adj)	**весняний**	[wɛs'nʲanij]
summer	**літо** (с)	['lito]

in summer	влітку	['wlitku]
summer (as adj)	літній	['litnij]
autumn	осінь (ж)	['ɔsinʲ]
in autumn	восени	[wosɛ'ni]
autumn (as adj)	осінній	[o'sinij]
winter	зима (ж)	[zi'ma]
in winter	взимку	['wzimku]
winter (as adj)	зимовий	[zi'mɔwij]
month	місяць (ч)	['misʲats]
this month	в цьому місяці (ч)	[w tsʲomu 'misʲatsi]
next month	в наступному місяці (ч)	[w na'stupnomu 'misʲatsi]
last month	в минулому місяці (ч)	[w mi'nulomu 'misʲatsi]
a month ago	місяць (ч) тому	['misʲats to'mu]
in a month (a month later)	через місяць	['tʃɛrɛz 'misʲats]
in 2 months (2 months later)	через 2 місяці	['tʃɛrɛz dwa 'misʲatsi]
the whole month	весь місяць (ч)	[wɛsʲ 'misʲats]
all month long	цілий місяць	['tsilij 'misʲats]
monthly (~ magazine)	щомісячний	[ɕo'misʲatʃnij]
monthly (adv)	щомісяця	[ɕo'misʲatsʲa]
every month	кожний місяць (ч)	['kɔʒnij 'misʲats]
twice a month	два рази на місяць	[dwa 'razɨ na 'misʲats]
year	рік (ч)	[rik]
this year	в цьому році	[w tsʲomu 'rɔtsi]
next year	в наступному році	[w na'stupnomu 'rɔtsi]
last year	в минулому році	[w mi'nulomu 'rɔtsi]
a year ago	рік тому	[rik 'tɔmu]
in a year	через рік	['tʃɛrɛz rik]
in two years	через два роки	['tʃɛrɛz dwa 'rɔki]
the whole year	увесь рік	[u'wɛsʲ rik]
all year long	цілий рік	['tsilij rik]
every year	кожен рік	['kɔʒɛn 'rik]
annual (adj)	щорічний	[ɕo'ritʃnij]
annually (adv)	щороку	[ɕo'rɔku]
4 times a year	чотири рази на рік	[tʃo'tiri 'razɨ na rik]
date (e.g. today's ~)	число (с)	[tʃis'lɔ]
date (e.g. ~ of birth)	дата (ж)	['data]
calendar	календар (ч)	[kalɛn'dar]
half a year	півроку	[piw'rɔku]
six months	піврічча (с)	[piw'ritʃʲa]
season (summer, etc.)	сезон (ч)	[sɛ'zɔn]
century	вік (ч)	[wik]

23. Time. Miscellaneous

time	час (с)	[tʃas]
moment	мить (ж)	[mitʲ]

instant (n)	момент (ч)	[mo'mɛnt]
instant (adj)	миттєвий	[mit'tɛwij]
lapse (of time)	відрізок (ч)	[wid'rizok]
life	життя (с)	[ʒit'tʲa]
eternity	вічність (ж)	['witʃnistʲ]
epoch	епоха (ж)	[ɛ'pɔha]
era	ера (ж)	['ɛra]
cycle	цикл (ч)	['ʦikl]
period	період (ч)	[pɛ'riod]
term (short-~)	термін (ч)	['tɛrmin]
the future	майбутнє (с)	[maj'butnɛ]
future (as adj)	майбутній	[maj'butnij]
next time	наступного разу (ч)	[na'stupnoɦo 'razu]
the past	минуле (с)	[mi'nulɛ]
past (recent)	минулий	[mi'nulij]
last time	минулого разу	[mi'nuloɦo 'razu]
later (adv)	пізніше	[piz'niʃɛ]
after (prep.)	після	['pislʲa]
nowadays (adv)	сьогодення	[sʲoɦo'dɛnʲa]
now (at this moment)	зараз	['zaraz]
immediately (adv)	негайно	[nɛ'ɦajno]
soon (adv)	незабаром	[nɛza'barom]
in advance (beforehand)	завчасно	[zaw'ʧasno]
a long time ago	давно	[daw'nɔ]
recently (adv)	нещодавно	[nɛɕo'dawno]
destiny	доля (ж)	['dɔlʲa]
recollections	пам'ять (ж)	['pamʲʲatʲ]
archives	архів (ч)	[ar'hiw]
during …	під час	[pid 'ʧas]
long, a long time (adv)	довго	['dɔwɦo]
not long (adv)	недовго	[nɛ'dɔwɦo]
early (in the morning)	рано	['rano]
late (not early)	пізно	['pizno]
forever (for good)	назавжди	[na'zawʒdi]
to start (begin)	починати	[poʧi'nati]
to postpone (vt)	перенести	[pɛrɛ'nɛsti]
at the same time	одночасно	[odno'ʧasno]
permanently (adv)	постійно	[pos'tijno]
constant (noise, pain)	постійний	[pos'tijnij]
temporary (adj)	тимчасовий	[timʧa'sɔwij]
sometimes (adv)	інколи	['inkoli]
rarely (adv)	рідко	['ridko]
often (adv)	часто	['ʧasto]

24. Lines and shapes

square	квадрат (ч)	[kwad'rat]
square (as adj)	квадратний	[kwad'ratnij]

circle	коло (с)	['kɔlo]
round (adj)	круглий	['kruɦlij]
triangle	трикутник (ч)	[tri'kutnik]
triangular (adj)	трикутний	[tri'kutnij]
oval	овал (ч)	[o'wal]
oval (as adj)	овальний	[o'walʲnij]
rectangle	прямокутник (ч)	[prʲamo'kutnik]
rectangular (adj)	прямокутний	[prʲamo'kutnij]
pyramid	піраміда (ж)	[pira'mida]
rhombus	ромб (ч)	[romb]
trapezium	трапеція (ж)	[tra'pɛtsiʲa]
cube	куб (ч)	[kub]
prism	призма (ж)	['prizma]
circumference	коло (с)	['kɔlo]
sphere	сфера (ж)	['sfɛra]
ball (solid sphere)	куля (ж)	['kulʲa]
diameter	діаметр (ч)	[di'amɛtr]
radius	радіус (ч)	['radius]
perimeter (circle's ~)	периметр (ч)	[pɛ'rimɛtr]
centre	центр (ч)	[ʦɛntr]
horizontal (adj)	горизонтальний	[ɦorizon'talʲnij]
vertical (adj)	вертикальний	[wɛrti'kalʲnij]
parallel (n)	паралель (ж)	[para'lɛlʲ]
parallel (as adj)	паралельний	[para'lɛlʲnij]
line	лінія (ж)	['liniʲa]
stroke	риса (ж)	['risa]
straight line	пряма (ж)	[prʲa'ma]
curve (curved line)	крива (ж)	[kri'wa]
thin (line, etc.)	тонкий	[ton'kij]
contour (outline)	контур (ч)	['kɔntur]
intersection	перетин (ч)	[pɛ'rɛtin]
right angle	прямий кут (ч)	[prʲa'mij kut]
segment	сегмент (ч)	[sɛɦ'mɛnt]
sector (circular ~)	сектор (ч)	['sɛktor]
side (of a triangle)	бік (ч)	[bik]
angle	кут (ч)	[kut]

25. Units of measurement

weight	вага (ж)	[wa'ɦa]
length	довжина (ж)	[dowʒi'na]
width	ширина (ж)	[ʃiri'na]
height	висота (ж)	[wiso'ta]
depth	глибина (ж)	[ɦlibi'na]
volume	об'єм (ч)	[o'bʲɛm]
area	площа (ж)	['plɔɕa]
gram	грам (ч)	[ɦram]
milligram	міліграм (ч)	[mili'ɦram]

kilogram	кілограм (ч)	[kilo'ɦram]
ton	тонна (ж)	['tɔna]
pound	фунт (ч)	['funt]
ounce	унція (ж)	['unʦiˈa]
metre	метр (ч)	[mɛtr]
millimetre	міліметр (ч)	[mili'mɛtr]
centimetre	сантиметр (ч)	[santi'mɛtr]
kilometre	кілометр (ч)	[kilo'mɛtr]
mile	миля (ж)	['miɫˈa]
inch	дюйм (ч)	[dˈujm]
foot	фут (ч)	[fut]
yard	ярд (ч)	[jard]
square metre	квадратний метр (ч)	[kwad'ratnij mɛtr]
hectare	гектар (ч)	[ɦɛk'tar]
litre	літр (ч)	[litr]
degree	градус (ч)	['ɦradus]
volt	вольт (ч)	[wolˈt]
ampere	ампер (ч)	[am'pɛr]
horsepower	кінська сила (ж)	['kinsˈka 'sila]
quantity	кількість (ж)	['kilˈkistˈ]
a little bit of …	небагато …	[nɛba'ɦato]
half	половина (ж)	[polo'wina]
dozen	дюжина (ж)	['dˈuʒina]
piece (item)	штука (ж)	['ʃtuka]
size	розмір (ч)	['rɔzmir]
scale (map ~)	масштаб (ч)	[masʃ'tab]
minimal (adj)	мінімальний	[mini'malˈnij]
the smallest (adj)	найменший	[naj'mɛnʃij]
medium (adj)	середній	[sɛ'rɛdnij]
maximal (adj)	максимальний	[maksi'malˈnij]
the largest (adj)	найбільший	[naj'bilˈʃij]

26. Containers

canning jar (glass ~)	банка (ж)	['banka]
tin, can	банка (ж)	['banka]
bucket	відро (с)	[wid'rɔ]
barrel	бочка (ж)	['bɔʧka]
wash basin (e.g., plastic ~)	таз (ч)	[taz]
tank (100L water ~)	бак (ч)	[bak]
hip flask	фляжка (ж)	['flˈaʒka]
jerrycan	каністра (ж)	[ka'nistra]
tank (e.g., tank car)	цистерна (ж)	[ʦis'tɛrna]
mug	кухоль (ч)	['kuholˈ]
cup (of coffee, etc.)	чашка (ж)	['ʧaʃka]

saucer	блюдце (с)	['blʲudtsɛ]
glass (tumbler)	склянка (ж)	['sklʲanka]
wine glass	келих (ч)	['kɛlih]
stock pot (soup pot)	каструля (ж)	[kas'trulʲa]

| bottle (~ of wine) | пляшка (ж) | ['plʲaʃka] |
| neck (of the bottle, etc.) | шийка (ж) | ['ʃijka] |

carafe (decanter)	карафа (ж)	[ka'rafa]
pitcher	глечик (ч)	['ɦlɛtʃik]
vessel (container)	посудина (ж)	[po'sudina]
pot (crock, stoneware ~)	горщик (ч)	['ɦorɕik]
vase	ваза (ж)	['waza]

flacon, bottle (perfume ~)	флакон (ч)	[fla'kɔn]
vial, small bottle	пляшечка (ж)	['plʲaʃɛtʃka]
tube (of toothpaste)	тюбик (ч)	['tʲubik]

sack (bag)	мішок (ч)	[mi'ʃɔk]
bag (paper ~, plastic ~)	пакет (ч)	[pa'kɛt]
packet (of cigarettes, etc.)	пачка (ж)	['patʃka]

box (e.g. shoebox)	коробка (ж)	[ko'rɔbka]
crate	ящик (ч)	['ʲaɕik]
basket	кошик (ч)	['kɔʃik]

27. Materials

material	матеріал (ч)	[matɛri'al]
wood (n)	дерево (с)	['dɛrɛwo]
wood-, wooden (adj)	дерев'яний	[dɛrɛ'wʲanij]

| glass (n) | скло (с) | ['sklo] |
| glass (as adj) | скляний | [sklʲa'nij] |

| stone (n) | камінь (ч) | ['kaminʲ] |
| stone (as adj) | кам'яний | [kamʲa'nij] |

| plastic (n) | пластмаса (ж) | [plast'masa] |
| plastic (as adj) | пластмасовий | [plast'masowij] |

| rubber (n) | гума (ж) | ['ɦuma] |
| rubber (as adj) | гумовий | ['ɦumowij] |

| cloth, fabric (n) | тканина (ж) | [tka'nina] |
| fabric (as adj) | з тканини | [z tka'nini] |

| paper (n) | папір (ч) | [pa'pir] |
| paper (as adj) | паперовий | [papɛ'rɔwij] |

cardboard (n)	картон (ч)	[kar'tɔn]
cardboard (as adj)	картоновий	[kar'tɔnowij]
polyethylene	поліетилен (ч)	[poliɛti'lɛn]
cellophane	целофан (ч)	[tsɛlo'fan]

plywood	фанера (ж)	[fa'nɛra]
porcelain (n)	фарфор (ч)	['farfor]
porcelain (as adj)	порцеляновий	[portsɛ'lʲanowij]
clay (n)	глина (ж)	['ɦlina]
clay (as adj)	глиняний	['ɦlinʲanij]
ceramic (n)	кераміка (ж)	[kɛ'ramika]
ceramic (as adj)	керамічний	[kɛra'mitʃnij]

28. Metals

metal (n)	метал (ч)	[mɛ'tal]
metal (as adj)	металевий	[mɛta'lɛwij]
alloy (n)	сплав (ч)	[splaw]

gold (n)	золото (с)	['zɔloto]
gold, golden (adj)	золотий	[zolo'tij]
silver (n)	срібло (с)	['sriblo]
silver (as adj)	срібний	['sribnij]

iron (n)	залізо (с)	[za'lizo]
iron-, made of iron (adj)	залізний	[za'liznij]
steel (n)	сталь (ж)	[stalʲ]
steel (as adj)	сталевий	[sta'lɛwij]
copper (n)	мідь (ж)	[midʲ]
copper (as adj)	мідний	['midnij]

aluminium (n)	алюміній (ч)	[alʲu'minij]
aluminium (as adj)	алюмінієвий	[alʲu'miniɛwij]
bronze (n)	бронза (ж)	['brɔnza]
bronze (as adj)	бронзовий	['brɔnzowij]

brass	латунь (ж)	[la'tunʲ]
nickel	нікель (ч)	['nikɛlʲ]
platinum	платина (ж)	['platina]
mercury	ртуть (ж)	[rtutʲ]
tin	олово (с)	['ɔlowo]
lead	свинець (ч)	[swi'nɛts]
zinc	цинк (ч)	['tsink]

HUMAN BEING

Human being. The body

human being	людина (ж)	[lʲu'dina]
man (adult male)	чоловік (ч)	[tʃolo'wik]
woman	жінка (ж)	['ʒinka]
child	дитина (ж)	[di'tina]
girl	дівчинка (ж)	['diwtʃinka]
boy	хлопчик (ч)	['hlɔptʃik]
teenager	підліток (ч)	['pidlitok]
old man	старий (ч)	[sta'rij]
old woman	стара (ж)	[sta'ra]

organism (body)	організм (ч)	[orɦa'nizm]
heart	серце (с)	['sɛrtsɛ]
blood	кров (ж)	[krow]
artery	артерія (ж)	[ar'tɛriʲa]
vein	вена (ж)	['wɛna]
brain	мозок (ч)	['mɔzok]
nerve	нерв (ч)	[nɛrw]
nerves	нерви (мн)	['nɛrwi]
vertebra	хребець (ч)	[hrɛ'bɛts]
spine (backbone)	хребет (ч)	[hrɛ'bɛt]
stomach (organ)	шлунок (ч)	['ʃlunok]
intestines, bowels	кишечник (ч)	[ki'ʃɛtʃnik]
intestine (e.g. large ~)	кишка (ж)	['kiʃka]
liver	печінка (ж)	[pɛ'tʃinka]
kidney	нирка (ж)	['nirka]
bone	кістка (ж)	['kistka]
skeleton	скелет (ч)	[skɛ'lɛt]
rib	ребро (с)	[rɛb'rɔ]
skull	череп (ч)	['tʃɛrɛp]
muscle	м'яз (ч)	['mʲʲaz]
biceps	біцепс (ч)	['bitsɛps]
triceps	трицепс (ч)	['tritsɛps]
tendon	сухожилля (с)	[suho'ʒilʲʲa]
joint	суглоб (ч)	[suɦ'lɔb]

lungs	легені (мн)	[lɛ'ɦɛni]
genitals	статеві органи (мн)	[sta'tɛwi 'ɔrɦani]
skin	шкіра (ж)	['ʃkira]

31. Head

head	голова (ж)	[ɦolo'wa]
face	обличчя (с)	[ob'litʃ'a]
nose	ніс (ч)	[nis]
mouth	рот (ч)	[rot]

eye	око (с)	['ɔko]
eyes	очі (мн)	['ɔtʃi]
pupil	зіниця (ч)	[zi'nits'a]
eyebrow	брова (ж)	[bro'wa]
eyelash	вія (ж)	['wi'a]
eyelid	повіка (ж)	[po'wika]

tongue	язик (ч)	[ja'zik]
tooth	зуб (ч)	[zub]
lips	губи (мн)	['ɦubi]
cheekbones	вилиці (мн)	['wilits'i]
gum	ясна (мн)	['ʲasna]
palate	піднебіння (с)	[pidnɛ'bin'a]

nostrils	ніздрі (мн)	['nizdri]
chin	підборіддя (с)	[pidbo'ridd'a]
jaw	щелепа (ж)	[ɕɛ'lɛpa]
cheek	щока (ж)	[ɕo'ka]

forehead	чоло (с)	[tʃo'lɔ]
temple	скроня (ж)	['skrɔn'a]
ear	вухо (с)	['wuho]
back of the head	потилиця (ж)	[po'tilits'a]
neck	шия (ж)	['ʃi'a]
throat	горло (с)	['ɦɔrlo]

hair	волосся (с)	[wo'lɔss'a]
hairstyle	зачіска (ж)	['zatʃiska]
haircut	стрижка (ж)	['striʒka]
wig	парик (ч)	[pa'rik]

moustache	вуса (мн)	['wusa]
beard	борода (ж)	[boro'da]
to have (a beard, etc.)	носити	[no'siti]
plait	коса (ж)	[ko'sa]
sideboards	бакенбарди (мн)	[bakɛn'bardi]

red-haired (adj)	рудий	[ru'dij]
grey (hair)	сивий	['siwij]
bald (adj)	лисий	['lisij]
bald patch	лисина (ж)	['lisina]
ponytail	хвіст (ч)	[hwist]
fringe	чубчик (ч)	['tʃubtʃik]

32. Human body

hand	кисть (ж)	[kistʲ]
arm	рука (ж)	[ruˈka]
finger	палець (ч)	[ˈpalɛʦ]
thumb	великий палець (ч)	[wɛˈlikij ˈpalɛʦ]
little finger	мізинець (ч)	[miˈzinɛʦ]
nail	ніготь (ч)	[ˈniɦotʲ]
fist	кулак (ч)	[kuˈlak]
palm	долоня (ж)	[doˈlɔnʲa]
wrist	зап'ясток (ч)	[zaˈpʲastok]
forearm	передпліччя (с)	[pɛrɛdpˈlitʃʲa]
elbow	лікоть (ч)	[ˈlikotʲ]
shoulder	плече (с)	[plɛˈtʃɛ]
leg	гомілка (ж)	[ɦoˈmilka]
foot	ступня (ж)	[stupˈnʲa]
knee	коліно (с)	[koˈlino]
calf	литка (ж)	[ˈlitka]
hip	стегно (с)	[stɛɦˈno]
heel	п'ятка (ж)	[ˈpʲatka]
body	тіло (с)	[ˈtilo]
stomach	живіт (ч)	[ʒiˈwit]
chest	груди (мн)	[ˈɦrudi]
breast	груди (мн)	[ˈɦrudi]
flank	бік (ч)	[bik]
back	спина (ж)	[ˈspina]
lower back	поперек (ч)	[popɛˈrɛk]
waist	талія (ж)	[ˈtalʲia]
navel (belly button)	пупок (ч)	[puˈpɔk]
buttocks	сідниці (мн)	[sidˈniʦi]
bottom	зад (ч)	[zad]
beauty spot	родимка (ж)	[ˈrɔdimka]
birthmark (café au lait spot)	родима пляма (ж)	[roˈdima ˈplʲama]
tattoo	татуювання (с)	[tatuʲuˈwanʲa]
scar	рубець (ч)	[ruˈbɛʦ]

Clothing & Accessories

33. Outerwear. Coats

clothes	**одяг** (ч)	['ɔdʲaĥ]
outerwear	**верхній одяг** (ч)	['wɛrhnij 'ɔdʲaĥ]
winter clothing	**зимовий одяг** (ч)	[zi'mɔwij 'ɔdʲaĥ]

coat (overcoat)	**пальто** (с)	[palʲ'tɔ]
fur coat	**шуба** (ж)	['ʃuba]
fur jacket	**кожушок** (ч)	[koʒu'ʃɔk]
down coat	**пуховик** (ч)	[puho'wik]

jacket (e.g. leather ~)	**куртка** (ж)	['kurtka]
raincoat (trenchcoat, etc.)	**плащ** (ч)	[plaɕ]
waterproof (adj)	**непромокальний**	[nɛpromo'kalʲnij]

34. Men's & women's clothing

shirt (button shirt)	**сорочка** (ж)	[so'rɔtʃka]
trousers	**штани** (мн)	[ʃta'ni]
jeans	**джинси** (мн)	['dʒinsi]
suit jacket	**піджак** (ч)	[pi'dʒak]
suit	**костюм** (ч)	[kos'tʲum]

dress (frock)	**сукня** (ж)	['suknʲa]
skirt	**спідниця** (ж)	[spid'nitsʲa]
blouse	**блузка** (ж)	['bluzka]
knitted jacket (cardigan, etc.)	**кофта** (ж)	['kɔfta]
jacket (of a woman's suit)	**жакет** (ч)	[ʒa'kɛt]

T-shirt	**футболка** (ж)	[fut'bɔlka]
shorts (short trousers)	**шорти** (мн)	['ʃɔrti]
tracksuit	**спортивний костюм** (ч)	[spor'tiwnij kos'tʲum]
bathrobe	**халат** (ч)	[ha'lat]
pyjamas	**піжама** (ж)	[pi'ʒama]

jumper (sweater)	**светр** (ч)	[swɛtr]
pullover	**пуловер** (ч)	[pulo'wɛr]

waistcoat	**жилет** (ч)	[ʒi'lɛt]
tailcoat	**фрак** (ч)	[frak]
dinner suit	**смокінг** (ч)	['smɔkinĥ]

uniform	**форма** (ж)	['fɔrma]
workwear	**робочий одяг** (ж)	[ro'bɔtʃij 'ɔdʲaĥ]
boiler suit	**комбінезон** (ч)	[kombinɛ'zɔn]
coat (e.g. doctor's smock)	**халат** (ч)	[ha'lat]

35. Clothing. Underwear

underwear	білизна (ж)	[bi'lizna]
vest (singlet)	майка (ж)	['majka]
socks	шкарпетки (мн)	[ʃkar'pɛtki]
nightdress	нічна сорочка (ж)	[nitʃ'na so'rɔtʃka]
bra	бюстгальтер (ч)	[bʲustʲhalʲtɛr]
knee highs (knee-high socks)	гольфи (мн)	['hɔlʲfi]
tights	колготки (мн)	[kol'hɔtki]
stockings (hold ups)	панчохи (мн)	[pan'tʃɔhi]
swimsuit, bikini	купальник (ч)	[ku'palʲnik]

36. Headwear

hat	шапка (ж)	['ʃapka]
trilby hat	капелюх (ч)	[kapɛ'lʲuh]
baseball cap	бейсболка (ж)	[bɛjs'bɔlka]
flatcap	кашкет (ч)	[kaʃ'kɛt]
beret	берет (ч)	[bɛ'rɛt]
hood	каптур (ч)	[kap'tur]
panama hat	панамка (ж)	[pa'namka]
knit cap (knitted hat)	в'язана шапочка (ж)	['wʲazana 'ʃapotʃka]
headscarf	хустка (ж)	['hustka]
women's hat	капелюшок (ч)	[kapɛ'lʲuʃok]
hard hat	каска (ж)	['kaska]
forage cap	пілотка (ж)	[pi'lɔtka]
helmet	шолом (ч)	[ʃo'lɔm]
bowler	котелок (ч)	[kotɛ'lɔk]
top hat	циліндр (ч)	[tsi'lindr]

37. Footwear

footwear	взуття (с)	[wzut'tʲa]
shoes (men's shoes)	черевики (мн)	[tʃɛrɛ'wiki]
shoes (women's shoes)	туфлі (мн)	['tufli]
boots (e.g., cowboy ~)	чоботи (мн)	['tʃɔboti]
carpet slippers	капці (мн)	['kaptsi]
trainers	кросівки (мн)	[kro'siwki]
trainers	кеди (мн)	['kɛdi]
sandals	сандалі (мн)	[san'dali]
cobbler (shoe repairer)	чоботар (ч)	[tʃobo'tar]
heel	каблук (ч)	[kab'luk]
pair (of shoes)	пара (ж)	['para]
lace (shoelace)	шнурок (ч)	[ʃnu'rɔk]

to lace up (vt)	шнурувати	[ʃnuru'wati]
shoehorn	ложка (ж)	['lɔʒka]
shoe polish	крем (ч) для взуття	[krɛm dlʲa wzut'tʲa]

38. Textile. Fabrics

cotton (n)	бавовна (ж)	[ba'wɔwna]
cotton (as adj)	з бавовни	[z ba'wɔwnɨ]
flax (n)	льон (ч)	[lʲon]
flax (as adj)	з льону	[z lʲonu]

silk (n)	шовк (ч)	['ʃɔwk]
silk (as adj)	шовковий	[ʃow'kɔwij]
wool (n)	вовна (ж)	['wɔwna]
wool (as adj)	вовняний	['wɔwnʲanij]

velvet	оксамит (ч)	[oksa'mit]
suede	замша (ж)	['zamʃa]
corduroy	вельвет (ч)	[wɛlʲ'wɛt]

nylon (n)	нейлон (ч)	[nɛj'lɔn]
nylon (as adj)	з нейлону	[z nɛj'lɔnu]
polyester (n)	поліестр (ч)	[poli'ɛstr]
polyester (as adj)	поліестровий	[poli'ɛstrowij]

leather (n)	шкіра (ж)	['ʃkira]
leather (as adj)	зі шкіри	[zi 'ʃkiri]
fur (n)	хутро (с)	['hutro]
fur (e.g. ~ coat)	хутряний	[hu'trʲanij]

39. Personal accessories

gloves	рукавички (мн)	[ruka'witʃki]
mittens	рукавиці (мн)	[ruka'witsi]
scarf (muffler)	шарф (ч)	[ʃarf]

glasses	окуляри (мн)	[oku'lʲari]
frame (eyeglass ~)	оправа (ж)	[op'rawa]
umbrella	парасолька (ж)	[para'sɔlʲka]
walking stick	ціпок (ч)	[tsi'pɔk]
hairbrush	щітка (ж) для волосся	['ɕitka dlʲa wo'lɔssʲa]
fan	віяло (с)	['wiʲalo]

tie (necktie)	краватка (ж)	[kra'watka]
bow tie	краватка-метелик (ж)	[kra'watka mɛ'tɛlik]
braces	шлейки (мн)	['ʃlɛjki]
handkerchief	носовичок (ч)	[nosowi'tʃɔk]

comb	гребінець (ч)	[hrɛbi'nɛts]
hair slide	заколка (ж)	[za'kɔlka]
hairpin	шпилька (ж)	['ʃpilʲka]
buckle	пряжка (ж)	['prʲaʒka]

belt	пасок (ч)	['pasok]
shoulder strap	ремінь (ч)	['rɛminʲ]
bag (handbag)	сумка (ж)	['sumka]
handbag	сумочка (ж)	['sumotʃka]
rucksack	рюкзак (ч)	[rʲuk'zak]

40. Clothing. Miscellaneous

fashion	мода (ж)	['mɔda]
in vogue (adj)	модний	['mɔdnij]
fashion designer	модельєр (ч)	[modɛ'ljɛr]
collar	комір (ч)	['kɔmir]
pocket	кишеня (ж)	[kiˈʃɛnʲa]
pocket (as adj)	кишеньковий	[kiʃɛnʲˈkɔwij]
sleeve	рукав (ч)	[ru'kaw]
hanging loop	петелька (ж)	[pɛ'tɛlʲka]
flies (on trousers)	ширінка (ж)	[ʃi'rinka]
zip (fastener)	змійка (ж)	['zmijka]
fastener	застібка (ж)	['zastibka]
button	ґудзик (ч)	['gudzik]
buttonhole	петля (ж)	[pɛt'lʲa]
to come off (ab. button)	відірватися	[widir'watisʲa]
to sew (vi, vt)	шити	['ʃiti]
to embroider (vi, vt)	вишивати	[wiʃi'wati]
embroidery	вишивка (ж)	['wiʃiwka]
sewing needle	голка (ж)	['ɦɔlka]
thread	нитка (ж)	['nitka]
seam	шов (ч)	[ʃow]
to get dirty (vi)	забруднитися	[zabrud'nitisʲa]
stain (mark, spot)	пляма (ж)	['plʲama]
to crease, to crumple	пом'ятися	[po'mʲatisʲa]
to tear, to rip (vt)	порвати	[por'wati]
clothes moth	міль (ж)	[milʲ]

41. Personal care. Cosmetics

toothpaste	зубна паста (ж)	[zub'na 'pasta]
toothbrush	зубна щітка (ж)	[zub'na 'ɕitka]
to clean one's teeth	чистити зуби	['tʃistiti 'zubi]
razor	бритва (ж)	['britwa]
shaving cream	крем (ч) для гоління	[krɛm dlʲa ɦo'linʲa]
to shave (vi)	голитися	[ɦo'litisʲa]
soap	мило (с)	['milo]
shampoo	шампунь (ч)	[ʃam'punʲ]
scissors	ножиці (мн)	['nɔʒitsi]

nail file	пилочка (ж) для нігтів	['pɪlotʃka dlʲa 'niɦtiw]
nail clippers	щипчики (мн)	['ɕiptʃiki]
tweezers	пінцет (ч)	[pin'tsɛt]

cosmetics	косметика (ж)	[kos'mɛtika]
face mask	маска (ж)	['maska]
manicure	манікюр (ч)	[mani'kʲur]
to have a manicure	робити манікюр	[ro'biti mani'kʲur]
pedicure	педикюр (ч)	[pɛdi'kʲur]

make-up bag	косметичка (ж)	[kosmɛ'titʃka]
face powder	пудра (ж)	['pudra]
powder compact	пудрениця (ж)	['pudrɛnitsʲa]
blusher	рум'яна (мн)	[ru'mʲʲana]

perfume (bottled)	парфуми (мн)	[par'fumi]
toilet water (lotion)	туалетна вода (ж)	[tua'lɛtna wo'da]
lotion	лосьйон (ч)	[lo'sjon]
cologne	одеколон (ч)	[odɛko'lɔn]

eyeshadow	тіні (мн) для повік	['tini dlʲa po'wik]
eyeliner	олівець (ч) для очей	[oli'wɛts dlʲa o'tʃɛj]
mascara	туш (ж)	[tuʃ]

lipstick	губна помада (ж)	[ɦub'na po'mada]
nail polish	лак (ч) для нігтів	[lak dlʲa 'niɦtiw]
hair spray	лак (ч) для волосся	[lak dlʲa wo'lɔssʲa]
deodorant	дезодорант (ч)	[dɛzodo'rant]

cream	крем (ч)	[krɛm]
face cream	крем (ч) для обличчя	[krɛm dlʲa ob'litʃʲa]
hand cream	крем (ч) для рук	[krɛm dlʲa ruk]
anti-wrinkle cream	крем (ч) проти зморшок	[krɛm 'prɔti 'zmɔrʃok]
day (as adj)	денний	['dɛnij]
night (as adj)	нічний	[nitʃ'nij]

tampon	тампон (ч)	[tam'pɔn]
toilet paper (toilet roll)	туалетний папір (ч)	[tua'lɛtnij pa'pir]
hair dryer	фен (ч)	[fɛn]

42. Jewellery

jewellery, jewels	коштовність (ж)	[koʃ'tɔwnistʲ]
precious (e.g. ~ stone)	коштовний	[koʃ'tɔwnij]
hallmark stamp	проба (ж)	['prɔba]

ring	каблучка (ж)	[kab'lutʃka]
wedding ring	обручка (ж)	[ob'rutʃka]
bracelet	браслет (ч)	[bras'lɛt]

earrings	сережки (мн)	[sɛ'rɛʒki]
necklace (~ of pearls)	намисто (с)	[na'misto]
crown	корона (ж)	[ko'rɔna]
bead necklace	буси (мн)	['busi]

diamond	діамант (ч)	[dia'mant]
emerald	смарагд (ч)	[sma'raɦd]
ruby	рубін (ч)	[ru'bin]
sapphire	сапфір (ч)	[sap'fir]
pearl	перли (мн)	['pɛrli]
amber	бурштин (ч)	[burʃ'tin]

43. Watches. Clocks

watch (wristwatch)	годинник (ч)	[ɦo'dinik]
dial	циферблат (ч)	[ʦifɛrb'lat]
hand (clock, watch)	стрілка (ж)	['strilka]
metal bracelet	браслет (ч)	[bras'lɛt]
watch strap	ремінець (ч)	[rɛmi'nɛʦ]

battery	батарейка (ж)	[bata'rɛjka]
to be flat (battery)	сісти	['sisti]
to change a battery	поміняти батарейку	[pomi'nʲati bata'rɛjku]
to run fast	поспішати	[pospi'ʃati]
to run slow	відставати	[widsta'wati]

wall clock	годинник (ч)	[ɦo'dinik]
hourglass	годинник (ч) пісковий	[ɦo'dinik pis'kɔwij]
sundial	годинник (ч) сонячний	[ɦo'dinik 'sɔnʲatʃnij]
alarm clock	будильник (ч)	[bu'dilʲnik]
watchmaker	годинникар (ч)	[ɦodini'kar]
to repair (vt)	ремонтувати	[rɛmontu'wati]

Food. Nutricion

meat	м'ясо (с)	['m^jaso]
chicken	курка (ж)	['kurka]
poussin	курча (с)	[kur'tʃa]
duck	качка (ж)	['katʃka]
goose	гусак (ч)	[ɦu'sak]
game	дичина (ж)	[ditʃi'na]
turkey	індичка (ж)	[in'ditʃka]

pork	свинина (ж)	[swi'nina]
veal	телятина (ж)	[tɛ'l^jatina]
lamb	баранина (ж)	[ba'ranina]
beef	яловичина (ж)	['^jalowitʃina]
rabbit	кріль (ч)	[kril^j]

sausage (bologna, etc.)	ковбаса (ж)	[kowba'sa]
vienna sausage (frankfurter)	сосиска (ж)	[so'siska]
bacon	бекон (ч)	[bɛ'kɔn]
ham	шинка (ж)	['ʃinka]
gammon	окіст (ч)	['ɔkist]

pâté	паштет (ч)	[paʃ'tɛt]
liver	печінка (ж)	[pɛ'tʃinka]
mince (minced meat)	фарш (ч)	[farʃ]
tongue	язик (ч)	[ja'zik]

egg	яйце (с)	[jaj'tsɛ]
eggs	яйця (мн)	['^jajts^ja]
egg white	білок (ч)	[bi'lɔk]
egg yolk	жовток (ч)	[ʒow'tɔk]

fish	риба (ж)	['riba]
seafood	морепродукти (мн)	[morɛpro'dukti]
caviar	ікра (ж)	[ik'ra]

crab	краб (ч)	[krab]
prawn	креветка (ж)	[krɛ'wɛtka]
oyster	устриця (ж)	['ustrits^ja]
spiny lobster	лангуст (ч)	[lan'ɦust]
octopus	восьминіг (ч)	[wos^jmi'niɦ]
squid	кальмар (ч)	[kal^j'mar]

sturgeon	осетрина (ж)	[osɛt'rina]
salmon	лосось (ч)	[lo'sɔs^j]
halibut	палтус (ч)	['paltus]
cod	тріска (ж)	[tris'ka]
mackerel	скумбрія (ж)	['skumbri^ja]

tuna	тунець (ч)	[tu'nɛʦ]
eel	вугор (ч)	[wu'ɦɔr]
trout	форель (ж)	[fo'rɛlʲ]
sardine	сардина (ж)	[sar'dina]
pike	щука (ж)	[ɕuka]
herring	оселедець (ч)	[osɛ'lɛdɛʦ]
bread	хліб (ч)	[hlib]
cheese	сир (ч)	[sir]
sugar	цукор (ч)	['ʦukor]
salt	сіль (ж)	[silʲ]
rice	рис (ч)	[ris]
pasta (macaroni)	макарони (мн)	[maka'rɔni]
noodles	локшина (ж)	[lokʃi'na]
butter	вершкове масло (с)	[wɛrʃ'kɔwɛ 'maslo]
vegetable oil	олія (ж) рослинна	[o'liʲa ros'lina]
sunflower oil	соняшникова олія (ж)	['sɔnʲaʃnikowa o'liʲa]
margarine	маргарин (ч)	[marɦa'rin]
olives	оливки (мн)	[o'liwki]
olive oil	олія (ж) оливкова	[o'liʲa o'liwkowa]
milk	молоко (с)	[molo'kɔ]
condensed milk	згущене молоко (с)	['zɦuɕɛnɛ molo'kɔ]
yogurt	йогурт (ч)	['jɔɦurt]
soured cream	сметана (ж)	[smɛ'tana]
cream (of milk)	вершки (мн)	[wɛrʃ'ki]
mayonnaise	майонез (ч)	[maʲo'nɛz]
buttercream	крем (ч)	[krɛm]
groats (barley ~, etc.)	крупа (ж)	[kru'pa]
flour	борошно (с)	['bɔroʃno]
tinned food	консерви (мн)	[kon'sɛrwi]
cornflakes	кукурудзяні пластівці (мн)	[kuku'rudzʲani plastiw'ʦi]
honey	мед (ч)	[mɛd]
jam	джем (ч)	[dʒɛm]
chewing gum	жувальна гумка (ж)	[ʒu'walʲna 'ɦumka]

45. Drinks

water	вода (ж)	[wo'da]
drinking water	питна вода (ж)	[pit'na wo'da]
mineral water	мінеральна вода (ж)	[minɛ'ralʲna wo'da]
still (adj)	без газу	[bɛz 'ɦazu]
carbonated (adj)	газований	[ɦa'zɔwanij]
sparkling (adj)	з газом	[z 'ɦazom]
ice	лід (ч)	[lid]
with ice	з льодом	[z lʲodom]

non-alcoholic (adj)	безалкогольний	[bɛzalko'ɦɔlʲnij]
soft drink	безалкогольний напій (ч)	[bɛzalko'ɦɔlʲnij na'pij]
refreshing drink	прохолодній напій (ч)	[proho'lɔdnij na'pij]
lemonade	лимонад (ч)	[limo'nad]

spirits	алкогольні напої (мн)	[alko'ɦɔlʲni na'pɔji]
wine	вино (с)	[wi'nɔ]
white wine	біле вино (с)	['bilɛ wi'nɔ]
red wine	червоне вино (с)	[ʧɛr'wɔnɛ wi'nɔ]

liqueur	лікер (ч)	[li'kɛr]
champagne	шампанське (с)	[ʃam'pansʲkɛ]
vermouth	вермут (ч)	['wɛrmut]

whisky	віскі (с)	['wiski]
vodka	горілка (ж)	[ɦo'rilka]
gin	джин (ч)	[dʒin]
cognac	коньяк (ч)	[ko'nʲak]
rum	ром (ч)	[rom]

coffee	кава (ж)	['kawa]
black coffee	чорна кава (ж)	['ʧɔrna 'kawa]
white coffee	кава (ж) з молоком	['kawa z molo'kɔm]
cappuccino	кава (ж) з вершками	['kawa z wɛrʃkami]
instant coffee	розчинна кава (ж)	[roz'ʧina 'kawa]

milk	молоко (с)	[molo'kɔ]
cocktail	коктейль (ч)	[kok'tɛjlʲ]
milkshake	молочний коктейль (ч)	[mo'lɔʧnij kok'tɛjlʲ]

juice	сік (ч)	[sik]
tomato juice	томатний сік (ч)	[to'matnij 'sik]
orange juice	апельсиновий сік (ч)	[apɛlʲ'sinowij sik]
freshly squeezed juice	свіжовижатий сік (ч)	[swiʐo'wiʐatij sik]

beer	пиво (с)	['piwo]
lager	світле пиво (с)	['switlɛ 'piwo]
bitter	темне пиво (с)	['tɛmnɛ 'piwo]

tea	чай (ч)	[ʧaj]
black tea	чорний чай (ч)	['ʧɔrnij ʧaj]
green tea	зелений чай (ч)	[zɛ'lɛnij ʧaj]

46. Vegetables

| vegetables | овочі (мн) | ['ɔwoʧi] |
| greens | зелень (ж) | ['zɛlɛnʲ] |

tomato	помідор (ч)	[pomi'dɔr]
cucumber	огірок (ч)	[oɦi'rɔk]
carrot	морква (ж)	['mɔrkwa]
potato	картопля (ж)	[kar'tɔplʲa]
onion	цибуля (ж)	[ʦi'bulʲa]
garlic	часник (ч)	[ʧas'nik]

cabbage	капуста (ж)	[ka'pusta]
cauliflower	кольорова капуста (ж)	[kolʲoˈrɔwa ka'pusta]
Brussels sprouts	брюссельська капуста (ж)	[brʲuˈsɛlʲsʲka ka'pusta]
broccoli	капуста броколі (ж)	[ka'pusta 'brɔkoli]
beetroot	буряк (ч)	[buˈrʲak]
aubergine	баклажан (ч)	[bakla'ʒan]
courgette	кабачок (ч)	[kabaˈʧɔk]
pumpkin	гарбуз (ч)	[ɦarˈbuz]
turnip	ріпа (ж)	['ripa]
parsley	петрушка (ж)	[pɛt'ruʃka]
dill	кріп (ч)	[krip]
lettuce	салат (ч)	[sa'lat]
celery	селера (ж)	[sɛ'lɛra]
asparagus	спаржа (ж)	['sparʒa]
spinach	шпинат (ч)	[ʃpiˈnat]
pea	горох (ч)	[ɦoˈrɔh]
beans	боби (мн)	[bo'bi]
maize	кукурудза (ж)	[kuku'rudza]
kidney bean	квасоля (ж)	[kwa'sɔlʲa]
sweet paper	перець (ч)	['pɛrɛʦ]
radish	редька (ж)	['rɛdʲka]
artichoke	артишок (ч)	[arti'ʃɔk]

47. Fruits. Nuts

fruit	фрукт (ч)	[frukt]
apple	яблуко (с)	['ʲabluko]
pear	груша (ж)	['ɦruʃa]
lemon	лимон (ч)	[li'mɔn]
orange	апельсин (ч)	[apɛlʲˈsin]
strawberry (garden ~)	полуниця (ж)	[polu'niʦʲa]
tangerine	мандарин (ч)	[manda'rin]
plum	слива (ж)	['sliwa]
peach	персик (ч)	['pɛrsik]
apricot	абрикос (ч)	[abri'kɔs]
raspberry	малина (ж)	[ma'lina]
pineapple	ананас (ч)	[ana'nas]
banana	банан (ч)	[ba'nan]
watermelon	кавун (ч)	[ka'wun]
grape	виноград (ч)	[wino'ɦrad]
sour cherry	вишня (ж)	['wiʃnʲa]
sweet cherry	черешня (ж)	[ʧɛ'rɛʃnʲa]
melon	диня (ж)	['dinʲa]
grapefruit	грейпфрут (ч)	[ɦrɛjpˈfrut]
avocado	авокадо (с)	[awo'kado]
papaya	папайя (ж)	[pa'paʲa]
mango	манго (с)	['manɦo]

pomegranate	гранат (ч)	[ɦraˈnat]
redcurrant	порічки (мн)	[poˈritʃki]
blackcurrant	чорна смородина (ж)	[ˈtʃɔrna smoˈrɔdina]
gooseberry	аґрус (ч)	[ˈagrus]
bilberry	чорниця (ж)	[tʃorˈnitsʲa]
blackberry	ожина (ж)	[oˈʒina]

raisin	родзинки (мн)	[roˈdzinki]
fig	інжир (ч)	[inˈʒir]
date	фінік (ч)	[ˈfinik]

peanut	арахіс (ч)	[aˈrahis]
almond	мигдаль (ч)	[miɦˈdalʲ]
walnut	горіх (ч) волоський	[ɦoˈrih woˈlɔsʲkij]
hazelnut	ліщина (ж)	[liˈɕina]
coconut	горіх (ч) кокосовий	[ɦoˈrih koˈkɔsowij]
pistachios	фісташки (мн)	[fisˈtaʃki]

48. Bread. Sweets

bakers' confectionery (pastry)	кондитерські вироби (мн)	[konˈditɛrsʲki ˈwirobi]
bread	хліб (ч)	[hlib]
biscuits	печиво (с)	[ˈpɛtʃiwo]

chocolate (n)	шоколад (ч)	[ʃokoˈlad]
chocolate (as adj)	шоколадний	[ʃokoˈladnij]
candy (wrapped)	цукерка (ж)	[tsuˈkɛrka]
cake (e.g. cupcake)	тістечко (с)	[ˈtistɛtʃko]
cake (e.g. birthday ~)	торт (ч)	[tort]

| pie (e.g. apple ~) | пиріг (ч) | [piˈriɦ] |
| filling (for cake, pie) | начинка (ж) | [naˈtʃinka] |

jam (whole fruit jam)	варення (с)	[waˈrɛnʲa]
marmalade	мармелад (ч)	[marmɛˈlad]
wafers	вафлі (мн)	[ˈwafli]
ice-cream	морозиво (с)	[moˈrɔziwo]

49. Cooked dishes

course, dish	страва (ж)	[ˈstrawa]
cuisine	кухня (ж)	[ˈkuhnʲa]
recipe	рецепт (ч)	[rɛˈtsɛpt]
portion	порція (ж)	[ˈpɔrtsiʲa]

| salad | салат (ч) | [saˈlat] |
| soup | юшка (ж) | [ˈʲuʃka] |

clear soup (broth)	бульйон (ч)	[bulʲon]
sandwich (bread)	канапка (ж)	[kaˈnapka]
fried eggs	яєчня (ж)	[jaˈɛnʲa]
hamburger (beefburger)	гамбургер (ч)	[ˈɦamburɦɛr]

beefsteak	біфштекс (ч)	[bif'ʃtɛks]
side dish	гарнір (ч)	[har'nir]
spaghetti	спагеті (мн)	[spa'hɛti]
mash	картопляне пюре (с)	[kartop'lʲanɛ pʲu'rɛ]
pizza	піца (ж)	['pitsa]
porridge (oatmeal, etc.)	каша (ж)	['kaʃa]
omelette	омлет (ч)	[om'lɛt]
boiled (e.g. ~ beef)	варений	[wa'rɛnij]
smoked (adj)	копчений	[kop'tʃɛnij]
fried (adj)	смажений	['smaʒɛnij]
dried (adj)	сушений	['suʃɛnij]
frozen (adj)	заморожений	[zamo'rɔʒɛnij]
pickled (adj)	маринований	[mari'nɔwanij]
sweet (sugary)	солодкий	[so'lɔdkij]
salty (adj)	солоний	[so'lɔnij]
cold (adj)	холодний	[ho'lɔdnij]
hot (adj)	гарячий	[ha'rʲatʃij]
bitter (adj)	гіркий	[hir'kij]
tasty (adj)	смачний	[smatʃ'nij]
to cook in boiling water	варити	[wa'riti]
to cook (dinner)	готувати	[hotu'wati]
to fry (vt)	смажити	['smaʒiti]
to heat up (food)	розігрівати	[rozihri'wati]
to salt (vt)	солити	[so'liti]
to pepper (vt)	перчити	[pɛr'tʃiti]
to grate (vt)	терти	['tɛrti]
peel (n)	шкірка (ж)	['ʃkirka]
to peel (vt)	чистити	['tʃistiti]

50. Spices

salt	сіль (ж)	[silʲ]
salty (adj)	солоний	[so'lɔnij]
to salt (vt)	солити	[so'liti]
black pepper	чорний перець (ч)	['tʃɔrnij 'pɛrɛts]
red pepper (milled ~)	червоний перець (ч)	[tʃɛr'wɔnij 'pɛrɛts]
mustard	гірчиця (ж)	[hir'tʃitsʲa]
horseradish	хрін (ч)	[hrin]
condiment	приправа (ж)	[prip'rawa]
spice	прянощі (мн)	[prʲa'nɔci]
sauce	соус (ч)	['sɔus]
vinegar	оцет (ч)	['ɔtsɛt]
anise	аніс (ч)	['anis]
basil	базилік (ч)	[bazi'lik]
cloves	гвоздика (ж)	[hwoz'dika]
ginger	імбир (ч)	[im'bir]
coriander	коріандр (ч)	[kori'andr]

cinnamon	кориця (ж)	[ko'ritsʲa]
sesame	кунжут (ч)	[kun'ʒut]
bay leaf	лавровий лист (ч)	[law'rɔwij list]
paprika	паприка (ж)	['paprika]
caraway	кмин (ч)	[kmin]
saffron	шафран (ч)	[ʃafʲran]

51. Meals

| food | їжа (ж) | ['jiʒa] |
| to eat (vi, vt) | їсти | ['jisti] |

breakfast	сніданок (ч)	[sni'danok]
to have breakfast	снідати	['snidati]
lunch	обід (ч)	[o'bid]
to have lunch	обідати	[o'bidati]
dinner	вечеря (ж)	[wɛ'ʧɛrʲa]
to have dinner	вечеряти	[wɛ'ʧɛrʲati]

| appetite | апетит (ч) | [apɛ'tit] |
| Enjoy your meal! | Смачного! | [smaʧ'nɔho] |

to open (~ a bottle)	відкривати	[widkri'wati]
to spill (liquid)	пролити	[pro'liti]
to spill out (vi)	пролитись	[pro'litisʲ]
to boil (vi)	кипіти	[ki'piti]
to boil (vt)	кип'ятити	[kipʲa'titi]
boiled (~ water)	кип'ячений	[kipʲa'ʧɛnij]
to chill, cool down (vt)	охолодити	[oholo'diti]
to chill (vi)	охолоджуватись	[oho'lɔdʒuwatisʲ]

| taste, flavour | смак (ч) | [smak] |
| aftertaste | присмак (ч) | ['prismak] |

to slim down (lose weight)	худнути	['hudnuti]
diet	дієта (ж)	[di'ɛta]
vitamin	вітамін (ч)	[wita'min]
calorie	калорія (ж)	[ka'lɔrʲia]
vegetarian (n)	вегетаріанець (ч)	[wɛɦɛtari'anɛts]
vegetarian (adj)	вегетаріанський	[wɛɦɛtari'ansʲkij]

fats (nutrient)	жири (мн)	[ʒi'ri]
proteins	білки (мн)	[bil'ki]
carbohydrates	вуглеводи (ч)	[wuɦlɛ'wɔdi]
slice (of lemon, ham)	скибка (ж)	['skibka]
piece (of cake, pie)	шматок (ч)	[ʃma'tɔk]
crumb (of bread, cake, etc.)	крихта (ж)	['krihta]

52. Table setting

| spoon | ложка (ж) | ['lɔʒka] |
| knife | ніж (ч) | [niʒ] |

fork	виделка (ж)	[wi'dɛlka]
cup (e.g., coffee ~)	чашка (ж)	['ʧaʃka]
plate (dinner ~)	тарілка (ж)	[ta'rilka]
saucer	блюдце (с)	['blʲudtsɛ]
serviette	серветка (ж)	[sɛr'wɛtka]
toothpick	зубочистка (ж)	[zubo'ʧistka]

53. Restaurant

restaurant	ресторан (ч)	[rɛsto'ran]
coffee bar	кав'ярня (ж)	[ka'w'ʲarnʲa]
pub, bar	бар (ч)	[bar]
tearoom	чайна (ж)	['ʧajna]

waiter	офіціант (ч)	[ofitsi'ant]
waitress	офіціантка (ж)	[ofitsi'antka]
barman	бармен (ч)	[bar'mɛn]

menu	меню (с)	[mɛ'nʲu]
wine list	карта (ж) вин	['karta win]
to book a table	забронювати столик	[zabronʲu'wati 'stɔlik]

course, dish	страва (ж)	['strawa]
to order (meal)	замовити	[za'mɔwiti]
to make an order	зробити замовлення	[zro'biti za'mɔwlɛnʲa]

aperitif	аперитив (ч)	[apɛri'tiw]
starter	закуска (ж)	[za'kuska]
dessert, pudding	десерт (ч)	[dɛ'sɛrt]

bill	рахунок (ч)	[ra'hunok]
to pay the bill	оплатити рахунок	[opla'titi ra'hunok]
to give change	дати решту	['dati 'rɛʃtu]
tip	чайові (мн)	[ʧaʲo'wi]

Family, relatives and friends

54. Personal information. Forms

name (first name)	**ім'я** (с)	[i'm'ʲa]
surname (last name)	**прізвище** (с)	['prizwiɕɛ]
date of birth	**дата** (ж) **народження**	['data na'rɔdʒɛnʲa]
place of birth	**місце** (с) **народження**	['mistsɛ na'rɔdʒɛnʲa]
nationality	**національність** (ж)	[natsio'nalʲnistʲ]
place of residence	**місце** (с) **проживання**	['mistsɛ proʒi'wanʲa]
country	**країна** (ж)	[kra'jina]
profession (occupation)	**професія** (ж)	[pro'fɛsiʲa]
gender, sex	**стать** (ж)	[statʲ]
height	**зріст** (ч)	[zrist]
weight	**вага** (ж)	[wa'ɦa]

55. Family members. Relatives

mother	**мати** (ж)	['mati]
father	**батько** (ч)	['batʲko]
son	**син** (ч)	[sin]
daughter	**дочка** (ж)	[dotʃ'ka]
younger daughter	**молодша дочка** (ж)	[mo'lɔdʃa dotʃ'ka]
younger son	**молодший син** (ч)	[mo'lɔdʃij sin]
eldest daughter	**старша дочка** (ж)	['starʃa dotʃ'ka]
eldest son	**старший син** (ч)	['starʃij sin]
brother	**брат** (ч)	[brat]
sister	**сестра** (ж)	[sɛst'ra]
cousin (masc.)	**двоюрідний брат** (ч)	[dwoʲu'ridnij brat]
cousin (fem.)	**двоюрідна сестра** (ж)	[dwoʲu'ridna sɛst'ra]
mummy	**мати** (ж)	['mati]
dad, daddy	**тато** (ч)	['tato]
parents	**батьки** (мн)	[batʲ'ki]
child	**дитина** (ж)	[di'tina]
children	**діти** (мн)	['diti]
grandmother	**бабуся** (ж)	[ba'busʲa]
grandfather	**дід** (ч)	['did]
grandson	**онук** (ч)	[o'nuk]
granddaughter	**онука** (ж)	[o'nuka]
grandchildren	**онуки** (мн)	[o'nuki]
uncle	**дядько** (ч)	['dʲadʲko]
aunt	**тітка** (ж)	['titka]

nephew	племінник (ч)	[plɛ'minik]
niece	племінниця (ж)	[plɛ'minitsʲa]
mother-in-law (wife's mother)	теща (ж)	['tɛɕa]
father-in-law (husband's father)	свекор (ч)	['swɛkor]
son-in-law (daughter's husband)	зять (ч)	[zʲatʲ]
stepmother	мачуха (ж)	['matʃuha]
stepfather	вітчим (ч)	['witʃim]
infant	немовля (с)	[nɛmow'lʲa]
baby (infant)	немовля (с)	[nɛmow'lʲa]
little boy, kid	малюк (ч)	[ma'lʲuk]
wife	дружина (ж)	[dru'ʒina]
husband	чоловік (ч)	[tʃolo'wik]
spouse (husband)	чоловік (ч)	[tʃolo'wik]
spouse (wife)	дружина (ж)	[dru'ʒina]
married (masc.)	одружений	[od'ruʒɛnij]
married (fem.)	заміжня	[za'miʒnʲa]
single (unmarried)	холостий	[holos'tij]
bachelor	холостяк (ч)	[holos'tʲak]
divorced (masc.)	розведений	[roz'wɛdɛnij]
widow	вдова (ж)	[wdo'wa]
widower	вдівець (ч)	[wdi'wɛts]
relative	родич (ч)	['roditʃ]
close relative	близький родич (ч)	[bliz'kij 'roditʃ]
distant relative	далекий родич (ч)	[da'lɛkij 'roditʃ]
relatives	рідні (мн)	['ridni]
orphan (boy or girl)	сирота (ч)	[siro'ta]
guardian (of a minor)	опікун (ч)	[opi'kun]
to adopt (a boy)	усиновити	[usino'witi]
to adopt (a girl)	удочерити	[udotʃɛ'riti]

56. Friends. Colleagues

friend (masc.)	товариш (ч)	[to'wariʃ]
friend (fem.)	подруга (ж)	['podruɦa]
friendship	дружба (ж)	['druʒba]
to be friends	дружити	[dru'ʒiti]
pal (masc.)	приятель (ч)	['prijatɛlʲ]
pal (fem.)	приятелька (ж)	['prijatɛlʲka]
partner	партнер (ч)	[part'nɛr]
chief (boss)	шеф (ч)	[ʃɛf]
superior (n)	начальник (ч)	[na'tʃalʲnik]
subordinate (n)	підлеглий (ч)	[pid'lɛɦlij]
colleague	колега (ч)	[ko'lɛɦa]

acquaintance (person)	знайомий (ч)	[zna'jɔmij]
fellow traveller	попутник (ч)	[po'putnik]
classmate	однокласник (ч)	[odno'klasnik]

neighbour (masc.)	сусід (ч)	[su'sid]
neighbour (fem.)	сусідка (ж)	[su'sidka]
neighbours	сусіди (мн)	[su'sidɨ]

57. Man. Woman

woman	жінка (ж)	['ʒinka]
girl (young woman)	дівчина (ж)	['diwtʃina]
bride	наречена (ж)	[narɛ'tʃɛna]

beautiful (adj)	гарна	['ɦarna]
tall (adj)	висока	[wi'sɔka]
slender (adj)	струнка	[stru'nka]
short (adj)	невисокого зросту	[nɛwi'sɔkoɦo 'zrɔstu]

| blonde (n) | блондинка (ж) | [blon'dinka] |
| brunette (n) | брюнетка (ж) | [brʲu'nɛtka] |

ladies' (adj)	дамський	['damsʲkij]
virgin (girl)	незаймана дівчина (ж)	[nɛ'zajmana 'diwtʃina]
pregnant (adj)	вагітна	[wa'ɦitna]

man (adult male)	чоловік (ч)	[tʃolo'wik]
blonde haired man	блондин (ч)	[blon'din]
dark haired man	брюнет (ч)	[brʲu'nɛt]
tall (adj)	високий	[wi'sɔkij]
short (adj)	невисокого зросту	[nɛwi'sɔkoɦo 'zrɔstu]

rude (rough)	брутальний	[bru'talʲnij]
stocky (adj)	кремезний	[krɛ'mɛznij]
robust (adj)	міцний	[mits'nij]
strong (adj)	сильний	['silʲnij]
strength	сила (ж)	['sila]

plump, fat (adj)	повний	['pɔwnij]
swarthy (dark-skinned)	смаглявий	[smaɦ'lʲawij]
slender (well-built)	стрункий	[stru'nkij]
elegant (adj)	елегантний	[ɛlɛ'ɦantnij]

58. Age

age	вік (ч)	[wik]
youth (young age)	юність (ж)	['ʲunistʲ]
young (adj)	молодий	[molo'dij]

younger (adj)	молодший	[mo'lɔdʃij]
older (adj)	старший	['starʃij]
young man	юнак (ч)	[ʲu'nak]

| teenager | підліток (ч) | ['pidlitok] |
| guy, fellow | хлопець (ч) | ['hlɔpɛts] |

| old man | старий (ч) | [sta'rij] |
| old woman | стара (ж) | [sta'ra] |

| adult (adj) | дорослий | [do'rɔslij] |
| middle-aged (adj) | середніх років | [sɛ'rɛdnih ro'kiw] |

| elderly (adj) | похилий | [po'hilij] |
| old (adj) | старий | [sta'rij] |

retirement	пенсія (ж)	['pɛnsiʲa]
to retire (from job)	вийти на пенсію	['wijti na 'pɛnsiʲu]
retiree, pensioner	пенсіонер (ч)	[pɛnsio'nɛr]

59. Children

child	дитина (ж)	[di'tina]
children	діти (мн)	['diti]
twins	близнюки (мн)	[blizn'u'ki]

cradle	колиска (ж)	[ko'liska]
rattle	брязкальце (с)	['brʲazkalʲtsɛ]
nappy	підгузок (ч)	[pid'ɦuzok]

| dummy, comforter | соска (ж) | ['sɔska] |
| pram | коляска (ж) | [ko'lʲaska] |

| nursery | дитячий садок (ч) | [di'tʲatʃij sa'dɔk] |
| babysitter | няня (ж) | ['nʲanʲa] |

| childhood | дитинство (с) | [di'tinstwo] |
| doll | лялька (ж) | ['lʲalʲka] |

| toy | іграшка (ж) | ['iɦraʃka] |
| construction set (toy) | конструктор (ч) | [kon'struktor] |

well-bred (adj)	вихований	['wihowanij]
ill-bred (adj)	невихований	[nɛ'wihowanij]
spoilt (adj)	розбещений	[roz'bɛɕɛnij]

| to be naughty | бешкетувати | [bɛʃkɛtu'wati] |
| mischievous (adj) | пустотливий | [pustot'liwij] |

| mischievousness | витівка (ж) | ['witiwka] |
| mischievous child | пустун (ч) | [pus'tun] |

| obedient (adj) | слухняний | [sluh'nʲanij] |
| disobedient (adj) | неслухняний | [nɛsluh'nʲanij] |

docile (adj)	розумний	[ro'zumnij]
clever (intelligent)	розумний	[ro'zumnij]
child prodigy	вундеркінд (ч)	[wundɛr'kind]

60. Married couples. Family life

to kiss (vt)	цілувати	[tsilu'wati]
to kiss (vi)	цілуватися	[tsilu'watisʲa]
family (n)	сім'я (ж)	[si'mʲia]
family (as adj)	сімейний	[si'mɛjnij]
couple	пара (ж)	['para]
marriage (state)	шлюб (ч)	[ʃlʲub]
hearth (home)	домашнє вогнище (с)	[do'maʃnɛ 'wɔɦniɕɛ]
dynasty	династія (ж)	[di'nastiʲa]
date	побачення (с)	[po'batʃɛnʲa]
kiss	поцілунок (ч)	[potsi'lunok]
love (for sb)	кохання (с)	[ko'hanʲa]
to love (sb)	кохати	[ko'hati]
beloved	кохана людина (ж)	[ko'hana lʲu'dina]
tenderness	ніжність (ж)	['niʒnistʲ]
tender (affectionate)	ніжний	['niʒnij]
faithfulness	незрадливість (ж)	[nɛzrad'liwistʲ]
faithful (adj)	незрадливий	[nɛzrad'liwij]
care (attention)	турбота (ж)	[tur'bɔta]
caring (~ father)	турботливий	[tur'bɔtliwij]
newlyweds	молодята (мн)	[molo'dʲata]
honeymoon	медовий місяць (ч)	[mɛ'dɔwij 'misʲats]
to get married (ab. woman)	вийти заміж	['wijti 'zamiʒ]
to get married (ab. man)	одружуватися	[od'ruʒuwatisʲa]
wedding	весілля (с)	[wɛ'silʲa]
golden wedding	золоте весілля (с)	[zolo'tɛ wɛ'silʲa]
anniversary	річниця (ж)	[ritʃ'nitsʲa]
lover (masc.)	коханець (ч)	[ko'hanɛts]
mistress (lover)	коханка (ж)	[ko'hanka]
adultery	зрада (ж)	['zrada]
to cheat on ... (commit adultery)	зрадити	['zraditi]
jealous (adj)	ревнивий	[rɛw'niwij]
to be jealous	ревнувати	[rɛwnu'wati]
divorce	розлучення (с)	[roz'lutʃɛnʲa]
to divorce (vi)	розлучитися	[rozlu'tʃitisʲa]
to quarrel (vi)	сваритися	[swa'ritisʲa]
to be reconciled (after an argument)	миритися	[mi'ritisʲa]
together (adv)	разом	['razom]
sex	секс (ч)	[sɛks]
happiness	щастя (с)	['ɕastʲa]
happy (adj)	щасливий	[ɕas'liwij]
misfortune (accident)	нещастя (с)	[nɛ'ɕastʲa]
unhappy (adj)	нещасний	[nɛ'ɕasnij]

Character. Feelings. Emotions

61. Feelings. Emotions

feeling (emotion)	**почуття** (с)	[pot͡ʃutˈtʲa]
feelings	**почуття** (мн)	[pot͡ʃutˈtʲa]
hunger	**голод** (ч)	[ˈɦɔlod]
to be hungry	**хотіти їсти**	[hoˈtiti ˈjisti]
thirst	**спрага** (ж)	[ˈspraɦa]
to be thirsty	**хотіти пити**	[hoˈtiti ˈpiti]
sleepiness	**сонливість** (ж)	[sonˈliwistʲ]
to feel sleepy	**хотіти спати**	[hoˈtiti ˈspati]
tiredness	**втома** (ж)	[ˈwtɔma]
tired (adj)	**втомлений**	[ˈwtɔmlɛnij]
to get tired	**втомитися**	[wtoˈmitisʲa]
mood (humour)	**настрій** (ч)	[ˈnastrij]
boredom	**нудьга** (ж)	[nudʲˈɦa]
to be bored	**нудьгувати**	[nudʲɦuˈwati]
seclusion	**самота** (ж)	[samoˈta]
to seclude oneself	**усамітнюватися**	[usaˈmitnʲuwatisʲa]
to worry (make anxious)	**хвилювати**	[hwilʲuˈwati]
to be worried	**хвилюватися**	[hwilʲuˈwatisʲa]
worrying (n)	**хвилювання** (с)	[hwilʲuˈwanʲa]
anxiety	**занепокоєння** (с)	[zanɛpoˈkɔɛnʲa]
preoccupied (adj)	**занепокоєний**	[zanɛpoˈkɔɛnij]
to be nervous	**нервуватися**	[nɛrwuˈwatisʲa]
to panic (vi)	**панікувати**	[panikuˈwati]
hope	**надія** (ж)	[naˈdiʲa]
to hope (vi, vt)	**сподіватися**	[spodiˈwatisʲa]
certainty	**упевненість** (ж)	[uˈpɛwnɛnistʲ]
certain, sure (adj)	**упевнений**	[uˈpɛwnɛnij]
uncertainty	**непевність** (ж)	[nɛˈpɛwnistʲ]
uncertain (adj)	**невпевнений**	[nɛwˈpɛwnɛnij]
drunk (adj)	**п'яний**	[ˈpʲʲanij]
sober (adj)	**тверезий**	[twɛˈrɛzij]
weak (adj)	**слабкий**	[slabˈkij]
happy (adj)	**щасливий**	[ɕasˈliwij]
to scare (vt)	**налякати**	[nalʲaˈkati]
fury (madness)	**шаленство** (с)	[ʃaˈlɛnstwo]
rage (fury)	**лють** (ж)	[lʲutʲ]
depression	**депресія** (ж)	[dɛˈprɛsiʲa]
discomfort (unease)	**дискомфорт** (ч)	[diskomˈfɔrt]

comfort	комфорт (ч)	[kɔm'fɔrt]
to regret (be sorry)	жалкувати	[ʒalku'wati]
regret	жаль (ч)	[ʒalʲ]
bad luck	невезіння (c)	[nɛwɛ'zinʲa]
sadness	прикрість (ж)	['prikristʲ]

shame (remorse)	сором (ч)	['sɔrom]
gladness	веселість (ж)	[wɛ'sɛlistʲ]
enthusiasm, zeal	ентузіазм (ч)	[ɛntuzi'azm]
enthusiast	ентузіаст (ч)	[ɛntuzi'ast]
to show enthusiasm	проявити ентузіазм	[proja'witi ɛntuzi'azm]

62. Character. Personality

character	характер (ч)	[ha'raktɛr]
character flaw	вада (ж)	['wada]
mind	ум (ч)	[um]
reason	розум (ч)	['rɔzum]

conscience	совість (ж)	['sɔwistʲ]
habit (custom)	звичка (ж)	['zwitʃka]
ability (talent)	здібність (ж)	['zdibnistʲ]
can (e.g. ~ swim)	уміти	[u'miti]

patient (adj)	терплячий	[tɛrp'lʲatʃij]
impatient (adj)	нетерплячий	[nɛtɛr'plʲatʃij]
curious (inquisitive)	допитливий	[do'pitliwij]
curiosity	цікавість (ж)	[tsi'kawistʲ]

modesty	скромність (ж)	['skrɔmnistʲ]
modest (adj)	скромний	['skrɔmnij]
immodest (adj)	нескромний	[nɛ'skrɔmnij]

laziness	лінь (ж)	[linʲ]
lazy (adj)	ледачий	[lɛ'datʃij]
lazy person (masc.)	ледар (ч)	['lɛdar]

cunning (n)	хитрість (ж)	['hitristʲ]
cunning (as adj)	хитрий	['hitrij]
distrust	недовіра (ж)	[nɛdo'wira]
distrustful (adj)	недовірливий	[nɛdo'wirliwij]

generosity	щедрість (ж)	['ɕɛdristʲ]
generous (adj)	щедрий	['ɕɛdrij]
talented (adj)	талановитий	[talano'witij]
talent	талант (ч)	[ta'lant]

courageous (adj)	сміливий	[smi'liwij]
courage	сміливість (ж)	[smi'liwistʲ]
honest (adj)	чесний	['tʃɛsnij]
honesty	чесність (ж)	['tʃɛsnistʲ]

| careful (cautious) | обережний | [obɛ'rɛʒnij] |
| brave (courageous) | відважний | [wid'waʒnij] |

| serious (adj) | серйозний | [sɛrˈoznij] |
| strict (severe, stern) | суворий | [suˈwɔrij] |

decisive (adj)	рішучий	[riˈʃutʃij]
indecisive (adj)	нерішучий	[nɛriˈʃutʃij]
shy, timid (adj)	сором'язливий	[soroˈmʲjazliwij]
shyness, timidity	сором'язливість (ж)	[soroˈmʲjazliwistʲ]

confidence (trust)	довіра (ж)	[doˈwira]
to believe (trust)	вірити	[ˈwiriti]
trusting (credulous)	довірливий	[doˈwirliwij]

sincerely (adv)	щиро	[ˈɕiro]
sincere (adj)	щирий	[ˈɕirij]
sincerity	щирість (ж)	[ˈɕiristʲ]
open (person)	відкритий	[widˈkritij]

calm (adj)	тихий	[ˈtihij]
frank (sincere)	відвертий	[widˈwɛrtij]
naïve (adj)	наївний	[naˈjiwnij]
absent-minded (adj)	неуважний	[nɛuˈwaʒnij]
funny (odd)	кумедний	[kuˈmɛdnij]

greed, stinginess	жадібність (ж)	[ˈʒadibnistʲ]
greedy, stingy (adj)	жадібний	[ˈʒadibnij]
stingy (adj)	скупий	[skuˈpij]
evil (adj)	злий	[ˈzlij]
stubborn (adj)	впертий	[ˈwpɛrtij]
unpleasant (adj)	неприємний	[nɛpriˈɛmnij]

selfish person (masc.)	егоїст (ч)	[ɛɦoˈjist]
selfish (adj)	егоїстичний	[ɛɦojisˈtitʃnij]
coward	боягуз (ч)	[bojaˈɦuz]
cowardly (adj)	боягузливий	[bojaˈɦuzliwij]

63. Sleep. Dreams

to sleep (vi)	спати	[ˈspati]
sleep, sleeping	сон (ч)	[son]
dream	сон (ч)	[son]
to dream (in sleep)	бачити сни	[ˈbatʃiti sni]
sleepy (adj)	сонний	[ˈsɔnij]

bed	ліжко (с)	[ˈliʒko]
mattress	матрац (ч)	[matˈrats]
blanket (eiderdown)	ковдра (ж)	[ˈkɔwdra]
pillow	подушка (ж)	[poˈduʃka]
sheet	простирадло (с)	[prostiˈradlo]

insomnia	безсоння (с)	[bɛzˈsɔnʲa]
sleepless (adj)	безсонний	[bɛzˈsɔnij]
sleeping pill	снодійне (с)	[snoˈdijnɛ]
to take a sleeping pill	прийняти снодійне	[prijˈnʲati snoˈdijnɛ]
to feel sleepy	хотіти спати	[hoˈtiti ˈspati]

to yawn (vi)	позіхати	[pozi'hati]
to go to bed	йти спати	[jti 'spati]
to make up the bed	стелити ліжко	[stɛ'liti 'liʒko]
to fall asleep	заснути	[zas'nuti]

nightmare	страхіття (c)	[stra'hittʲa]
snore, snoring	хропіння (c)	[hro'pinʲa]
to snore (vi)	хропіти	[hro'piti]

alarm clock	будильник (ч)	[bu'diɫʲnik]
to wake (vt)	розбудити	[rozbu'diti]
to wake up	прокидатися	[proki'datisʲa]
to get up (vi)	вставати	[wsta'wati]
to have a wash	умитися	[u'mitisʲa]

64. Humour. Laughter. Gladness

humour (wit, fun)	гумор (ч)	['humor]
sense of humour	почуття (c)	[potʃut'tʲa]
to enjoy oneself	веселитися	[wɛsɛ'litisʲa]
cheerful (merry)	веселий	[wɛ'sɛlij]
merriment (gaiety)	веселощі (мн)	[wɛ'sɛloɕi]

smile	посмішка (ж)	['pɔsmiʃka]
to smile (vi)	посміхатися	[posmi'hatisʲa]
to start laughing	засміятися	[zasmiʲ'atisʲa]
to laugh (vi)	сміятися	[smiʲ'atisʲa]
laugh, laughter	сміх (ч)	[smih]

anecdote	анекдот (ч)	[anɛk'dɔt]
funny (anecdote, etc.)	смішний	[smiʃ'nij]
funny (odd)	кумедний	[ku'mɛdnij]

to joke (vi)	жартувати	[ʒartu'wati]
joke (verbal)	жарт (ч)	[ʒart]
joy (emotion)	радість (ж)	['radistʲ]
to rejoice (vi)	радіти	[ra'diti]
joyful (adj)	радісний	['radisnij]

65. Discussion, conversation. Part 1

| communication | спілкування (c) | [spilku'wanʲa] |
| to communicate | спілкуватися | [spilku'watisʲa] |

conversation	розмова (ж)	[roz'mɔwa]
dialogue	діалог (ч)	[dia'lɔh]
discussion (discourse)	дискусія (ж)	[dis'kusiʲa]
dispute (debate)	суперечка (ч)	[supɛ'rɛtʃka]
to dispute, to debate	сперечатися	[spɛrɛ'tʃatisʲa]

| interlocutor | співрозмовник (ч) | [spiwroz'mɔwnik] |
| topic (theme) | тема (ж) | ['tɛma] |

point of view	точка (ж) зору	['tɔtʃka 'zɔru]
opinion (point of view)	погляд (ч)	['pɔɦlʲad]
speech (talk)	промова (ж)	[pro'mɔwa]
discussion (of a report, etc.)	обговорення (с)	[obɦo'wɔrɛnʲa]
to discuss (vt)	обговорювати	[obɦo'wɔrʲuwati]
talk (conversation)	бесіда (ж)	['bɛsida]
to talk (to chat)	розмовляти	[rozmow'lʲati]
meeting (encounter)	зустріч (ж)	['zustritʃ]
to meet (vi, vt)	зустрічатися	[zustri'tʃatisʲa]
proverb	прислів'я (с)	[pris'liwˀʲa]
saying	приказка (ж)	['prikazka]
riddle (poser)	загадка (ж)	['zaɦadka]
to pose a riddle	загадувати загадку	[za'ɦaduwati 'zaɦadku]
password	пароль (ч)	[pa'rɔlʲ]
secret	секрет (ч)	[sɛk'rɛt]
oath (vow)	клятва (ж)	['klʲatwa]
to swear (an oath)	клястися	['klʲastisʲa]
promise	обіцянка (ж)	[obi'tsʲanka]
to promise (vt)	обіцяти	[obi'tsʲati]
advice (counsel)	порада (ж)	[po'rada]
to advise (vt)	радити	['raditi]
to listen to … (obey)	слухатись	['sluhatisʲ]
news	новина (ж)	[nowi'na]
sensation (news)	сенсація (ж)	[sɛn'satsiʲa]
information (report)	відомості (мн)	[wi'dɔmosti]
conclusion (decision)	висновок (ч)	['wisnowok]
voice	голос (ч)	['ɦolos]
compliment	комплімент (ч)	[kompli'mɛnt]
kind (nice)	люб'язний	[lʲu'bˀʲaznij]
word	слово (с)	['slɔwo]
phrase	фраза (ж)	['fraza]
answer	відповідь (ж)	['widpowidʲ]
truth	правда (ж)	['prawda]
lie	брехня (ж)	[brɛh'nʲa]
thought	думка (ж)	['dumka]
idea (inspiration)	думка (ж)	['dumka]
fantasy	вигадка (ж)	['wiɦadka]

66. Discussion, conversation. Part 2

respected (adj)	шановний	[ʃa'nɔwnij]
to respect (vt)	поважати	[powa'ʒati]
respect	повага (ж)	[po'waɦa]
Dear … (letter)	Шановний …	[ʃa'nɔwnij]
to introduce (sb to sb)	познайомити	[pozna'jomiti]
intention	намір (ч)	['namir]

to intend (have in mind)	мати наміри	['matɪ 'namiri]
wish	побажання (c)	[poba'ʒanʲa]
to wish (~ good luck)	побажати	[poba'ʒati]
surprise (astonishment)	здивування (c)	[zdɪwu'wanʲa]
to surprise (amaze)	дивувати	[dɪwu'wati]
to be surprised	дивуватись	[dɪwu'watisʲ]
to give (vt)	дати	['dati]
to take (get hold of)	взяти	['wzʲati]
to give back	повернути	[powɛr'nuti]
to return (give back)	віддати	[wid'dati]
to apologize (vi)	вибачатися	[wiba'tʃatisʲa]
apology	вибачення (c)	['wibatʃɛnʲa]
to forgive (vt)	прощати	[pro'çati]
to talk (speak)	розмовляти	[rozmow'lʲati]
to listen (vi)	слухати	['sluhati]
to hear out	вислухати	['wisluhati]
to understand (vt)	зрозуміти	[zrozu'miti]
to show (to display)	показати	[poka'zati]
to look at …	дивитися	[dɪ'witisʲa]
to call (yell for sb)	покликати	[pok'likati]
to disturb (vt)	заважати	[zawa'ʒati]
to pass (to hand sth)	передати	[pɛrɛ'dati]
demand (request)	прохання (c)	[pro'hanʲa]
to request (ask)	просити	[pro'siti]
demand (firm request)	вимога (ж)	[wi'moɦa]
to demand (request firmly)	вимагати	[wima'ɦati]
to tease (call names)	дражнити	[draʒ'niti]
to mock (make fun of)	насміхатися	[nasmi'hatisʲa]
mockery, derision	насмішка (ж)	[na'smiʃka]
nickname	прізвисько (c)	['prizwisʲko]
insinuation	натяк (ч)	['natʲak]
to insinuate (imply)	натякати	[natʲa'kati]
to mean (vt)	мати на увазі	['matɪ na u'wazi]
description	опис (ч)	['ɔpis]
to describe (vt)	описати	[opi'sati]
praise (compliments)	похвала (ж)	[pohwa'la]
to praise (vt)	похвалити	[pohwa'liti]
disappointment	розчарування (c)	[roztʃaru'wanʲa]
to disappoint (vt)	розчарувати	[roztʃaru'wati]
to be disappointed	розчаруватися	[roztʃaru'watisʲa]
supposition	припущення (c)	[pri'puçɛnʲa]
to suppose (assume)	припускати	[pripus'kati]
warning (caution)	застереження (c)	[zastɛ'rɛʒɛnʲa]
to warn (vt)	застерегти	[zastɛrɛɦ'ti]

67. Discussion, conversation. Part 3

to talk into (convince)	умовити	[u'mɔwiti]
to calm down (vt)	заспокоювати	[zaspo'kɔʲuwati]
silence (~ is golden)	мовчання (c)	[mow'ʧanʲa]
to be silent (not speaking)	мовчати	[mow'ʧati]
to whisper (vi, vt)	шепнути	[ʃɛp'nuti]
whisper	шепіт (ч)	['ʃɛpit]
frankly, sincerely (adv)	відверто	[wid'wɛrto]
in my opinion …	на мою думку …	[na mo'ʲu 'dumku]
detail (of the story)	подробиця (ж)	[pod'rɔbitsʲa]
detailed (adj)	докладний	[do'kladnij]
in detail (adv)	докладно	[do'kladno]
hint, clue	підказка (ж)	[pid'kazka]
to give a hint	підказувати	[pid'kazuwati]
look (glance)	погляд (ч)	['pɔɦlʲad]
to have a look	поглянути	[poɦ'lʲanuti]
fixed (look)	нерухомий	[nɛru'ɦɔmij]
to blink (vi)	кліпати	['klipati]
to wink (vi)	підморгнути	[pidmorɦ'nuti]
to nod (in assent)	кивнути	[kiw'nuti]
sigh	зітхання (c)	[zit'ɦanʲa]
to sigh (vi)	зітхнути	[zitɦ'nuti]
to shudder (vi)	здригатися	[zdri'ɦatisʲa]
gesture	жест (ч)	[ʒɛst]
to touch (one's arm, etc.)	доторкнутися	[dotor'knutisʲa]
to seize (e.g., ~ by the arm)	хапати	[ha'pati]
to tap (on the shoulder)	плескати	[plɛs'kati]
Look out!	Обережно!	[obɛ'rɛʒno]
Really?	Невже?	[nɛw'ʒɛ]
Are you sure?	Ти впевнений?	[ti 'wpɛwnɛnij]
Good luck!	Хай щастить!	[haj ɕas'titʲ]
I see!	Зрозуміло!	[zrozu'milo]
What a pity!	Шкода!	['ʃkɔda]

68. Agreement. Refusal

consent	згода (ж)	['zɦɔda]
to consent (vi)	погоджуватися	[po'ɦɔdʒuwatisʲa]
approval	схвалення (c)	[sh'walɛnʲa]
to approve (vt)	схвалити	[shwa'liti]
refusal	відмова (ж)	[wid'mɔwa]
to refuse (vi, vt)	відмовлятися	[widmow'lʲatisʲa]
Great!	Чудово!	[ʧu'dɔwo]
All right!	Добре!	['dɔbrɛ]

Okay! (I agree)	Згода!	['zɦɔda]
forbidden (adj)	заборонений	[zabo'rɔnɛnij]
it's forbidden	не можна	[nɛ 'mɔʒna]
it's impossible	неможливо	[nɛmɔʒ'liwo]
incorrect (adj)	помилковий	[pomil'kɔwij]
to reject (~ a demand)	відхилити	[widhi'liti]
to support (cause, idea)	підтримати	[pid'trimati]
to accept (~ an apology)	прийняти	[prij'nʲati]
to confirm (vt)	підтвердити	[pid'twɛrditi]
confirmation	підтвердження (c)	[pid'twɛrdʒɛnʲa]
permission	дозвіл (ч)	['dɔzwil]
to permit (vt)	дозволити	[doz'wɔliti]
decision	рішення (c)	['riʃɛnʲa]
to say nothing (hold one's tongue)	промовчати	[promow'tʃati]
condition (term)	умова (ж)	[u'mɔwa]
excuse (pretext)	відмовка (ж)	[wid'mɔwka]
praise (compliments)	похвала (ж)	[pohwa'la]
to praise (vt)	хвалити	[hwa'liti]

69. Success. Good luck. Failure

success	успіх (ч)	['uspih]
successfully (adv)	успішно	[us'piʃno]
successful (adj)	успішний	[us'piʃnij]
luck (good luck)	везіння (c)	[wɛ'zinʲa]
Good luck!	Хай щастить!	[haj ɕas'titʲ]
lucky (e.g. ~ day)	вдалий	['wdalij]
lucky (fortunate)	щасливий	[ɕas'liwij]
failure	невдача (ж)	[nɛw'datʃa]
misfortune	невдача (ж)	[nɛw'datʃa]
bad luck	невезіння (c)	[nɛwɛ'zinʲa]
unsuccessful (adj)	невдалий	[nɛw'dalij]
catastrophe	катастрофа (ж)	[kata'strɔfa]
pride	гордість (ж)	['hɔrdistʲ]
proud (adj)	гордовитий	[hordo'witij]
to be proud	пишатися	[pi'ʃatisʲa]
winner	переможець (ч)	[pɛrɛ'mɔʒɛʦ]
to win (vi)	перемогти	[pɛrɛmoɦ'ti]
to lose (not win)	програти	[proɦ'rati]
try	спроба (ж)	['sprɔba]
to try (vi)	намагатися	[nama'ɦatisʲa]
chance (opportunity)	шанс (ч)	[ʃans]

70. Quarrels. Negative emotions

shout (scream)	крик (ч)	[krik]
to shout (vi)	кричати	[kri'tʃati]
to start to cry out	закричати	[zakri'tʃati]
quarrel	сварка (ж)	['swarka]
to quarrel (vi)	сваритися	[swa'ritisʲa]
fight (squabble)	скандал (ч)	[skan'dal]
to make a scene	сваритися	[swa'ritisʲa]
conflict	конфлікт (ч)	[kon'flikt]
misunderstanding	непорозуміння (с)	[nɛporozu'minʲa]
insult	образа (ж)	[ob'raza]
to insult (vt)	ображати	[obra'ʒati]
insulted (adj)	ображений	[ob'raʒɛnij]
resentment	образа (ж)	[ob'raza]
to offend (vt)	образити	[ob'raziti]
to take offence	образитись	[ob'razitisʲ]
indignation	обурення (с)	[o'burɛnʲa]
to be indignant	обурюватися	[o'burʲuwatisʲa]
complaint	скарга (ж)	['skarɦa]
to complain (vi, vt)	скаржитися	['skarʒitisʲa]
apology	вибачення (с)	['wibatʃɛnʲa]
to apologize (vi)	вибачатися	[wiba'tʃatisʲa]
to beg pardon	просити вибачення	[pro'siti 'wibatʃɛnʲa]
criticism	критика (ж)	['kritika]
to criticize (vt)	критикувати	[kritiku'wati]
accusation (charge)	обвинувачення (с)	[obwinu'watʃɛnʲa]
to accuse (vt)	звинувачувати	[zwinu'watʃuwati]
revenge	помста (ж)	['pomsta]
to avenge (get revenge)	мстити	['mstiti]
to pay back	помститися	[poms'titisʲa]
disdain	зневага (ж)	[znɛ'waɦa]
to despise (vt)	зневажати	[znɛwa'ʒati]
hatred, hate	ненависть (ж)	[nɛ'nawistʲ]
to hate (vt)	ненавидіти	[nɛna'widiti]
nervous (adj)	нервовий	[nɛr'wɔwij]
to be nervous	нервувати	[nɛrwu'wati]
angry (mad)	сердитий	[sɛr'ditij]
to make angry	розсердити	[roz'sɛrditi]
humiliation	приниження (с)	[pri'niʒɛnʲa]
to humiliate (vt)	принижувати	[pri'niʒuwati]
to humiliate oneself	принижуватись	[pri'niʒuwatisʲ]
shock	шок (ч)	[ʃok]
to shock (vt)	шокувати	[ʃoku'wati]
trouble (e.g. serious ~)	неприємність (ж)	[nɛpri'ɛmnistʲ]

unpleasant (adj)	**неприємний**	[nɛpriˈɛmnij]
fear (dread)	**страх** (ч)	[strah]
terrible (storm, heat)	**страшний**	[ˈstraʃnij]
scary (e.g. ~ story)	**страшний**	[ˈstraʃnij]
horror	**жах** (ч)	[ʒah]
awful (crime, news)	**жахливий**	[ʒahˈliwij]
to cry (weep)	**плакати**	[ˈplakati]
to start crying	**заплакати**	[zaˈplakati]
tear	**сльоза** (ж)	[slʲoˈza]
fault	**вина** (ж)	[wiˈna]
guilt (feeling)	**провина** (ж)	[proˈwina]
dishonor (disgrace)	**ганьба** (ж)	[hanʲˈba]
protest	**протест** (ч)	[proˈtɛst]
stress	**стрес** (ч)	[ˈstrɛs]
to disturb (vt)	**заважати**	[zawaˈʒati]
to be furious	**лютувати**	[lʲutuˈwati]
angry (adj)	**злий**	[ˈzlij]
to end (~ a relationship)	**припиняти**	[pripiˈnʲati]
to swear (at sb)	**лаятися**	[ˈlaʲatisʲa]
to scare (become afraid)	**лякатися**	[lʲaˈkatisʲa]
to hit (strike with hand)	**ударити**	[uˈdariti]
to fight (street fight, etc.)	**битися**	[ˈbitisʲa]
to settle (a conflict)	**урегулювати**	[urɛhulʲuˈwati]
discontented (adj)	**незадоволений**	[nɛzadoˈwɔlɛnij]
furious (adj)	**розлючений**	[rozˈlʲutʃɛnij]
It's not good!	**Це недобре!**	[tsɛ nɛˈdɔbrɛ]
It's bad!	**Це погано!**	[tsɛ poˈhano]

Medicine

71. Diseases

illness	хвороба (ж)	[hwoˈrɔba]
to be ill	хворіти	[hwoˈriti]
health	здоров'я (с)	[zdoˈrɔwⁿa]
runny nose (coryza)	нежить (ч)	[ˈnɛʒitʲ]
tonsillitis	ангіна (ж)	[anˈɦina]
cold (illness)	застуда (ж)	[zaˈstuda]
to catch a cold	застудитися	[zastuˈditisʲa]
bronchitis	бронхіт (ч)	[bronˈhit]
pneumonia	запалення (с) легенів	[zaˈpalɛnja lɛˈɦɛniw]
flu, influenza	грип (ч)	[ɦrip]
shortsighted (adj)	короткозорий	[korotkoˈzɔrij]
longsighted (adj)	далекозорий	[dalɛkoˈzɔrij]
strabismus (crossed eyes)	косоокість (ж)	[kosoˈɔkistʲ]
squint-eyed (adj)	косоокий	[kosoˈɔkij]
cataract	катаракта (ж)	[kataˈrakta]
glaucoma	глаукома (ж)	[ɦlauˈkɔma]
stroke	інсульт (ч)	[inˈsulʲt]
heart attack	інфаркт (ч)	[inˈfarkt]
myocardial infarction	інфаркт (ч) міокарду	[inˈfarkt mioˈkardu]
paralysis	параліч (ч)	[paraˈlitʃ]
to paralyse (vt)	паралізувати	[paralizuˈwati]
allergy	алергія (ж)	[alɛrˈɦiʲa]
asthma	астма (ж)	[ˈastma]
diabetes	діабет (ч)	[diaˈbɛt]
toothache	зубний біль (ч)	[zubˈnij bilʲ]
caries	карієс (ч)	[ˈkariɛs]
diarrhoea	діарея (ж)	[diaˈrɛʲa]
constipation	запор (ч)	[zaˈpɔr]
stomach upset	розлад (ч) шлунку	[ˈrɔzlad ˈʃlunku]
food poisoning	отруєння (с)	[otˈruɛnʲa]
to get food poisoning	отруїтись	[otruˈjitisʲ]
arthritis	артрит (ч)	[artˈrit]
rickets	рахіт (ч)	[raˈhit]
rheumatism	ревматизм (ч)	[rɛwmaˈtizm]
atherosclerosis	атеросклероз (ч)	[atɛrosklɛˈrɔz]
gastritis	гастрит (ч)	[ɦastˈrit]
appendicitis	апендицит (ч)	[apɛndiˈtsit]

| cholecystitis | холецистит (ч) | [holɛtsis'tit] |
| ulcer | виразка (ж) | ['wirazka] |

measles	кір (ч)	[kir]
rubella (German measles)	краснуха (ж)	[kras'nuha]
jaundice	жовтуха (ж)	[ʒow'tuha]
hepatitis	гепатит (ч)	[ɦɛpa'tit]

schizophrenia	шизофренія (ж)	[ʃizofrɛ'niʲa]
rabies (hydrophobia)	сказ (ч)	[skaz]
neurosis	невроз (ч)	[nɛw'rɔz]
concussion	струс (ч) мозку	['strus 'mɔzku]

cancer	рак (ч)	[rak]
sclerosis	склероз (ч)	[sklɛ'rɔz]
multiple sclerosis	розсіяний склероз (ч)	[roz'siʲanij sklɛ'rɔz]

alcoholism	алкоголізм (ч)	[alkoɦo'lizm]
alcoholic (n)	алкоголік (ч)	[alko'ɦolik]
syphilis	сифіліс (ч)	['sifilis]
AIDS	СНІД (ч)	[snid]

tumour	пухлина (ж)	[puh'lina]
malignant (adj)	злоякісна	[zlo'ʲakisna]
benign (adj)	доброякісний	[dobro'ʲakisnij]

fever	гарячка (ж)	[ɦa'rʲatʃka]
malaria	малярія (ж)	[malʲa'riʲa]
gangrene	гангрена (ж)	[ɦan'ɦrɛna]
seasickness	морська хвороба (ж)	[morsʲ'ka hwo'rɔba]
epilepsy	епілепсія (ж)	[ɛpi'lɛpsiʲa]

epidemic	епідемія (ж)	[ɛpi'dɛmiʲa]
typhus	тиф (ч)	[tif]
tuberculosis	туберкульоз (ч)	[tubɛrku'lʲoz]
cholera	холера (ж)	[ho'lɛra]
plague (bubonic ~)	чума (ж)	[tʃu'ma]

72. Symptoms. Treatments. Part 1

symptom	симптом (ч)	[simp'tɔm]
temperature	температура (ж)	[tɛmpɛra'tura]
high temperature (fever)	висока температура (ж)	[wi'sɔka tɛmpɛra'tura]
pulse (heartbeat)	пульс (ч)	[pulʲs]

dizziness (vertigo)	запаморочення (с)	[za'pamorotʃɛnʲa]
hot (adj)	гарячий	[ɦa'rʲatʃij]
shivering	озноб (ч)	[oz'nɔb]
pale (e.g. ~ face)	блідий	[bli'dij]

cough	кашель (ч)	['kaʃɛlʲ]
to cough (vi)	кашляти	['kaʃlʲati]
to sneeze (vi)	чхати	['tʃhati]
faint	непритомність (ж)	[nɛpri'tɔmnistʲ]

to faint (vi)	знепритомніти	[znɛpriˈtɔmniti]
bruise (hématome)	синець (ч)	[siˈnɛts]
bump (lump)	гуля (ж)	[ˈɦulʲa]
to bang (bump)	ударитись	[uˈdaritisʲ]
contusion (bruise)	забите місце (с)	[zaˈbitɛ ˈmistsɛ]
to get a bruise	забитися	[zaˈbitisʲa]
to limp (vi)	кульгати	[kulʲˈɦati]
dislocation	вивих (ч)	[ˈwiwih]
to dislocate (vt)	вивихнути	[ˈwiwihnuti]
fracture	перелом (ч)	[pɛrɛˈlɔm]
to have a fracture	дістати перелом	[disˈtati pɛrɛˈlɔm]
cut (e.g. paper ~)	поріз (ч)	[poˈriz]
to cut oneself	порізатися	[poˈrizatisʲa]
bleeding	кровотеча (ж)	[krowoˈtɛtʃa]
burn (injury)	опік (ч)	[ˈɔpik]
to get burned	обпектися	[obpɛkˈtisʲa]
to prick (vt)	уколоти	[ukoˈlɔti]
to prick oneself	уколотися	[ukoˈlɔtisʲa]
to injure (vt)	пошкодити	[poʃˈkɔditi]
injury	ушкодження (с)	[uʃˈkɔdʒɛnʲa]
wound	рана (ж)	[ˈrana]
trauma	травма (ж)	[ˈtrawma]
to be delirious	марити	[ˈmariti]
to stutter (vi)	заїкатися	[zajiˈkatisʲa]
sunstroke	сонячний удар (ч)	[ˈsɔnʲatʃnij uˈdar]

73. Symptoms. Treatments. Part 2

pain, ache	біль (ч)	[bilʲ]
splinter (in foot, etc.)	скалка (ж)	[ˈskalka]
sweat (perspiration)	піт (ч)	[pit]
to sweat (perspire)	спітніти	[spitˈniti]
vomiting	блювота (ж)	[blʲuˈwɔta]
convulsions	судома (ж)	[suˈdɔma]
pregnant (adj)	вагітна	[waˈɦitna]
to be born	народитися	[naroˈditisʲa]
delivery, labour	пологи (мн)	[poˈlɔɦi]
to deliver (~ a baby)	народжувати	[naˈrɔdʒuwati]
abortion	аборт (ч)	[aˈbɔrt]
breathing, respiration	дихання (с)	[ˈdihanʲa]
in-breath (inhalation)	вдих (ч)	[wdih]
out-breath (exhalation)	видих (ч)	[ˈwidih]
to exhale (breathe out)	видихнути	[ˈwidihnuti]
to inhale (vi)	зробити вдих	[zroˈbiti wdih]
disabled person	інвалід (ч)	[inwaˈlid]
cripple	каліка (ч)	[kaˈlika]

drug addict	наркоман (ч)	[narko'man]
deaf (adj)	глухий (ч)	[ɦlu'hij]
mute (adj)	німий (ч)	[ni'mij]
deaf mute (adj)	глухонімий (ч)	[ɦluhoni'mij]

mad, insane (adj)	божевільний	[boʒɛ'wilʲnij]
madman	божевільний (ч)	[boʒɛ'wilʲnij]
(demented person)		
madwoman	божевільна (ж)	[boʒɛ'wilʲna]
to go insane	збожеволіти	[zboʒɛ'wɔliti]

gene	ген (ч)	[ɦɛn]
immunity	імунітет (ч)	[imuni'tɛt]
hereditary (adj)	спадковий	[spad'kɔwij]
congenital (adj)	вроджений	['wrɔdʒɛnij]

virus	вірус (ч)	['wirus]
microbe	мікроб (ч)	[mik'rɔb]
bacterium	бактерія (ж)	[bak'tɛriʲa]
infection	інфекція (ж)	[in'fɛktsiʲa]

74. Symptoms. Treatments. Part 3

| hospital | лікарня (ж) | [li'karnʲa] |
| patient | пацієнт (ч) | [patsi'ɛnt] |

diagnosis	діагноз (ч)	[di'aɦnoz]
cure	лікування (с)	[liku'wanʲa]
medical treatment	лікування (с)	[liku'wanʲa]
to get treatment	лікуватися	[liku'watisʲa]
to treat (~ a patient)	лікувати	[liku'wati]
to nurse (look after)	доглядати	[doɦlʲa'dati]
care (nursing ~)	догляд (ч)	['dɔɦlʲad]

operation, surgery	операція (ж)	[opɛ'ratsiʲa]
to bandage (head, limb)	перев'язати	[pɛrɛw'ʲa'zati]
bandaging	перев'язка (ж)	[pɛrɛ'w'ʲazka]

vaccination	щеплення (с)	['ɕɛplɛnʲa]
to vaccinate (vt)	робити щеплення	[ro'biti 'ɕɛplɛnʲa]
injection	ін'єкція (ж)	[i'nʲɛktsiʲa]
to give an injection	робити укол	[ro'biti u'kɔl]

amputation	ампутація (ж)	[ampu'tatsiʲa]
to amputate (vt)	ампутувати	[amputu'wati]
coma	кома (ж)	['kɔma]
to be in a coma	бути в комі	['buti w 'kɔmi]
intensive care	реанімація (ж)	[rɛani'matsiʲa]

to recover (~ from flu)	видужувати	[wɨ'duʒuwati]
condition (patient's ~)	стан (ч)	['stan]
consciousness	свідомість (ж)	[swi'dɔmistʲ]
memory (faculty)	пам'ять (ж)	['pamʲatʲ]
to pull out (tooth)	видалити	['widaliti]

| filling | пломба (ж) | ['plɔmba] |
| to fill (a tooth) | пломбувати | [plɔmbu'wati] |

| hypnosis | гіпноз (ч) | [ɦip'nɔz] |
| to hypnotize (vt) | гіпнотизувати | [ɦipnotizu'wati] |

75. Doctors

doctor	лікар (ч)	['likar]
nurse	медсестра (ж)	[mɛdsɛst'ra]
personal doctor	особистий лікар (ч)	[oso'bistij 'likar]

dentist	дантист (ч)	[dan'tist]
optician	окуліст (ч)	[oku'list]
general practitioner	терапевт (ч)	[tɛra'pɛwt]
surgeon	хірург (ч)	[hi'rurɦ]

psychiatrist	психіатр (ч)	[psihi'atr]
paediatrician	педіатр (ч)	[pɛdi'atr]
psychologist	психолог (ч)	[psi'ɦɔlɔɦ]
gynaecologist	гінеколог (ч)	[ɦinɛ'kɔlɔɦ]
cardiologist	кардіолог (ч)	[kardi'ɔlɔɦ]

76. Medicine. Drugs. Accessories

medicine, drug	ліки (мн)	['liki]
remedy	засіб (ч)	['zasib]
to prescribe (vt)	прописати	[propi'sati]
prescription	рецепт (ч)	[rɛ'ʦɛpt]

tablet, pill	пігулка (ж)	[pi'ɦulka]
ointment	мазь (ж)	[mazʲ]
ampoule	ампула (ж)	['ampula]
mixture, solution	мікстура (ж)	[miks'tura]
syrup	сироп (ч)	[si'rɔp]
capsule	пілюля (ж)	[pi'lʲulʲa]
powder	порошок (ч)	[poro'ʃɔk]

gauze bandage	бинт (ч)	[bint]
cotton wool	вата (ж)	['wata]
iodine	йод (ч)	[ʲod]

plaster	лейкопластир (ч)	[lɛjko'plastir]
eyedropper	піпетка (ж)	[pi'pɛtka]
thermometer	градусник (ч)	['ɦradusnik]
syringe	шприц (ч)	[ʃpriʦ]

| wheelchair | коляска (ж) | [ko'lʲaska] |
| crutches | милиці (мн) | ['miliʦi] |

| painkiller | знеболювальне (с) | [znɛ'bɔlʲuwalʲnɛ] |
| laxative | проносне (с) | [pronos'nɛ] |

spirits (ethanol)	спирт (ч)	[spirt]
medicinal herbs	трава (ж)	[tra'wa]
herbal (~ tea)	трав'яний	[traw'ʲa'nij]

77. Smoking. Tobacco products

tobacco	тютюн (ч)	[tʲu'tʲun]
cigarette	цигарка (ж)	[tsi'harka]
cigar	сигара (ж)	[si'hara]
pipe	люлька (ж)	['lʲulʲka]
packet (of cigarettes)	пачка (ж)	['patʃka]

matches	сірники (мн)	[sirni'ki]
matchbox	сірникова коробка (ж)	[sirni'kowa ko'rɔbka]
lighter	запальничка (ж)	[zapalʲ'nitʃka]
ashtray	попільниця (ж)	[popilʲ'nitsʲa]
cigarette case	портсигар (ч)	[portsi'har]

| cigarette holder | мундштук (ч) | [mund'ʃtuk] |
| filter (cigarette tip) | фільтр (ч) | ['filʲtr] |

to smoke (vi, vt)	палити	[pa'liti]
to light a cigarette	запалити	[zapa'liti]
smoking	паління (с)	[pa'linʲa]
smoker	курець (ч)	[ku'rɛts]

cigarette end	недопалок (ч)	[nɛdo'palok]
smoke, fumes	дим (ч)	[dim]
ash	попіл (ч)	['pɔpil]

HUMAN HABITAT

City

city, town	**місто** (с)	['misto]
capital city	**столиця** (ж)	[stoˈliʦʲa]
village	**село** (с)	[sɛˈlɔ]
city map	**план** (ч) **міста**	[plan ˈmista]
city centre	**центр** (ч) **міста**	[ʦɛntr ˈmista]
suburb	**передмістя** (с)	[pɛrɛdˈmistʲa]
suburban (adj)	**приміський**	[primisʲˈkij]
outskirts	**околиця** (ж)	[oˈkɔliʦʲa]
environs (suburbs)	**околиці** (мн)	[oˈkɔliʦi]
city block	**квартал** (ч)	[kwarˈtal]
residential block (area)	**житловий квартал** (ч)	[ʒitloˈwij kwarˈtal]
traffic	**рух** (ч)	[ruh]
traffic lights	**світлофор** (ч)	[switloˈfɔr]
public transport	**міський транспорт** (ч)	[misʲˈkij ˈtransport]
crossroads	**перехрестя** (с)	[pɛrɛhˈrɛstʲa]
zebra crossing	**перехід** (ч)	[pɛrɛˈhid]
pedestrian subway	**підземний перехід** (ч)	[piˈdzɛmnij pɛrɛˈhid]
to cross (~ the street)	**переходити**	[pɛrɛˈhɔditi]
pedestrian	**пішохід** (ч)	[piʃoˈhid]
pavement	**тротуар** (ч)	[trotuˈar]
bridge	**міст** (ч)	[mist]
embankment (river walk)	**набережна** (ж)	['nabɛrɛʒna]
fountain	**фонтан** (ч)	[fonˈtan]
allée (garden walkway)	**алея** (ж)	[aˈlɛʲa]
park	**парк** (ч)	[park]
boulevard	**бульвар** (ч)	[bulʲˈwar]
square	**площа** (ж)	['plɔɕa]
avenue (wide street)	**проспект** (ч)	[prosˈpɛkt]
street	**вулиця** (ж)	['wuliʦʲa]
side street	**провулок** (ч)	[proˈwulok]
dead end	**глухий кут** (ч)	[ɦluˈhij kut]
house	**будинок** (ч)	[buˈdinok]
building	**споруда** (ж)	[spoˈruda]
skyscraper	**хмарочос** (ч)	[hmaroˈʧɔs]
facade	**фасад** (ч)	[faˈsad]
roof	**дах** (ч)	[dah]

window	вікно (с)	[wik'nɔ]
arch	арка (ж)	['arka]
column	колона (ж)	[ko'lɔna]
corner	ріг (ч)	[riɦ]

shop window	вітрина (ж)	[wi'trina]
signboard (store sign, etc.)	вивіска (ж)	['wiwiska]
poster (e.g., playbill)	афіша (ж)	[a'fiʃa]
advertising poster	рекламний плакат (ч)	[rɛk'lamnij pla'kat]
hoarding	рекламний щит (ч)	[rɛk'lamnij ɕit]

rubbish	сміття (с)	[smit'tʲa]
rubbish bin	урна (ж)	['urna]
to litter (vi)	смітити	[smi'titi]
rubbish dump	смітник (ч)	[smit'nik]

telephone box	телефонна будка (ж)	[tɛlɛ'fɔna 'budka]
lamppost	ліхтарний стовп (ч)	[lih'tarnij stowp]
bench (park ~)	лавка (ж)	['lawka]

police officer	поліцейський (ч)	[poli'tsɛjsʲkij]
police	поліція (ж)	[po'litsiʲa]
beggar	жебрак (ч)	[ʒɛb'rak]
homeless (n)	безпритульний (ч)	[bɛzpri'tulʲnij]

79. Urban institutions

shop	магазин (ч)	[maɦa'zin]
chemist, pharmacy	аптека (ж)	[ap'tɛka]
optician (spectacles shop)	оптика (ж)	['ɔptika]
shopping centre	торгівельний центр (ч)	[torɦi'wɛlʲnij 'tsɛntr]
supermarket	супермаркет (ч)	[supɛr'markɛt]

bakery	булочна (ж)	['bulotʃna]
baker	пекар (ч)	['pɛkar]
cake shop	кондитерська (ж)	[kon'ditɛrsʲka]
grocery shop	бакалія (ж)	[baka'liʲa]
butcher shop	м'ясний магазин (ч)	[mʲas'nij maɦa'zin]

| greengrocer | овочевий магазин (ч) | [owo'tʃɛwij maɦa'zin] |
| market | ринок (ч) | ['rinok] |

coffee bar	кав'ярня (ж)	[ka'wʲarnʲa]
restaurant	ресторан (ч)	[rɛsto'ran]
pub, bar	пивна (ж)	[piw'na]
pizzeria	піцерія (ж)	[pitsɛ'riʲa]

hairdresser	перукарня (ж)	[pɛru'karnʲa]
post office	пошта (ж)	['pɔʃta]
dry cleaners	хімчистка (ж)	[him'tʃistka]
photo studio	фотоательє (с)	[fotoatɛ'ljɛ]

| shoe shop | взуттєвий магазин (ч) | [wzut'tɛwij maɦa'zin] |
| bookshop | книгарня (ж) | [kni'ɦarnʲa] |

sports shop	спортивний магазин (ч)	[spor'tiwnij maɦa'zin]
clothes repair shop	ремонт (ч) одягу	[rɛ'mɔnt 'ɔdʲaɦu]
formal wear hire	прокат (ч) одягу	[pro'kat 'ɔdʲaɦu]
video rental shop	прокат (ч) фільмів	[pro'kat 'filʲmiw]

circus	цирк (ч)	[ʦirk]
zoo	зоопарк (ч)	[zoo'park]
cinema	кінотеатр (ч)	[kinotɛ'atr]
museum	музей (ч)	[mu'zɛj]
library	бібліотека (ж)	[biblio'tɛka]

theatre	театр (ч)	[tɛ'atr]
opera (opera house)	опера (ж)	['ɔpɛra]
nightclub	нічний клуб (ч)	[niʧ'nij klub]
casino	казино (с)	[kazi'nɔ]

mosque	мечеть (ж)	[mɛ'ʧɛtʲ]
synagogue	синагога (ж)	[sina'ɦɔɦa]
cathedral	собор (ч)	[so'bɔr]
temple	храм (ч)	[hram]
church	церква (ж)	['ʦɛrkwa]

college	інститут (ч)	[insti'tut]
university	університет (ч)	[uniwɛrsi'tɛt]
school	школа (ж)	['ʃkɔla]

prefecture	префектура (ж)	[prɛfɛk'tura]
town hall	мерія (ж)	['mɛriʲa]
hotel	готель (ч)	[ɦo'tɛlʲ]
bank	банк (ч)	[bank]

embassy	посольство (с)	[po'sɔlʲstwo]
travel agency	турагентство (с)	[tura'ɦɛnʦtwo]
information office	довідкове бюро (с)	[dowid'kɔwɛ bʲu'rɔ]
currency exchange	обмінний пункт (ч)	[ob'minij punkt]

| underground, tube | метро (с) | [mɛt'rɔ] |
| hospital | лікарня (ж) | [li'karnʲa] |

| petrol station | бензоколонка (ж) | [bɛnzoko'lɔnka] |
| car park | стоянка (ж) | [sto'ʲanka] |

80. Signs

signboard (store sign, etc.)	вивіска (ж)	['wiwiska]
notice (door sign, etc.)	напис (ч)	['napis]
poster	плакат (ч)	[pla'kat]
direction sign	дороговказ (ч)	[doroɦow'kaz]
arrow (sign)	стрілка (ж)	['strilka]

caution	застереження (с)	[zastɛ'rɛʒɛnʲa]
warning sign	попередження (с)	[popɛ'rɛʤɛnʲa]
to warn (vt)	попереджувати	[popɛ'rɛʤuwati]
rest day (weekly ~)	вихідний день (ч)	[wihid'nij dɛnʲ]

| timetable (schedule) | розклад (ч) | ['rɔzklad] |
| opening hours | години (мн) роботи | [ɦo'dini ro'bɔti] |

WELCOME!	ЛАСКАВО ПРОСИМО!	[las'kawo 'prɔsimo]
ENTRANCE	ВХІД	[whid]
WAY OUT	ВИХІД	['wihid]

PUSH	ВІД СЕБЕ	[wid 'sɛbɛ]
PULL	ДО СЕБЕ	[do 'sɛbɛ]
OPEN	ВІДЧИНЕНО	[wid'ʧinɛno]
CLOSED	ЗАЧИНЕНО	[za'ʧinɛno]

| WOMEN | ДЛЯ ЖІНОК | [dlʲa ʒi'nɔk] |
| MEN | ДЛЯ ЧОЛОВІКІВ | [dlʲa ʧolowi'kiw] |

DISCOUNTS	ЗНИЖКИ	['zniʒki]
SALE	РОЗПРОДАЖ	[rozp'rɔdaʒ]
NEW!	НОВИНКА!	[no'winka]
FREE	БЕЗКОШТОВНО	[bɛzkoʃ'tɔwno]

ATTENTION!	УВАГА!	[u'waɦa]
NO VACANCIES	МІСЦЬ НЕМАЄ	[misʦ nɛ'maɛ]
RESERVED	ЗАРЕЗЕРВОВАНО	[zarɛzɛr'wɔwano]

| ADMINISTRATION | АДМІНІСТРАЦІЯ | [admini'straʦiʲa] |
| STAFF ONLY | ТІЛЬКИ ДЛЯ ПЕРСОНАЛУ | ['tilʲki dlʲa pɛrso'nalu] |

BEWARE OF THE DOG!	ОБЕРЕЖНО! ЗЛИЙ ПЕС	[obɛ'rɛʒno! zlij pɛs]
NO SMOKING	ПАЛИТИ ЗАБОРОНЕНО	[pa'liti zabo'rɔnɛno]
DO NOT TOUCH!	НЕ ТОРКАТИСЯ!	[nɛ tor'katisʲa]

DANGEROUS	НЕБЕЗПЕЧНО	[nɛbɛz'pɛʧno]
DANGER	НЕБЕЗПЕКА	[nɛbɛz'pɛka]
HIGH VOLTAGE	ВИСОКА НАПРУГА	[wi'sɔka na'pruɦa]
NO SWIMMING!	КУПАТИСЯ ЗАБОРОНЕНО	[ku'patisʲa zabo'rɔnɛno]
OUT OF ORDER	НЕ ПРАЦЮЄ	[nɛ pra'ʦʲuɛ]

FLAMMABLE	ВОГНЕНЕБЕЗПЕЧНО	[woɦnɛnɛbɛz'pɛʧno]
FORBIDDEN	ЗАБОРОНЕНО	[zabo'rɔnɛno]
NO TRESPASSING!	ПРОХІД ЗАБОРОНЕНО	[pro'hid zabo'rɔnɛno]
WET PAINT	ПОФАРБОВАНО	[pofar'bɔwano]

81. Urban transport

bus, coach	автобус (ч)	[aw'tɔbus]
tram	трамвай (ч)	[tram'waj]
trolleybus	тролейбус (ч)	[tro'lɛjbus]
route (bus ~)	маршрут (ч)	[marʃ'rut]
number (e.g. bus ~)	номер (ч)	['nɔmɛr]

to go by ...	їхати на ...	['jihati na]
to get on (~ the bus)	сісти	['sisti]
to get off ...	зійти	[zij'ti]
stop (e.g. bus ~)	зупинка (ж)	[zu'pinka]

next stop	наступна зупинка (ж)	[na'stupna zu'pinka]
terminus	кінцева зупинка (ж)	[kin'tsɛwa zu'pinka]
timetable	розклад (ч)	['rɔzklad]
to wait (vt)	чекати	[ʧɛ'kati]

| ticket | квиток (ч) | [kwi'tɔk] |
| fare | вартість (ж) квитка | ['wartistʲ kwit'ka] |

cashier (ticket seller)	касир (ч)	[ka'sir]
ticket inspection	контроль (ч)	[kon'trɔlʲ]
ticket inspector	контролер (ч)	[kontro'lɛr]

to be late (for …)	запізнюватися	[za'piznʲuwatisʲa]
to miss (~ the train, etc.)	спізнитися	[spiz'nitisʲa]
to be in a hurry	поспішати	[pospi'ʃati]

taxi, cab	таксі (с)	[tak'si]
taxi driver	таксист (ч)	[tak'sist]
by taxi	на таксі	[na tak'si]
taxi rank	стоянка (с) таксі	[stoʲ'anka tak'si]
to call a taxi	викликати таксі	['wiklikati tak'si]
to take a taxi	взяти таксі	['wzʲati tak'si]

traffic	вуличний рух (ч)	['wuliʧnij ruh]
traffic jam	пробка (ж)	['prɔbka]
rush hour	години (мн) пік	[ɦo'dini pik]
to park (vi)	паркуватися	[parku'watisʲa]
to park (vt)	паркувати	[parku'wati]
car park	стоянка (ж)	[stoʲ'anka]

underground, tube	метро (с)	[mɛt'rɔ]
station	станція (ж)	['stantsiʲa]
to take the tube	їхати в метро	['jihati w mɛt'rɔ]
train	поїзд (ч)	['pɔjizd]
train station	вокзал (ч)	[wok'zal]

82. Sightseeing

monument	пам'ятник (ч)	['pamʲʲatnik]
fortress	фортеця (ж)	[for'tɛtsʲa]
palace	палац (ч)	[pa'lats]
castle	замок (ч)	['zamok]
tower	вежа (ж)	['wɛʒa]
mausoleum	мавзолей (ч)	[mawzo'lɛj]

architecture	архітектура (ж)	[arhitɛk'tura]
medieval (adj)	середньовічний	[sɛrɛdnʲo'wiʧnij]
ancient (adj)	старовинний	[staro'winij]
national (adj)	національний	[natsio'nalʲnij]
famous (monument, etc.)	відомий	[wi'dɔmij]

tourist	турист (ч)	[tu'rist]
guide (person)	гід (ч)	[ɦid]
excursion, sightseeing tour	екскурсія (ж)	[ɛks'kursiʲa]

| to show (vt) | показувати | [po'kazuwati] |
| to tell (vt) | розповідати | [rozpowi'dati] |

to find (vt)	знайти	[znaj'ti]
to get lost (lose one's way)	загубитися	[zaɦu'bitisʲa]
map (e.g. underground ~)	схема (ж)	['sɦɛma]
map (e.g. city ~)	план (ч)	[plan]

souvenir, gift	сувенір (ч)	[suwɛ'nir]
gift shop	магазин (ч) сувенірів	[maɦa'zin suwɛ'niriw]
to take pictures	фотографувати	[fotoɦrafu'wati]
to have one's picture taken	фотографуватися	[fotoɦrafu'watisʲa]

83. Shopping

to buy (purchase)	купляти	[kup'lʲati]
shopping	покупка (ж)	[po'kupka]
to go shopping	робити покупки	[ro'biti po'kupki]
shopping	шопінг (ч)	['ʃopinɦ]

| to be open (ab. shop) | працювати | [pratsʲu'wati] |
| to be closed | зачинитися | [zatʃi'nitisʲa] |

footwear, shoes	взуття (с)	[wzut'tʲa]
clothes, clothing	одяг (ч)	['ɔdʲaɦ]
cosmetics	косметика (ж)	[kos'mɛtika]
food products	продукти (мн)	[pro'dukti]
gift, present	подарунок (ч)	[poda'runok]

| shop assistant (masc.) | продавець (ч) | [proda'wɛts] |
| shop assistant (fem.) | продавщиця (ж) | [prodaw'çitsʲa] |

cash desk	каса (ж)	['kasa]
mirror	дзеркало (с)	['dzɛrkalo]
counter (shop ~)	прилавок (ч)	[pri'lawok]
fitting room	примірочна (ж)	[pri'mirotʃna]

to try on	приміряти	[pri'mirʲati]
to fit (ab. dress, etc.)	пасувати	[pasu'wati]
to fancy (vt)	подобатися	[po'dobatisʲa]

price	ціна (ж)	[tsi'na]
price tag	цінник (ч)	['tsinik]
to cost (vt)	коштувати	['koʃtuwati]
How much?	Скільки?	['skilʲki]
discount	знижка (ж)	['zniʒka]

inexpensive (adj)	недорогий	[nɛdoro'ɦij]
cheap (adj)	дешевий	[dɛ'ʃewij]
expensive (adj)	дорогий	[doro'ɦij]
It's expensive	Це дорого.	[tsɛ 'dɔroɦo]

| hire (n) | прокат (ч) | [pro'kat] |
| to hire (~ a dinner jacket) | взяти напрокат | ['wzʲati napro'kat] |

| credit (trade credit) | кредит (ч) | [krɛ'dit] |
| on credit (adv) | в кредит (ч) | [w krɛ'dit] |

84. Money

money	гроші (мн)	['ɦrɔʃi]
currency exchange	обмін (ч)	['ɔbmin]
exchange rate	курс (ч)	[kurs]
cashpoint	банкомат (ч)	[banko'mat]
coin	монета (ж)	[mo'nɛta]

| dollar | долар (ч) | ['dɔlar] |
| euro | євро (ч) | ['ɛwro] |

lira	ліра (ж)	['lira]
Deutschmark	марка (ж)	['marka]
franc	франк (ч)	['frank]
pound sterling	фунт (ч)	['funt]
yen	ієна (ж)	[i'ɛna]

debt	борг (ч)	['bɔrɦ]
debtor	боржник (ч)	[borʒ'nik]
to lend (money)	позичити	[po'zitʃiti]
to borrow (vi, vt)	взяти в борг	['wzʲati w borɦ]

bank	банк (ч)	[bank]
account	рахунок (ч)	[ra'hunok]
to deposit into the account	покласти на рахунок	[pok'lasti na ra'hunok]
to withdraw (vt)	зняти з рахунку	['znʲati z ra'hunku]

credit card	кредитна картка (ж)	[krɛ'ditna 'kartka]
cash	готівка (ж)	[ɦo'tiwka]
cheque	чек (ч)	[tʃɛk]
to write a cheque	виписати чек	['wipisati 'tʃɛk]
chequebook	чекова книжка (ж)	['tʃɛkowa 'kniʒka]

wallet	гаманець (ч)	[ɦama'nɛts]
purse	гаманець (ч)	[ɦama'nɛts]
safe	сейф (ч)	[sɛjf]

heir	спадкоємець (ч)	[spadko'ɛmɛts]
inheritance	спадщина (с)	['spadɕina]
fortune (wealth)	статок (ч)	['statok]

lease	оренда (ж)	[o'rɛnda]
rent (money)	квартирна плата (ж)	[kwar'tirna 'plata]
to rent (sth from sb)	наймати	[naj'mati]

price	ціна (ж)	[tsi'na]
cost	вартість (ж)	['wartistʲ]
sum	сума (ж)	['suma]

| to spend (vt) | витрачати | [witra'tʃati] |
| expenses | витрати (мн) | ['witrati] |

| to economize (vi, vt) | економити | [ɛko'nɔmiti] |
| economical | економний | [ɛko'nɔmnij] |

to pay (vi, vt)	платити	[pla'titi]
payment	оплата (ж)	[op'lata]
change (give the ~)	решта (ж)	['rɛʃta]

tax	податок (ч)	[po'datok]
fine	штраф (ч)	[ʃtraf]
to fine (vt)	штрафувати	[ʃtrafu'wati]

85. Post. Postal service

post office	пошта (ж)	['pɔʃta]
post (letters, etc.)	пошта (ж)	['pɔʃta]
postman	листоноша (ч)	[listo'nɔʃa]
opening hours	години (мн) роботи	[ɦo'dini ro'bɔti]

letter	лист (ч)	[list]
registered letter	рекомендований лист (ч)	[rɛkomɛn'dɔwanij list]
postcard	листівка (ж)	[lis'tiwka]
telegram	телеграма (ж)	[tɛlɛ'ɦrama]
parcel	посилка (ж)	[po'silka]
money transfer	грошовий переказ (ч)	[ɦroʃo'wij pɛ'rɛkaz]

to receive (vt)	отримати	[ot'rimati]
to send (vt)	відправити	[wid'prawiti]
sending	відправлення (с)	[wid'prawlɛnʲa]

address	адреса (ж)	[ad'rɛsa]
postcode	індекс (ч)	['indɛks]
sender	відправник (ч)	[wid'prawnik]
receiver	одержувач (ч)	[o'dɛrʒuwatʃ]

| name (first name) | ім'я (с) | [i'mʲʲa] |
| surname (last name) | прізвище (с) | ['prizwiçɛ] |

postage rate	тариф (ч)	[ta'rif]
standard (adj)	звичайний	[zwi'tʃajnij]
economical (adj)	економічний	[ɛkono'mitʃnij]

weight	вага (ж)	[wa'ɦa]
to weigh (~ letters)	важити	['waʒiti]
envelope	конверт (ч)	[kon'wɛrt]
postage stamp	марка (ж)	['marka]

Dwelling. House. Home

86. House. Dwelling

house	будинок (ч)	[bu'dinok]
at home (adv)	вдома	['wdɔma]
yard	двір (ч)	[dwir]
fence (iron ~)	грати (мн)	['ɦrati]
brick (n)	цегла (ж)	['tsɛɦla]
brick (as adj)	цегляний	[tsɛɦlʲa'nij]
stone (n)	камінь (ч)	['kaminʲ]
stone (as adj)	кам'яний	[kamʲa'nij]
concrete (n)	бетон (ч)	[bɛ'tɔn]
concrete (as adj)	бетонний	[bɛ'tɔnij]
new (new-built)	новий	[no'wij]
old (adj)	старий	[sta'rij]
decrepit (house)	старий, ветхий	[sta'rij], ['wɛthij]
modern (adj)	сучасний	[su'tʃasnij]
multistorey (adj)	багатоповерховий	[ba'ɦato powɛr'ɦowij]
tall (~ building)	високий	[wi'sɔkij]
floor, storey	поверх (ч)	['pɔwɛrh]
single-storey (adj)	одноповерховий	[odnopowɛr'ɦowij]
ground floor	нижній поверх (ч)	['niʒnij 'pɔwɛrh]
top floor	верхній поверх (ч)	['wɛrhnij 'pɔwɛrh]
roof	дах (ч)	[dah]
chimney	труба (ж)	[tru'ba]
roof tiles	черепиця (ж)	[tʃɛrɛ'pitsʲa]
tiled (adj)	черепичний	[tʃɛrɛ'pitʃnij]
loft (attic)	горище (с)	[ɦo'riɕɛ]
window	вікно (с)	[wik'nɔ]
glass	скло (с)	['sklo]
window ledge	підвіконня (с)	[pidwi'kɔnʲa]
shutters	віконниці (мн)	[wi'kɔnitsi]
wall	стіна (ж)	[sti'na]
balcony	балкон (ч)	[bal'kɔn]
downpipe	ринва (ж)	['rinwa]
upstairs (to be ~)	нагорі	[naɦo'ri]
to go upstairs	підніматися	[pidni'matisʲa]
to come down (the stairs)	спускатися	[spus'katisʲa]
to move (to new premises)	переїздити	[pɛrɛjiz'diti]

87. House. Entrance. Lift

entrance	під'їзд (ч)	[pid"jizd]
stairs (stairway)	сходи (мн)	['shɔdi]
steps	сходинки (мн)	['shɔdinki]
banisters	поруччя (мн)	[po'rutʃʲa]
lobby (hotel ~)	хол (ч)	[hol]
postbox	поштова скринька (ж)	[poʃ'tɔwa sk'rinʲka]
waste bin	бак (ч) для сміття	[bak dlʲa smit'tʲa]
refuse chute	сміттєпровід (ч)	[smittɛ'prɔwid]
lift	ліфт (ч)	[lift]
goods lift	вантажний ліфт (ч)	[wan'taʒnij lift]
lift cage	кабіна (ж)	[ka'bina]
to take the lift	їхати в ліфті	['jihati w 'lifti]
flat	квартира (ж)	[kwar'tira]
residents (~ of a building)	мешканці (мн)	['mɛʃkanʦi]
neighbour (masc.)	сусід (ч)	[su'sid]
neighbour (fem.)	сусідка (ж)	[su'sidka]
neighbours	сусіди (мн)	[su'sidi]

88. House. Electricity

electricity	електрика (ж)	[ɛ'lɛktrika]
light bulb	лампочка (ж)	['lampoʧka]
switch	вимикач (ч)	[wimi'kaʧ]
fuse (plug fuse)	пробка (ж)	['prɔbka]
cable, wire (electric ~)	провід (ч)	['prɔwid]
wiring	проводка (ж)	[pro'wɔdka]
electricity meter	лічильник (ч)	[li'ʧilʲnik]
readings	показання (с)	[poka'zanʲa]

89. House. Doors. Locks

door	двері (мн)	['dwɛri]
gate (vehicle ~)	брама (ж)	['brama]
handle, doorknob	ручка (ж)	['ruʧka]
to unlock (unbolt)	відкрити	[wid'kriti]
to open (vt)	відкривати	[widkri'wati]
to close (vt)	закривати	[zakri'wati]
key	ключ (ч)	[klʲuʧ]
bunch (of keys)	в'язка (ж)	['wʲazka]
to creak (door, etc.)	скрипіти	[skri'piti]
creak	скрипіння (с)	[skri'pinʲa]
hinge (door ~)	петля (ж)	[pɛt'lʲa]
doormat	килимок (ч)	[kili'mɔk]
door lock	замок (ч)	[za'mɔk]

keyhole	замкова щілина (ж)	[zam'kɔwa ɕi'lina]
crossbar (sliding bar)	засув (ч)	['zasuw]
door latch	засувка (ж)	['zasuwka]
padlock	навісний замок (ч)	[nawis'nij za'mɔk]

to ring (~ the door bell)	дзвонити	[dʑwo'niti]
ringing (sound)	дзвінок (ч)	[dʑwi'nɔk]
doorbell	дзвінок (ч)	[dʑwi'nɔk]
doorbell button	кнопка (ж)	['knɔpka]
knock (at the door)	стукіт (ч)	['stukit]
to knock (vi)	стукати	['stukati]

code	код (ч)	[kod]
combination lock	кодовий замок (ч)	['kɔdowij za'mɔk]
intercom	домофон (ч)	[domo'fɔn]
number (on the door)	номер (ч)	['nɔmɛr]
doorplate	табличка (ж)	[tab'litʃka]
peephole	вічко (с)	['witʃko]

90. Country house

village	село (с)	[sɛ'lɔ]
vegetable garden	город (ч)	[ɦo'rɔd]
fence	паркан (ч)	[par'kan]
picket fence	тин (ч)	[tin]
wicket gate	хвіртка (ж)	['hwirtka]

granary	комора (ж)	[ko'mɔra]
cellar	льох (ч)	[lʲoh]
shed (garden ~)	сарай (ч)	[sa'raj]
water well	криниця (ж)	[kri'nitsʲa]

stove (wood-fired ~)	піч (ж)	[pitʃ]
to stoke the stove	палити	[pa'liti]
firewood	дрова (мн)	['drɔwa]
log (firewood)	поліно (с)	[po'lino]

veranda	веранда (ж)	[wɛ'randa]
deck (terrace)	тераса (ж)	[tɛ'rasa]
stoop (front steps)	ганок (ч)	['ɦanok]
swing (hanging seat)	гойдалка (ж)	['ɦɔjdalka]

91. Villa. Mansion

country house	будинок (ч) за містом	[bu'dinok za 'mistom]
country-villa	вілла (ж)	['willa]
wing (~ of a building)	крило (с)	[kri'lɔ]

garden	сад (ч)	[sad]
park	парк (ч)	[park]
conservatory (greenhouse)	оранжерея (ж)	[oranʒɛ'rɛʲa]
to look after (garden, etc.)	доглядати	[doɦlʲa'dati]

swimming pool	басейн (ч)	[ba'sɛjn]
gym (home gym)	спортивний зал (ч)	[spor'tiwnij 'zal]
tennis court	тенісний корт (ч)	['tɛnisnij 'kɔrt]
home theater (room)	кінотеатр (ч)	[kinotɛ'atr]
garage	гараж (ч)	[ɦa'raʒ]

| private property | приватна власність (ж) | [pri'watna 'wlasnistⁱ] |
| private land | приватні володіння (мн) | [pri'watni wolo'dinⁱa] |

| warning (caution) | попередження (с) | [popɛ'rɛdʒɛnⁱa] |
| warning sign | попереджувальний напис (ч) | [popɛ'rɛdʒuwalⁱnij 'napis] |

security	охорона (ж)	[oho'rɔna]
security guard	охоронник (ч)	[oho'rɔnik]
burglar alarm	сигналізація (ж)	[siɦnali'zatsiⁱa]

92. Castle. Palace

castle	замок (ч)	['zamok]
palace	палац (ч)	[pa'lats]
fortress	фортеця (ж)	[for'tɛtsⁱa]
wall (round castle)	стіна (ж)	[sti'na]
tower	вежа (ж)	['wɛʒa]
keep, donjon	головна вежа (ж)	[ɦolow'na 'wɛʒa]

portcullis	підйомна брама (ж)	[pid'jomna 'brama]
subterranean passage	підземний хід (ч)	[pi'dzɛmnij hid]
moat	рів (ч)	[riw]
chain	ланцюг (ч)	[lan'tsⁱuɦ]
arrow loop	бійниця (ж)	[bij'nitsⁱa]

magnificent (adj)	пишний	['piʃnij]
majestic (adj)	величний	[wɛ'litʃnij]
impregnable (adj)	неприступний	[nɛpri'stupnij]
medieval (adj)	середньовічний	[sɛrɛdnⁱo'witʃnij]

93. Flat

flat	квартира (ж)	[kwar'tira]
room	кімната (ж)	[kim'nata]
bedroom	спальня (ж)	['spalⁱnⁱa]
dining room	їдальня (ж)	['jidalⁱnⁱa]
living room	вітальня (ж)	[wi'talⁱnⁱa]
study (home office)	кабінет (ч)	[kabi'nɛt]

entry room	передпокій (ч)	[pɛrɛd'pɔkij]
bathroom	ванна кімната (ж)	['wana kim'nata]
water closet	туалет (ч)	[tua'lɛt]
ceiling	стеля (ж)	['stɛlⁱa]
floor	підлога (ж)	[pid'lɔɦa]
corner	куток (ч)	[ku'tɔk]

94. Flat. Cleaning

to clean (vi, vt)	прибирати	[pribi'rati]
to put away (to stow)	прибирати	[pribi'rati]
dust	пил (ч)	[pil]
dusty (adj)	курний	[kur'nij]
to dust (vt)	витирати пил	[witi'rati pil]
vacuum cleaner	пилосос (ч)	[pilo'sɔs]
to vacuum (vt)	пилососити	[pilo'sɔsiti]
to sweep (vi, vt)	підмітати	[pidmi'tati]
sweepings	сміття (с)	[smit'tʲa]
order	лад (ч)	[lad]
disorder, mess	безлад (ч)	['bɛzlad]
mop	швабра (ж)	['ʃwabra]
duster	ганчірка (ж)	[ɦan'tʃirka]
short broom	віник (ч)	['winik]
dustpan	совок (ч) для сміття	[so'wɔk dlʲa smit'tʲa]

95. Furniture. Interior

furniture	меблі (мн)	['mɛbli]
table	стіл (ч)	[stil]
chair	стілець (ч)	[sti'lɛts]
bed	ліжко (с)	['liʒko]
sofa, settee	диван (ч)	[di'wan]
armchair	крісло (с)	['krislo]
bookcase	шафа (ж)	['ʃafa]
shelf	полиця (ж)	[po'litsʲa]
wardrobe	шафа (ж)	['ʃafa]
coat rack (wall-mounted ~)	вішалка (ж)	['wiʃalka]
coat stand	вішак (ч)	[wi'ʃak]
chest of drawers	комод (ч)	[ko'mɔd]
coffee table	журнальний столик (ч)	[ʒur'nalʲnij 'stɔlik]
mirror	дзеркало (с)	['dzɛrkalo]
carpet	килим (ч)	['kilim]
small carpet	килимок (ч)	[kili'mɔk]
fireplace	камін (ч)	[ka'min]
candle	свічка (ж)	['switʃka]
candlestick	свічник (ч)	[switʃ'nik]
drapes	штори (мн)	['ʃtɔri]
wallpaper	шпалери (мн)	[ʃpa'lɛri]
blinds (jalousie)	жалюзі (мн)	['ʒalʲuzi]
table lamp	настільна лампа (ж)	[na'stilʲna 'lampa]
wall lamp (sconce)	світильник (ч)	[swi'tilʲnik]

standard lamp	торшер (ч)	[tor'ʃɛr]
chandelier	люстра (ж)	['lʲustra]

leg (of a chair, table)	ніжка (ж)	['niʒka]
armrest	підлокітник (ч)	[pidlo'kitnik]
back (backrest)	спинка (ж)	['spinka]
drawer	шухляда (ж)	[ʃuh'lʲada]

96. Bedding

bedclothes	білизна (ж)	[bi'lizna]
pillow	подушка (ж)	[po'duʃka]
pillowslip	наволочка (ж)	['nawolotʃka]
duvet	ковдра (ж)	['kɔwdra]
sheet	простирадло (с)	[prosti'radlo]
bedspread	покривало (с)	[pokri'walo]

97. Kitchen

kitchen	кухня (ж)	['kuhnʲa]
gas	газ (ч)	[ħaz]
gas cooker	плита (ж) газова	[pli'ta 'ħazowa]
electric cooker	плита (ж) електрична	[pli'ta ɛlɛkt'ritʃna]
oven	духовка (ж)	[du'hɔwka]
microwave oven	мікрохвильова піч (ж)	[mikrohwilʲo'wa pitʃ]

refrigerator	холодильник (ч)	[holo'dilʲnik]
freezer	морозильник (ч)	[moro'zilʲnik]
dishwasher	посудомийна машина (ж)	[posudo'mijna ma'ʃina]

mincer	м'ясорубка (ж)	[mʲʲaso'rubka]
juicer	соковижималка (ж)	[sokowiʒi'malka]
toaster	тостер (ч)	['tɔstɛr]
mixer	міксер (ч)	['miksɛr]

coffee machine	кавоварка (ж)	[kawo'warka]
coffee pot	кавник (ч)	[kaw'nik]
coffee grinder	кавомолка (ж)	[kawo'mɔlka]

kettle	чайник (ч)	['tʃajnik]
teapot	заварник (ч)	[za'warnik]
lid	кришка (ж)	['kriʃka]
tea strainer	ситечко (с)	['sitɛtʃko]

spoon	ложка (ж)	['lɔʒka]
teaspoon	чайна ложка (ж)	['tʃajna 'lɔʒka]
soup spoon	столова ложка (ж)	[sto'lɔwa 'lɔʒka]
fork	виделка (ж)	[wi'dɛlka]
knife	ніж (ч)	[niʒ]

tableware (dishes)	посуд (ч)	['pɔsud]
plate (dinner ~)	тарілка (ж)	[ta'rilka]

saucer	блюдце (с)	['blʲudʦɛ]
shot glass	чарка (ж)	['ʧarka]
glass (tumbler)	склянка (ж)	['sklʲanka]
cup	чашка (ж)	['ʧaʃka]

sugar bowl	цукорниця (ж)	['ʦukornitsʲa]
salt cellar	сільничка (ж)	[silʲ'niʧka]
pepper pot	перечниця (ж)	['pɛrɛʧnitsʲa]
butter dish	маслянка (ж)	['maslʲanka]

stock pot (soup pot)	каструля (ж)	[kas'trulʲa]
frying pan (skillet)	сковорідка (ж)	[skowo'ridka]
ladle	черпак (ч)	[ʧɛr'pak]
colander	друшляк (ч)	[druʃ'lʲak]
tray (serving ~)	піднос (ч)	[pid'nɔs]

bottle	пляшка (ж)	['plʲaʃka]
jar (glass)	банка (ж)	['banka]
tin (can)	банка (ж)	['banka]

bottle opener	відкривачка (ж)	[widkri'waʧka]
tin opener	відкривачка (ж)	[widkri'waʧka]
corkscrew	штопор (ч)	['ʃtɔpor]
filter	фільтр (ч)	['filʲtr]
to filter (vt)	фільтрувати	[filʲtru'wati]

| waste (food ~, etc.) | сміття (с) | [smit'tʲa] |
| waste bin (kitchen ~) | відро (с) для сміття | [wid'ro dlʲa smit'tʲa] |

98. Bathroom

bathroom	ванна кімната (ж)	['wana kim'nata]
water	вода (ж)	[wo'da]
tap	кран (ч)	[kran]
hot water	гаряча вода (ж)	[ɦa'rʲaʧa wo'da]
cold water	холодна вода (ж)	[ho'lɔdna wo'da]

| toothpaste | зубна паста (ж) | [zub'na 'pasta] |
| to clean one's teeth | чистити зуби | ['ʧistiti 'zubi] |

to shave (vi)	голитися	[ɦo'litisʲa]
shaving foam	піна (ж) для гоління	['pina dlʲa ɦo'linʲa]
razor	бритва (ж)	['britwa]

to wash (one's hands, etc.)	мити	['miti]
to have a bath	митися	['mitisʲa]
shower	душ (ч)	[duʃ]
to have a shower	приймати душ	[prij'mati duʃ]

bath	ванна (ж)	['wana]
toilet (toilet bowl)	унітаз (ч)	[uni'taz]
sink (washbasin)	раковина (ж)	['rakowina]
soap	мило (с)	['miɫo]
soap dish	мильниця (ж)	['milʲnitsʲa]

sponge	губка (ж)	['hubka]
shampoo	шампунь (ч)	[ʃam'punʲ]
towel	рушник (ч)	[ruʃ'nik]
bathrobe	халат (ч)	[ha'lat]

laundry (laundering)	прання (с)	[pra'nʲa]
washing machine	пральна машина (ж)	['pralʲna ma'ʃina]
to do the laundry	прати білизну	['prati bi'liznu]
washing powder	пральний порошок (ч)	['pralʲnij poro'ʃok]

99. Household appliances

TV, telly	телевізор (ч)	[tɛlɛ'wizor]
tape recorder	магнітофон (ч)	[mahnito'fɔn]
video	відеомагнітофон (ч)	['widɛo mahnito'fɔn]
radio	приймач (ч)	[prij'matʃ]
player (CD, MP3, etc.)	плеєр (ч)	['plɛɛr]

video projector	відеопроектор (ч)	['widɛo pro'ɛktor]
home cinema	домашній кінотеатр (ч)	[do'maʃnij kinotɛ'atr]
DVD player	програвач (ч) DVD	[prohra'watʃ diwi'di]
amplifier	підсилювач (ч)	[pid'silʲuwatʃ]
video game console	гральна приставка (ж)	['hralʲna pri'stawka]

video camera	відеокамера (ж)	['widɛo 'kamɛra]
camera (photo)	фотоапарат (ч)	[fotoapa'rat]
digital camera	цифровий фотоапарат (ч)	[tsifro'wij fotoapa'rat]

vacuum cleaner	пилосос (ч)	[pilo'sɔs]
iron (e.g. steam ~)	праска (ж)	['praska]
ironing board	дошка (ж) для прасування	['dɔʃka dlʲa prasu'wanʲa]

telephone	телефон (ч)	[tɛlɛ'fɔn]
mobile phone	мобільний телефон (ч)	[mo'bilʲnij tɛlɛ'fɔn]
typewriter	машинка (ж)	[ma'ʃinka]
sewing machine	швейна машинка (ж)	['ʃwɛjna ma'ʃinka]

microphone	мікрофон (ч)	[mikro'fɔn]
headphones	навушники (мн)	[na'wuʃniki]
remote control (TV)	пульт (ч)	[pulʲt]

CD, compact disc	CD-диск (ч)	[si'di disk]
cassette, tape	касета (ж)	[ka'sɛta]
vinyl record	платівка (ж)	[pla'tiwka]

100. Repairs. Renovation

renovations	ремонт (ч)	[rɛ'mɔnt]
to renovate (vt)	робити ремонт	[ro'biti rɛ'mɔnt]
to repair, to fix (vt)	ремонтувати	[rɛmontu'wati]
to put in order	привести до ладу	[pri'wɛsti do 'ladu]
to redo (do again)	переробляти	[pɛrɛrob'lʲati]

paint	фарба (ж)	['farba]
to paint (~ a wall)	фарбувати	[farbu'wati]
house painter	маляр (ж)	['malʲar]
paintbrush	щітка (ж)	['ɕitka]

| whitewash | побілка (ж) | [po'bilka] |
| to whitewash (vt) | білити | [bi'liti] |

wallpaper	шпалери (мн)	[ʃpa'lɛri]
to wallpaper (vt)	поклеїти шпалерами	[pok'lɛjiti ʃpa'lɛrami]
varnish	лак (ч)	[lak]
to varnish (vt)	покривати лаком	[pokri'wati 'lakom]

101. Plumbing

water	вода (ж)	[wo'da]
hot water	гаряча вода (ж)	[ɦa'rʲatʃa wo'da]
cold water	холодна вода (ж)	[ho'lɔdna wo'da]
tap	кран (ч)	[kran]

drop (of water)	крапля (ж)	['kraplʲa]
to drip (vi)	крапати	['krapati]
to leak (ab. pipe)	текти	[tɛk'ti]
leak (pipe ~)	теча (ж)	['tɛtʃa]
puddle	калюжа (ж)	[ka'lʲuʒa]

pipe	труба (ж)	[tru'ba]
valve (e.g., ball ~)	вентиль (ч)	['wɛntilʲ]
to be clogged up	забитись	[za'bitisʲ]

tools	інструменти (мн)	[instru'mɛnti]
adjustable spanner	розвідний ключ (ч)	[roz'widnij klʲutʃ]
to unscrew (lid, filter, etc.)	відкрутити	[widkru'titi]
to screw (tighten)	закручувати	[za'krutʃuwati]

to unclog (vt)	прочищати	[protʃi'ɕati]
plumber	сантехнік (ч)	[san'tɛhnik]
basement	підвал (ч)	[pid'wal]
sewerage (system)	каналізація (ж)	[kanali'zatsiʲa]

102. Fire. Conflagration

fire (accident)	вогонь (ч)	[wo'ɦonʲ]
flame	полум'я (с)	['polumʲa]
spark	іскра (ж)	['iskra]
smoke (from fire)	дим (ч)	[dim]
torch (flaming stick)	смолоскип (ч)	[smolos'kip]
campfire	багаття (с)	[ba'ɦatʲa]

petrol	бензин (ч)	[bɛn'zin]
paraffin	керосин (ч)	[kɛro'sin]
flammable (adj)	горючий	[ɦo'rʲutʃij]

| explosive (adj) | вибухонебезпечний | [wibuhonɛbɛz'pɛʧnij] |
| NO SMOKING | ПАЛИТИ ЗАБОРОНЕНО | [pa'liti zabo'rɔnɛno] |

safety	безпека (ж)	[bɛz'pɛka]
danger	небезпека (ж)	[nɛbɛz'pɛka]
dangerous (adj)	небезпечний	[nɛbɛz'pɛʧnij]

to catch fire	загорітися	[zaɦo'ritisʲa]
explosion	вибух (ч)	['wibuh]
to set fire	підпалити	[pidpa'liti]
arsonist	підпалювач (ч)	[pid'palʲuwaʧ]
arson	підпал (ч)	['pidpal]

to blaze (vi)	палати	[pa'lati]
to burn (be on fire)	горіти	[ɦo'riti]
to burn down	згоріти	[zɦo'riti]

firefighter, fireman	пожежник (ч)	[po'ʒɛʒnik]
fire engine	пожежна машина (ж)	[po'ʒɛʒna ma'ʃina]
fire brigade	пожежна команда (ж)	[po'ʒɛʒna ko'manda]
fire engine ladder	драбина (ж)	[dra'bina]

fire hose	шланг (ч)	[ʃlanɦ]
fire extinguisher	вогнегасник (ч)	[woɦnɛ'ɦasnik]
helmet	каска (ж)	['kaska]
siren	сирена (ж)	[si'rɛna]

to cry (for help)	кричати	[kri'ʧati]
to call for help	кликати на допомогу	['klikati na dopo'mɔɦu]
rescuer	рятувальник (ч)	[rʲatu'walʲnik]
to rescue (vt)	рятувати	[rʲatu'wati]

to arrive (vi)	приїхати	[pri'jihati]
to extinguish (vt)	тушити	[tu'ʃiti]
water	вода (ж)	[wo'da]
sand	пісок (ч)	[pi'sɔk]

ruins (destruction)	руїни (мн)	[ru'jini]
to collapse (building, etc.)	повалитися	[powa'litisʲa]
to fall down (vi)	обвалитися	[obwalitisʲa]
to cave in (ceiling, floor)	завалитися	[zawa'litisʲa]

| piece of debris | уламок (ч) | [u'lamok] |
| ash | попіл (ч) | ['pɔpil] |

| to suffocate (die) | задихнутися | [zadih'nutisʲa] |
| to be killed (perish) | загинути | [za'ɦinuti] |

HUMAN ACTIVITIES

Job. Business. Part 1

103.   Office. Working in the office

office (company ~)	**офіс** (ч)	['ɔfis]
office (director's ~)	**кабінет** (ч)	[kabi'nɛt]
reception desk	**ресепшн** (ч)	[rɛ'sɛpʃn]
secretary	**секретар** (ч)	[sɛkrɛ'tar]
secretary (fem.)	**секретарка** (ж)	[sɛkrɛ'tarka]
director	**директор** (ч)	[di'rɛktor]
manager	**менеджер** (ч)	['mɛnɛdʒɛr]
accountant	**бухгалтер** (ч)	[buh'ɦaltɛr]
employee	**робітник** (ч)	[ro'bitnik]
furniture	**меблі** (мн)	['mɛbli]
desk	**стіл** (ч)	[stil]
desk chair	**крісло** (с)	['krislo]
drawer unit	**тумбочка** (ч)	['tumbotʃka]
coat stand	**вішак** (ч)	[wi'ʃak]
computer	**комп'ютер** (ч)	[kom'pʲiutɛr]
printer	**принтер** (ч)	['printɛr]
fax machine	**факс** (ч)	[faks]
photocopier	**копіювальний апарат** (ч)	[kopiʲu'walʲnij apa'rat]
paper	**папір** (ч)	[pa'pir]
office supplies	**канцелярське приладдя** (с)	[kantsɛ'lʲarsʲkɛ pri'laddʲa]
mouse mat	**килимок** (ч)	[kiłi'mɔk]
sheet of paper	**аркуш** (ч)	['arkuʃ]
binder	**папка** (ж)	['papka]
catalogue	**каталог** (ч)	[kata'lɔɦ]
phone directory	**довідник** (ч)	[do'widnik]
documentation	**документація** (ж)	[dokumɛn'tatsiʲa]
brochure (e.g. 12 pages ~)	**брошура** (ж)	[bro'ʃura]
leaflet (promotional ~)	**листівка** (ж)	[lis'tiwka]
sample	**зразок** (ч)	[zra'zɔk]
training meeting	**тренінг** (ч)	['trɛninɦ]
meeting (of managers)	**нарада** (ж)	[na'rada]
lunch time	**перерва** (ж) **на обід**	[pɛ'rɛrwa na o'bid]
to make a copy	**робити копію**	[ro'biti 'kɔpiʲu]
to make multiple copies	**розмножити**	[rozm'nɔʒiti]
to receive a fax	**отримувати факс**	[ot'rimuwati faks]
to send a fax	**відправити факс**	[wid'prawiti faks]

to call (by phone)	подзвонити	[podzwo'niti]
to answer (vt)	відповісти	[widpo'wisti]
to put through	з'єднати	[z'ɛd'nati]

to arrange, to set up	призначити	[priz'natʃiti]
to demonstrate (vt)	демонструвати	[dɛmonstru'wati]
to be absent	бути відсутнім	['buti wid'sutnim]
absence	пропуск (ч)	['prɔpusk]

104. Business processes. Part 1

occupation	справа (ж)	['sprawa]
firm	фірма (ж)	['firma]
company	компанія (ж)	[kom'paniˡa]
corporation	корпорація (ж)	[korpo'ratsiˡa]
enterprise	підприємство (с)	[pidpri'ɛmstwo]
agency	агентство (с)	[a'ɦɛntstwo]

agreement (contract)	договір (ч)	['dɔɦowir]
contract	контракт (ч)	[kon'trakt]
deal	угода (ж)	[u'ɦɔda]
order (to place an ~)	замовлення (с)	[za'mɔwlɛnˡa]
terms (of the contract)	умова (ж)	[u'mɔwa]

wholesale (adv)	оптом	['ɔptom]
wholesale (adj)	оптовий	[op'tɔwij]
wholesale (n)	оптова торгівля (ж)	[op'tɔwa tor'ɦiwlˡa]
retail (adj)	роздрібний	[rozd'ribnij]
retail (n)	продаж (ч) в роздріб	['prɔdaʒ w 'rɔzdrib]

competitor	конкурент (ч)	[konku'rɛnt]
competition	конкуренція (ж)	[konku'rɛntsiˡa]
to compete (vi)	конкурувати	[konkuru'wati]

| partner (associate) | партнер (ч) | [part'nɛr] |
| partnership | партнерство (с) | [part'nɛrstwo] |

crisis	криза (ж)	['kriza]
bankruptcy	банкрутство (с)	[ban'krutstwo]
to go bankrupt	збанкрутувати	[zbankrutu'wati]
difficulty	складність (ж)	['skladnistˡ]
problem	проблема (ж)	[prob'lɛma]
catastrophe	катастрофа (ж)	[kata'strɔfa]

economy	економіка (ж)	[ɛko'nɔmika]
economic (~ growth)	економічний	[ɛkono'mitʃnij]
economic recession	економічний спад (ч)	[ɛkono'mitʃnij spad]

| goal (aim) | мета (ж) | [mɛ'ta] |
| task | завдання (с) | [zaw'danˡa] |

to trade (vi)	торгувати	[torɦu'wati]
network (distribution ~)	мережа (ж)	[mɛ'rɛʒa]
inventory (stock)	склад (ч)	['sklad]

range (assortment)	асортимент (ч)	[asorti'mɛnt]
leader (leading company)	лідер (ч)	['lidɛr]
large (~ company)	великий	[wɛ'likij]
monopoly	монополія (ж)	[mono'pɔliʲa]

theory	теорія (ж)	[tɛ'ɔriʲa]
practice	практика (ж)	['praktika]
experience (in my ~)	досвід (ч)	['dɔswid]
trend (tendency)	тенденція (ж)	[tɛn'dɛntsiʲa]
development	розвиток (ч)	['rɔzwitok]

105. Business processes. Part 2

| profit (foregone ~) | вигода (ж) | ['wiɦoda] |
| profitable (~ deal) | вигідний | ['wiɦidnij] |

delegation (group)	делегація (ж)	[dɛlɛ'ɦatsiʲa]
salary	заробітна платня (ж)	[zaro'bitna plat'nʲa]
to correct (an error)	виправляти	[wipraw'lʲati]
business trip	відрядження (с)	[wid'rʲadʒɛnʲa]
commission	комісія (ж)	[ko'misiʲa]

to control (vt)	контролювати	[kontrolʲu'wati]
conference	конференція (ж)	[konfɛ'rɛntsiʲa]
licence	ліцензія (ж)	[li'tsɛnziʲa]
reliable (~ partner)	надійний	[na'dijnij]

initiative (undertaking)	починання (с)	[potʃi'nanʲa]
norm (standard)	норма (ж)	['nɔrma]
circumstance	обставина (ж)	[ob'stawina]
duty (of an employee)	обов'язок (ч)	[o'bowʲazok]

organization (company)	організація (ж)	[orɦani'zatsiʲa]
organization (process)	організація (ж)	[orɦani'zatsiʲa]
organized (adj)	організований	[orɦani'zɔwanij]
cancellation	скасування (с)	[skasu'wanʲa]
to cancel (call off)	скасувати	[skasu'wati]
report (official ~)	звіт (ч)	[zwit]

patent	патент (ч)	[pa'tɛnt]
to patent (obtain patent)	патентувати	[patɛntu'wati]
to plan (vt)	планувати	[planu'wati]

bonus (money)	премія (ж)	['prɛmiʲa]
professional (adj)	професійний	[profɛ'sijnij]
procedure	процедура (ж)	[protsɛ'dura]

to examine (contract, etc.)	розглянути	[rozɦ'lʲanuti]
calculation	розрахунок (ч)	[rozra'hunok]
reputation	репутація (ж)	[rɛpu'tatsiʲa]
risk	ризик (ч)	['rizik]

| to manage, to run | керувати | [kɛru'wati] |
| information (report) | відомості (мн) | [wi'dɔmosti] |

| property | власність (ж) | ['wlasnistʲ] |
| union | союз (ч) | [soˈʲuz] |

life insurance	страхування (с) життя	[strahu'wanja ʒit't'a]
to insure (vt)	страхувати	[strahu'wati]
insurance	страхування (с)	[strahu'wanʲa]

auction (~ sale)	торги (мн)	[tor'ɦi]
to notify (inform)	повідомити	[powi'dɔmiti]
management (process)	управління (с)	[upraw'linʲa]
service (~ industry)	послуга (ж)	['pɔsluɦa]

forum	форум (ч)	['fɔrum]
to function (vi)	функціонувати	[funktsionu'wati]
stage (phase)	етап (ч)	[ɛ'tap]
legal (~ services)	юридичний	[ʲuri'ditʃnij]
lawyer (legal advisor)	юрист (ч)	[ʲu'rist]

106. Production. Works

plant	завод (ч)	[za'wɔd]
factory	фабрика (ж)	['fabrika]
workshop	цех (ч)	[tsɛh]
works, production site	виробництво (с)	[wirob'nitstwo]

industry (manufacturing)	промисловість (ж)	[promis'lɔwistʲ]
industrial (adj)	промисловий	[promis'lɔwij]
heavy industry	важка промисловість (ж)	[waʒ'ka promis'lɔwistʲ]
light industry	легка промисловість (ж)	[lɛɦ'ka promis'lɔwistʲ]

products	продукція (ж)	[pro'duktsiʲa]
to produce (vt)	виробляти	[wirob'lʲati]
raw materials	сировина (ж)	[sirowi'na]

foreman (construction ~)	бригадир (ч)	[briɦa'dir]
workers team (crew)	бригада (ж)	[bri'ɦada]
worker	робочий (ч)	[ro'bɔtʃij]

working day	робочий день (ч)	[ro'bɔtʃij dɛnʲ]
pause (rest break)	перерва (ж)	[pɛ'rɛrwa]
meeting	збори (мн)	['zbɔri]
to discuss (vt)	обговорювати	[obɦo'wɔrʲuwati]

plan	план (ч)	[plan]
to fulfil the plan	виконати план	['wikonati plan]
rate of output	норма (ж)	['nɔrma]
quality	якість (ж)	['ʲakistʲ]
control (checking)	контроль (ч)	[kon'trɔlʲ]
quality control	контроль (ч) якості	[kon'trɔlʲ 'jakosti]

workplace safety	безпека (ж) праці	[bɛz'pɛka 'pratsi]
discipline	дисципліна (ж)	[distsip'lina]
violation (of safety rules, etc.)	порушення (с)	[po'ruʃɛnʲa]
to violate (rules)	порушувати	[po'ruʃuwati]

strike	страйк (ч)	['strajk]
striker	страйкар (ч)	[straj'kar]
to be on strike	страйкувати	[strajku'wati]
trade union	профспілка (ж)	[profs'pilka]
to invent (machine, etc.)	винайти	['winajti]
invention	винахід (ч)	['winahid]
research	дослідження (с)	[do'slidʒɛnʲa]
to improve (make better)	покращувати	[pok'raɕuwati]
technology	технологія (ж)	[tɛhno'lɔɦiʲa]
technical drawing	креслення (с)	['krɛslɛnʲa]
load, cargo	вантаж (ч)	[wan'taʒ]
loader (person)	вантажник (ч)	[wan'taʒnik]
to load (vehicle, etc.)	вантажити	[wan'taʒiti]
loading (process)	завантаження (с)	[zawan'taʒɛnʲa]
to unload (vi, vt)	розвантажувати	[rozwan'taʒuwati]
unloading	розвантаження (с)	[rozwan'taʒɛnʲa]
transport	транспорт (ч)	['transport]
transport company	транспортна компанія (ж)	['transportna kom'paniʲa]
to transport (vt)	транспортувати	[transportu'wati]
wagon	товарний вагон (ч)	[to'warnij wa'ɦɔn]
tank (e.g., oil ~)	цистерна (ж)	[tsis'tɛrna]
lorry	вантажівка (ж)	[wanta'ʒiwka]
machine tool	станок (ч)	[sta'nɔk]
mechanism	механізм (ч)	[mɛha'nizm]
industrial waste	відходи (мн)	[wid'hɔdi]
packing (process)	пакування (с)	[paku'wanʲa]
to pack (vt)	упакувати	[upaku'wati]

107. Contract. Agreement

contract	контракт (ч)	[kon'trakt]
agreement	угода (ж)	[u'ɦɔda]
addendum	додаток (ч)	[do'datok]
to sign a contract	укласти контракт	[uk'lasti kon'trakt]
signature	підпис (ч)	['pidpis]
to sign (vt)	підписати	[pidpi'sati]
seal (stamp)	печатка (ж)	[pɛ'tʃatka]
subject of the contract	предмет (ч) договору	[prɛd'mɛt 'dɔɦoworu]
clause	пункт (ч)	[punkt]
parties (in contract)	сторони (мн)	['stɔroni]
legal address	юридична адреса (ж)	[ʲuri'ditʃna ad'rɛsa]
to violate the contract	порушити контракт	[po'ruʃiti kon'trakt]
commitment (obligation)	зобов'язання (с)	[zobo'wʲazanʲa]
responsibility	відповідальність (ж)	[widpowi'dalʲnistʲ]
force majeure	форс-мажор (ч)	[fors ma'ʒɔr]

| dispute | суперечка (ж) | [supɛ'rɛʧka] |
| penalties | штрафні санкції (мн) | [ʃtrafʼni 'sanktsiji] |

108. Import & Export

import	імпорт (ч)	['import]
importer	імпортер (ч)	[impor'tɛr]
to import (vt)	імпортувати	[importu'wati]
import (as adj.)	імпортний	['importnij]

| exporter | експортер (ч) | [ɛkspor'tɛr] |
| to export (vt) | експортувати | [ɛksportu'wati] |

| goods (merchandise) | товар (ч) | [to'war] |
| consignment, lot | партія (ж) | ['partiʲa] |

weight	вага (ж)	[wa'ɦa]
volume	об'єм (ч)	[o'bʲɛm]
cubic metre	кубічний метр (ч)	[ku'biʧnij mɛtr]

manufacturer	виробник (ч)	[wirob'nik]
transport company	транспортна компанія (ж)	['transportna kom'paniʲa]
container	контейнер (ч)	[kon'tɛjnɛr]

border	кордон (ч)	[kor'dɔn]
customs	митниця (ж)	['mitnitsʲa]
customs duty	митний збір (ч)	['mitnij zbir]
customs officer	митник (ч)	['mitnik]
smuggling	контрабанда (ж)	[kontra'banda]
contraband (smuggled goods)	контрабанда (ж)	[kontra'banda]

109. Finances

share, stock	акція (ж)	['aktsiʲa]
bond (certificate)	облігація (ж)	[obli'ɦatsiʲa]
promissory note	вексель (ч)	['wɛksɛlʲ]

| stock exchange | біржа (ж) | ['birʒa] |
| stock price | курс (ч) акцій | [kurs 'aktsij] |

| to go down (become cheaper) | подешевшати | [podɛ'ʃɛwʃati] |
| to go up (become more expensive) | подорожчати | [podo'rɔʒʧati] |

controlling interest	контрольний пакет (ч)	[kon'trɔlʲnij pa'kɛt]
investment	інвестиції (мн)	[inwɛs'titsiji]
to invest (vt)	інвестувати	[inwɛstu'wati]
percent	відсоток (ч)	[wid'sɔtok]
interest (on investment)	відсотки (мн)	[wid'sɔtki]
profit	прибуток (ч)	[pri'butok]

| profitable (adj) | прибутковий | [pribut'kɔwij] |
| tax | податок (ч) | [po'datok] |

currency (foreign ~)	валюта (ж)	[wa'lʲuta]
national (adj)	національний	[natsio'nalʲnij]
exchange (currency ~)	обмін (ч)	['ɔbmin]

| accountant | бухгалтер (ч) | [buh'ɦaltɛr] |
| accounting | бухгалтерія (ж) | [buhɦal'tɛriʲa] |

bankruptcy	банкрутство (с)	[ban'krutstwo]
collapse, ruin	крах (ч)	[krah]
ruin	розорення (с)	[ro'zorɛnʲa]
to be ruined (financially)	розоритися	[rozo'ritisʲa]
inflation	інфляція (ж)	[infʲlʲatsiʲa]
devaluation	девальвація (ж)	[dɛwalʲ'watsiʲa]

capital	капітал (ч)	[kapi'tal]
income	прибуток (ч)	[pri'butok]
turnover	обіг (ч)	['ɔbiɦ]
resources	ресурси (мн)	[rɛ'sursi]
monetary resources	кошти (мн)	['kɔʃti]
to reduce (expenses)	скоротити	[skoro'titi]

110. Marketing

marketing	маркетинг (ч)	[mar'kɛtinɦ]
market	ринок (ч)	['rinok]
market segment	сегмент (ч) ринку	[sɛɦ'mɛnt 'rinku]

| product | продукт (ч) | [pro'dukt] |
| goods (merchandise) | товар (ч) | [to'war] |

| brand | марка (ж), бренд (ч) | ['marka], ['brɛnd] |
| trademark | торгова марка (ж) | [tor'ɦowa 'marka] |

| logotype | фірмовий знак (ч) | ['firmowij 'znak] |
| logo | логотип (ч) | [loɦo'tip] |

| demand | попит (ч) | ['pɔpit] |
| supply | пропозиція (ж) | [propo'zitsiʲa] |

| need | потреба (ж) | [pot'rɛba] |
| consumer | споживач (ч) | [spoʒi'watʃ] |

| analysis | аналіз (ч) | [a'naliz] |
| to analyse (vt) | аналізувати | [analizu'wati] |

| positioning | позиціонування (с) | [pozitsionu'wanʲa] |
| to position (vt) | позиціонувати | [pozitsionu'wati] |

price	ціна (ж)	[tsi'na]
pricing policy	цінова політика (ж)	[tsino'wa po'litika]
price formation	ціноутворення (с)	[tsinout'worɛnʲa]

111. Advertising

advertising	реклама (ж)	[rɛk'lama]
to advertise (vt)	рекламувати	[rɛklamu'wati]
budget	бюджет (ч)	[bʲu'dʒɛt]

ad, advertisement	реклама (ж)	[rɛk'lama]
TV advertising	телереклама (ж)	['tɛlɛ rɛk'lama]
radio advertising	реклама (ж) на радіо	[rɛk'lama na 'radio]
outdoor advertising	зовнішня реклама (ж)	['zɔwniʃnʲa rɛklama]

mass medias	засоби (мн) масової інформації	['zasɔbi 'masɔwojɨ infor'matsiji]
periodical (n)	періодичне видання (с)	[pɛrio'ditʃnɛ wida'nʲa]
image (public appearance)	імідж (ч)	['imidʒ]

| slogan | гасло (с) | ['ɦaslo] |
| motto (maxim) | девіз (ч) | [dɛ'wiz] |

campaign	кампанія (ж)	[kam'paniʲa]
advertising campaign	рекламна кампанія (ж)	[rɛk'lamna kam'paniʲa]
target group	цільова аудиторія (ж)	[tsilʲo'wa audi'tɔriʲa]

business card	візитка (ж)	[wi'zitka]
leaflet (promotional ~)	листівка (ж)	[lis'tiwka]
brochure (e.g. 12 pages ~)	брошура (ж)	[bro'ʃura]
pamphlet	буклет (ч)	[buk'lɛt]
newsletter	бюлетень (ч)	[bʲulɛ'tɛnʲ]

signboard (store sign, etc.)	вивіска (ж)	['wiwiska]
poster	плакат (ч)	[pla'kat]
hoarding	щит (ч)	[ɕit]

112. Banking

| bank | банк (ч) | [bank] |
| branch (of a bank) | відділення (с) | [wid'dilɛnʲa] |

| consultant | консультант (ч) | [konsulʲ'tant] |
| manager (director) | управляючий (ч) | [upraw'lʲaʲutʃij] |

bank account	рахунок (ч)	[ra'hunok]
account number	номер (ч) рахунка	['nɔmɛr ra'hunka]
current account	поточний рахунок (ч)	[po'tɔtʃnij ra'hunok]
deposit account	накопичувальний рахунок (ч)	[nako'pitʃuwalʲnij ra'hunok]

to open an account	відкрити рахунок	[wid'kriti ra'hunok]
to close the account	закрити рахунок	[za'kriti ra'hunok]
to deposit into the account	покласти на рахунок	[pok'lasti na ra'hunok]
to withdraw (vt)	зняти з рахунку	['znʲati z ra'hunku]
deposit	внесок (ч)	['wnɛsok]
to make a deposit	зробити внесок	[zro'biti 'wnɛsok]

98

| wire transfer | переказ (ч) | [pɛˈrɛkaz] |
| to wire, to transfer | зробити переказ | [zroˈbiti pɛˈrɛkaz] |

| sum | сума (ж) | [ˈsuma] |
| How much? | Скільки? | [ˈskilʲki] |

| signature | підпис (ч) | [ˈpidpis] |
| to sign (vt) | підписати | [pidpiˈsati] |

credit card	кредитна картка (ж)	[krɛˈditna ˈkartka]
code (PIN code)	код (ч)	[kod]
credit card number	номер (ч) кредитної картки	[ˈnɔmɛr krɛˈditnoji ˈkartki]
cashpoint	банкомат (ч)	[bankoˈmat]

cheque	чек (ч)	[ʧɛk]
to write a cheque	виписати чек	[ˈwipisati ˈʧɛk]
chequebook	чекова книжка (ж)	[ˈʧɛkowa ˈkniʒka]

loan (bank ~)	кредит (ч)	[krɛˈdit]
to apply for a loan	звертатися за кредитом	[zwɛrˈtatisʲa za krɛˈditom]
to get a loan	брати кредит	[ˈbrati krɛˈdit]
to give a loan	надавати кредит	[nadaˈwati krɛˈdit]
guarantee	застава (ж)	[zaˈstawa]

113. Telephone. Phone conversation

telephone	телефон (ч)	[tɛlɛˈfon]
mobile phone	мобільний телефон (ч)	[moˈbilʲnij tɛlɛˈfon]
answerphone	автовідповідач (ч)	[awtowidpowiˈdaʧ]

| to call (by phone) | телефонувати | [tɛlɛfonuˈwati] |
| call, ring | дзвінок (ч) | [ʣwiˈnɔk] |

to dial a number	набрати номер	[nabˈrati ˈnɔmɛr]
Hello!	Алло!	[aˈlɔ]
to ask (vt)	запитати	[zapiˈtati]
to answer (vi, vt)	відповісти	[widpoˈwisti]

to hear (vt)	чути	[ˈʧuti]
well (adv)	добре	[ˈdɔbrɛ]
not well (adv)	погано	[poˈɦano]
noises (interference)	перешкоди (мн)	[pɛrɛʃˈkɔdi]

receiver	трубка (ж)	[ˈtrubka]
to pick up (~ the phone)	зняти трубку	[ˈznʲati ˈtrubku]
to hang up (~ the phone)	покласти трубку	[pokˈlasti tˈrubku]

busy (engaged)	зайнятий	[ˈzajnʲatij]
to ring (ab. phone)	дзвонити	[ʣwoˈniti]
telephone book	телефонна книга (ж)	[tɛlɛˈfona ˈkniɦa]

local (adj)	місцевий	[misˈtsɛwij]
local call	місцевий зв'язок (ч)	[misˈtsɛwij ˈzwʲazok]
trunk (e.g. ~ call)	міжміський	[miʒmisˈʲkij]

trunk call	міжміський зв'язок (ч)	[miʒmisˈˈkij ˈzwˈazok]
international (adj)	міжнародний	[miʒnaˈrɔdnij]
international call	міжнародний зв'язок (ч)	[miʒnaˈrɔdnij ˈzwˈazok]

114. Mobile telephone

mobile phone	мобільний телефон (ч)	[moˈbilˈnij tɛlɛˈfɔn]
display	дисплей (ч)	[disˈplɛj]
button	кнопка (ж)	[ˈknɔpka]
SIM card	SIM-карта (ж)	[sim ˈkarta]

battery	батарея (ж)	[bataˈrɛˈa]
to be flat (battery)	розрядитися	[rozrˈaˈditisˈa]
charger	зарядний пристрій (ч)	[zaˈrˈadnij ˈpristrij]

menu	меню (с)	[mɛˈnˈu]
settings	настройки (мн)	[naˈstrɔjki]
tune (melody)	мелодія (ж)	[mɛˈlɔdiˈa]
to select (vt)	вибрати	[ˈwɨbrati]

calculator	калькулятор (ч)	[kalˈkuˈlˈator]
voice mail	автовідповідач (ч)	[awtowidpowiˈdatʃ]
alarm clock	будильник (ч)	[buˈdiˈlˈnik]
contacts	телефонна книга (ж)	[tɛlɛˈfɔna ˈkniɦa]

| SMS (text message) | SMS-повідомлення (с) | [ɛsɛˈmɛs powiˈdɔmlɛnˈa] |
| subscriber | абонент (ч) | [aboˈnɛnt] |

115. Stationery

| ballpoint pen | авторучка (ж) | [awtoˈrutʃka] |
| fountain pen | ручка-перо (с) | [ˈrutʃka pɛˈrɔ] |

pencil	олівець (ч)	[oliˈwɛts]
highlighter	маркер (ч)	[ˈmarkɛr]
felt-tip pen	фломастер (ч)	[floˈmastɛr]

| notepad | блокнот (ч) | [blokˈnɔt] |
| diary | щоденник (ч) | [ɕoˈdɛnik] |

ruler	лінійка (ж)	[liˈnijka]
calculator	калькулятор (ч)	[kalˈkuˈlˈator]
rubber	гумка (ж)	[ˈɦumka]

| drawing pin | кнопка (ж) | [ˈknɔpka] |
| paper clip | скріпка (ж) | [ˈskripka] |

| glue | клей (ч) | [klɛj] |
| stapler | степлер (ч) | [ˈstɛplɛr] |

| hole punch | діркопробивач (ч) | [dirkoprobiˈwatʃ] |
| pencil sharpener | стругачка (ж) | [struˈɦatʃka] |

116. Various kinds of documents

account (report)	звіт (ч)	[zwit]
agreement	угода (ж)	[u'ɦɔda]
application form	заявка (ж)	[za'lawka]
authentic (adj)	оригінальний	[oriɦi'nalʲnij]
badge (identity tag)	бедж (ч)	[bɛdʒ]
business card	візитка (ж)	[wi'zitka]
certificate (~ of quality)	сертифікат (ч)	[sɛrtifi'kat]
cheque (e.g. draw a ~)	чек (ч)	[tʃɛk]
bill (in restaurant)	рахунок (ч)	[ra'hunok]
constitution	конституція (ж)	[konsti'tutsiʲa]
contract (agreement)	договір (ч)	['dɔɦowir]
copy	копія (ж)	['kɔpiʲa]
copy (of a contract, etc.)	примірник (ч)	[pri'mirnik]
customs declaration	декларація (ж)	[dɛkla'ratsiʲa]
document	документ (ч)	[doku'mɛnt]
driving licence	посвідчення (с) водія	[pos'widtʃɛnja wodiʲʲa]
addendum	додаток (ч)	[do'datok]
form	анкета (ж)	[an'kɛta]
ID card (e.g., warrant card)	посвідчення (с)	[pos'widtʃɛnʲia]
inquiry (request)	запит (ч)	['zapit]
invitation card	запрошення (с)	[za'prɔʃɛnʲia]
invoice	рахунок (ч)	[ra'hunok]
law	закон (ч)	[za'kɔn]
letter (mail)	лист (ч)	[list]
letterhead	бланк (ч)	[blank]
list (of names, etc.)	список (ч)	['spisok]
manuscript	рукопис (ч)	[ru'kɔpis]
newsletter	бюлетень (ч)	[bʲulɛ'tɛnʲ]
note (short letter)	записка (ж)	[za'piska]
pass (for worker, visitor)	перепустка (ж)	[pɛ'rɛpustka]
passport	паспорт (ч)	['pasport]
permit	дозвіл (ч)	['dɔzwil]
curriculum vitae, CV	резюме (с)	[rɛzʲu'mɛ]
debt note, IOU	розписка (ж)	[roz'piska]
receipt (for purchase)	квитанція (ж)	[kwi'tantsiʲa]
till receipt	чек (ч)	[tʃɛk]
report (mil.)	рапорт (ч)	['raport]
to show (ID, etc.)	пред'являти	[prɛdʲʲaw'lʲati]
to sign (vt)	підписати	[pidpi'sati]
signature	підпис (ч)	['pidpis]
seal (stamp)	печатка (ж)	[pɛ'tʃatka]
text	текст (ч)	[tɛkst]
ticket (for entry)	квиток (ч)	[kwi'tɔk]
to cross out	закреслити	[za'krɛsliti]
to fill in (~ a form)	заповнити	[za'pɔwniti]

| waybill (shipping invoice) | накладна (ж) | [naklad'na] |
| will (testament) | заповіт (ч) | [zapo'wit] |

117. Kinds of business

accounting services	бухгалтерські послуги (мн)	[buh'haltɛrsʲki 'pɔsluhi]
advertising	реклама (ж)	[rɛk'lama]
advertising agency	рекламне агентство (с)	[rɛk'lamnɛ a'hɛntstwo]
air-conditioners	кондиціонери (мн)	[konditsiʲɔnɛri]
airline	авіакомпанія (ж)	[awiakom'paniʲa]

alcoholic beverages	спиртні напої (мн)	[spirt'ni na'pɔji]
antiques (antique dealers)	антикваріат (ч)	[antikwari'at]
art gallery (contemporary ~)	галерея (ж)	[halɛ'rɛʲa]
audit services	аудиторські послуги (мн)	[au'ditorsʲki 'pɔsluhi]

banking industry	банківський бізнес (ч)	['bankiwsʲkij 'biznɛs]
beauty salon	салон (ч) краси	[sa'lɔn kra'si]
bookshop	книгарня (ж)	[kni'harnʲa]
brewery	броварня (ж)	[bro'warnʲa]
business centre	бізнес-центр (ч)	['biznɛs 'tsɛntr]
business school	бізнес-школа (ж)	['biznɛs 'ʃkɔla]

casino	казино (с)	[kazi'nɔ]
chemist, pharmacy	аптека (ж)	[ap'tɛka]
cinema	кінотеатр (ч)	[kinotɛ'atr]
construction	будівництво (с)	[budiw'nitstwo]
consulting	консалтинг (ч)	[kon'saltinɦ]

dental clinic	стоматологія (ж)	[stomato'lɔɦiʲa]
design	дизайн (ч)	[di'zajn]
dry cleaners	хімчистка (ж)	[him'tʃistka]

employment agency	кадрове агентство (с)	['kadrowɛ a'hɛntstwo]
financial services	фінансові послуги (мн)	[fi'nansowi 'pɔsluhi]
food products	продукти (мн) харчування	[pro'dukti hartʃu'wanʲa]
furniture (e.g. house ~)	меблі (мн)	['mɛbli]
clothing, garment	одяг (ч)	['ɔdʲaɦ]
hotel	готель (ч)	[ɦo'tɛlʲ]

ice-cream	морозиво (с)	[mo'rɔziwo]
industry (manufacturing)	промисловість (ж)	[promis'lɔwistʲ]
insurance	страхування (с)	[strahu'wanʲa]
Internet	інтернет (ч)	[intɛr'nɛt]
investments (finance)	інвестиції (мн)	[inwɛs'titsiji]
jeweller	ювелір (ч)	[ʲuwɛ'lir]
jewellery	ювелірні вироби (мн)	[ʲuwɛ'lirni 'wirobi]

laundry (shop)	пральня (ж)	['pralʲnʲa]
legal adviser	юридичні послуги (мн)	[ʲuri'ditʃni 'pɔsluhi]
light industry	легка промисловість (ж)	[lɛɦ'ka promis'lɔwistʲ]

| magazine | журнал (ч) | [ʒur'nal] |
| mail order selling | торгівля (ж) за каталогом | [tor'ɦiwlʲa za kata'lɔɦom] |

medicine	**медицина** (ж)	[mɛdi'ʦina]
museum	**музей** (ч)	[mu'zɛj]
news agency	**інформаційне агентство** (с)	[informa'ʦijnɛ a'ɦɛnʦtwo]
newspaper	**газета** (ж)	[ɦa'zɛta]
nightclub	**нічний клуб** (ч)	[niʧ'nij klub]
oil (petroleum)	**нафта** (ж)	['nafta]
courier services	**кур'єрська служба** (ж)	[ku'rʲɛrsʲka 'sluʒba]
pharmaceutics	**фармацевтика** (ж)	[farma'ʦɛwtika]
printing (industry)	**поліграфія** (ж)	[poliɦra'fiʲa]
pub	**бар** (ч)	[bar]
publishing house	**видавництво** (с)	[widaw'niʦtwo]
radio (~ station)	**радіо** (с)	['radio]
real estate	**нерухомість** (ж)	[nɛru'ɦɔmistʲ]
restaurant	**ресторан** (ч)	[rɛsto'ran]
security company	**охоронне агентство** (с)	[oɦo'rɔnɛ a'ɦɛnʦtwo]
shop	**магазин** (ч)	[maɦa'zin]
sport	**спорт** (ч)	[sport]
stock exchange	**біржа** (ж)	['birʒa]
supermarket	**супермаркет** (ч)	[supɛr'markɛt]
swimming pool (public ~)	**басейн** (ч)	[ba'sɛjn]
tailor shop	**ательє** (с)	[atɛ'ljɛ]
television	**телебачення** (с)	[tɛlɛ'baʧɛnʲa]
theatre	**театр** (ч)	[tɛ'atr]
trade (commerce)	**торгівля** (ж)	[tor'ɦiwlʲa]
transport companies	**перевезення** (с)	[pɛrɛ'wɛzɛnʲa]
travel	**туризм** (ч)	[tu'rizm]
undertakers	**похоронне бюро** (с)	[poɦo'rɔnɛ bʲuro]
veterinary surgeon	**ветеринар** (ч)	[wɛtɛri'nar]
warehouse	**склад** (ч)	['sklad]
waste collection	**вивіз** (ч) **сміття**	['wiwiz smit'tʲa]

Job. Business. Part 2

exhibition, show	виставка (ж)	['wistawka]
trade show	торгівельна виставка (ж)	[torɦi'wɛlʲna 'wistawka]
participation	участь (ж)	['utʃastʲ]
to participate (vi)	брати участь	['brati 'utʃastʲ]
participant (exhibitor)	учасник (ч)	[u'tʃasnik]
director	директор (ч)	[di'rɛktor]
organizers' office	дирекція (ж)	[diˈrɛktsiʲa]
organizer	організатор (ч)	[orɦani'zator]
to organize (vt)	організовувати	[orɦani'zɔwuwati]
participation form	заявка (ж) на участь	[za'ʲawka na 'utʃastʲ]
to fill in (vt)	заповнити	[za'pɔwniti]
details	деталі (мн)	[dɛ'tali]
information	інформація (ж)	[infor'matsiʲa]
price (cost, rate)	ціна (ж)	[tsi'na]
including	включно	['wklʲutʃno]
to include (vt)	включати	[wklʲu'tʃati]
to pay (vi, vt)	платити	[pla'titi]
registration fee	реєстраційний внесок (ч)	[rɛɛstra'tsijnij 'wnɛsok]
entrance	вхід (ч)	[whid]
pavilion, hall	павільйон (ч)	[pawilʲ'ʲɔn]
to register (vt)	реєструвати	[rɛɛstru'wati]
badge (identity tag)	бедж (ч)	[bɛdʒ]
stand	стенд (ч)	['stɛnd]
to reserve, to book	резервувати	[rɛzɛrwu'wati]
display case	вітрина (ж)	[wi'trina]
spotlight	світильник (ч)	[swi'tilʲnik]
design	дизайн (ч)	[di'zajn]
to place (put, set)	розташовувати	[rozta'ʃɔwuwati]
distributor	дистриб'ютор (ч)	[distri'bʲutor]
supplier	постачальник (ч)	[posta'tʃalʲnik]
country	країна (ж)	[kra'jina]
foreign (adj)	іноземний	[ino'zɛmnij]
product	продукт (ч)	[pro'dukt]
association	асоціація (ж)	[asotsi'atsiʲa]
conference hall	конференц-зал (ч)	[konfɛ'rɛnts zal]
congress	конгрес (ч)	[kon'ɦrɛs]

contest (competition)	конкурс (ч)	['kɔnkurs]
visitor (attendee)	відвідувач (ч)	[wid'widuwatʃ]
to visit (attend)	відвідувати	[wid'widuwati]
customer	замовник (ч)	[za'mɔwnik]

119. Mass Media

newspaper	газета (ж)	[ɦa'zɛta]
magazine	журнал (ч)	[ʒur'nal]
press (printed media)	преса (ж)	['prɛsa]
radio	радіо (с)	['radio]
radio station	радіостанція (ж)	[radios'tantsiˈa]
television	телебачення (с)	[tɛlɛ'batʃɛniˈa]

presenter, host	ведучий (ч)	[wɛ'dutʃij]
newsreader	диктор (ч)	['diktor]
commentator	коментатор (ч)	[komɛn'tator]

journalist	журналіст (ч)	[ʒurna'list]
correspondent (reporter)	кореспондент (ч)	[korɛspon'dɛnt]
press photographer	фотокореспондент (ч)	['foto korɛspon'dɛnt]
reporter	репортер (ч)	[rɛpor'tɛr]

editor	редактор (ч)	[rɛ'daktor]
editor-in-chief	головний редактор (ч)	[ɦolow'nij rɛ'daktor]
to subscribe (to …)	передплатити	[pɛrɛdpla'titi]
subscription	передплата (ж)	[pɛrɛdp'lata]
subscriber	передплатник (ч)	[pɛrɛdp'latnik]
to read (vi, vt)	читати	[tʃi'tati]
reader	читач (ч)	[tʃi'tatʃ]

circulation (of a newspaper)	наклад (ч)	['naklad]
monthly (adj)	щомісячний	[ɕo'misˈatʃnij]
weekly (adj)	щотижневий	[ɕotiʒ'nɛwij]
issue (edition)	номер (ч)	['nɔmɛr]
new (~ issue)	свіжий	['swiʒij]

headline	заголовок (ч)	[zaɦo'lɔwok]
short article	замітка (ж)	[za'mitka]
column (regular article)	рубрика (ж)	['rubrika]
article	стаття (ж)	[stat'tˈa]
page	сторінка (ж)	[sto'rinka]

reportage, report	репортаж (ч)	[rɛpor'taʒ]
event (happening)	подія (ж)	[po'diˈa]
sensation (news)	сенсація (ж)	[sɛn'satsiˈa]
scandal	скандал (ч)	[skan'dal]
scandalous (adj)	скандальний	[skan'dalˈnij]
great (~ scandal)	гучний	[ɦutʃ'nij]

programme (e.g. cooking ~)	передача (ж)	[pɛrɛ'datʃa]
interview	інтерв'ю (с)	[intɛr'wˀu]
live broadcast	пряма трансляція (ж)	[prˈa'ma trans'lˈatsiˈa]
channel	канал (ч)	[ka'nal]

120. Agriculture

agriculture	сільське господарство (c)	[silʲsʲˈkɛ ɦospoˈdarstwo]
peasant (masc.)	селянин (ч)	[sɛlʲaˈnin]
peasant (fem.)	селянка (ж)	[sɛˈlʲanka]
farmer	фермер (ч)	[ˈfɛrmɛr]
tractor	трактор (ч)	[ˈtraktor]
combine, harvester	комбайн (ч)	[komˈbajn]
plough	плуг (ч)	[pluɦ]
to plough (vi, vt)	орати	[oˈrati]
ploughland	рілля (ж)	[riˈlʲa]
furrow (in field)	борозна (ж)	[borozˈna]
to sow (vi, vt)	сіяти	[ˈsiʲati]
seeder	сівалка (ж)	[siˈwalka]
sowing (process)	посів (ч)	[poˈsiw]
scythe	коса (ж)	[koˈsa]
to mow, to scythe	косити	[koˈsiti]
spade (tool)	лопата (ж)	[loˈpata]
to till (vt)	копати	[koˈpati]
hoe	сапка (ж)	[ˈsapka]
to hoe, to weed	полоти	[poˈlɔti]
weed (plant)	бур'ян (ч)	[buˈrʲian]
watering can	лійка (ж)	[ˈlijka]
to water (plants)	поливати	[poliˈwati]
watering (act)	поливання (c)	[poliˈwanʲa]
pitchfork	вила (мн)	[ˈwila]
rake	граблі (мн)	[ɦraˈbli]
fertiliser	добриво (c)	[ˈdɔbriwo]
to fertilise (vt)	удобрювати	[uˈdɔbrʲuwati]
manure (fertiliser)	гній (ч)	[ɦnij]
field	поле (c)	[ˈpɔlɛ]
meadow	лука (ж)	[ˈluka]
vegetable garden	город (ч)	[ɦoˈrɔd]
orchard (e.g. apple ~)	сад (ч)	[sad]
to graze (vt)	пасти	[ˈpasti]
herdsman	пастух (ч)	[pasˈtuɦ]
pasture	пасовище (c)	[pasoˈwiɕɛ]
cattle breeding	тваринництво (c)	[twaˈrinitstwo]
sheep farming	вівчарство (c)	[wiwˈt͡ʃarstwo]
plantation	плантація (ж)	[planˈtat͡siʲa]
row (garden bed ~s)	грядка (ж)	[ˈɦrʲadka]
hothouse	парник (ч)	[parˈnik]

drought (lack of rain)	посуха (ж)	['pɔsuha]
dry (~ summer)	посушливий	[po'suʃliwij]
cereal crops	зернові (мн)	[zɛrno'wi]
to harvest, to gather	збирати	[zbi'rati]
miller (person)	мірошник (ч)	[mi'rɔʃnik]
mill (e.g. gristmill)	млин (ч)	[mlin]
to grind (grain)	молотити зерно	[molo'titi zɛr'nɔ]
flour	борошно (с)	['bɔroʃno]
straw	солома (ж)	[so'lɔma]

121. Building. Building process

building site	будівництво (с)	[budiw'nitstwo]
to build (vt)	будувати	[budu'wati]
building worker	будівельник (ч)	[budi'wɛlʲnik]
project	проект (ч)	[pro'ɛkt]
architect	архітектор (ч)	[arhi'tɛktor]
worker	робочий (ч)	[ro'bɔtʃij]
foundations (of a building)	фундамент (ч)	[fun'damɛnt]
roof	дах (ч)	[dah]
foundation pile	паля (ж)	['palʲa]
wall	стіна (ж)	[sti'na]
reinforcing bars	арматура (ж)	[arma'tura]
scaffolding	риштування (мн)	[riʃtu'wanʲa]
concrete	бетон (ч)	[bɛ'tɔn]
granite	граніт (ч)	[ɦra'nit]
stone	камінь (ч)	['kaminʲ]
brick	цегла (ж)	['tsɛɦla]
sand	пісок (ч)	[pi'sɔk]
cement	цемент (ч)	[tsɛ'mɛnt]
plaster (for walls)	штукатурка (ж)	[ʃtuka'turka]
to plaster (vt)	штукатурити	[ʃtuka'turiti]
paint	фарба (ж)	['farba]
to paint (~ a wall)	фарбувати	[farbu'wati]
barrel	бочка (ж)	['bɔtʃka]
crane	кран (ч)	[kran]
to lift, to hoist (vt)	піднімати	[pidni'mati]
to lower (vt)	опускати	[opus'kati]
bulldozer	бульдозер (ч)	[bulʲ'dɔzɛr]
excavator	екскаватор (ч)	[ɛkska'wator]
scoop, bucket	ківш (ч)	[kiwʃ]
to dig (excavate)	копати	[ko'pati]
hard hat	каска (ж)	['kaska]

122. Science. Research. Scientists

science	наука (ж)	[na'uka]
scientific (adj)	науковий	[nau'kɔwij]
scientist	вчений (ч)	['wtʃɛnij]
theory	теорія (ж)	[tɛ'ɔriʲa]

axiom	аксіома (ж)	[aksi'ɔma]
analysis	аналіз (ч)	[a'naliz]
to analyse (vt)	аналізувати	[analizu'wati]
argument (strong ~)	аргумент (ч)	[arɦu'mɛnt]
substance (matter)	речовина (ж)	[rɛtʃowi'na]

hypothesis	гіпофіз (ч)	[hi'pɔfiz]
dilemma	дилема (ж)	[di'lɛma]
dissertation	дисертація (ж)	[disɛr'tatsiʲa]
dogma	догма (ж)	['dɔɦma]

doctrine	доктрина (ж)	[dok'trina]
research	дослідження (с)	[do'slidʒɛnʲa]
to research (vt)	досліджувати	[do'slidʒuwati]
tests (laboratory ~)	контроль (ч)	[kon'trɔlʲ]
laboratory	лабораторія (ж)	[labora'tɔriʲa]

method	метод (ч)	['mɛtod]
molecule	молекула (ж)	[mo'lɛkula]
monitoring	моніторинг (ч)	[moni'tɔrinɦ]
discovery (act, event)	відкриття (с)	[widkrit'tʲa]

postulate	постулат (ч)	[postu'lat]
principle	принцип (ч)	['printsip]
forecast	прогноз (ч)	[proɦ'nɔz]
to forecast (vt)	прогнозувати	[proɦnozu'wati]

synthesis	синтез (ч)	['sintɛz]
trend (tendency)	тенденція (ж)	[tɛn'dɛntsiʲa]
theorem	теорема (ж)	[tɛo'rɛma]

teachings	вчення (с)	['wtʃɛnʲa]
fact	факт (ч)	[fakt]
expedition	експедиція (ж)	[ɛkspɛ'ditsiʲa]
experiment	експеримент (ч)	[ɛkspɛri'mɛnt]

academician	академік (ч)	[aka'dɛmik]
bachelor (e.g. ~ of Arts)	бакалавр (ч)	[baka'lawr]
doctor (PhD)	доктор (ч)	['dɔktor]
Associate Professor	доцент (ч)	[do'tsɛnt]
Master (e.g. ~ of Arts)	магістр (ч)	[ma'ɦistr]
professor	професор (ч)	[pro'fɛsor]

Professions and occupations

123. Job search. Dismissal

job	робота (ж)	[ro'bɔta]
staff (work force)	колектив, штат (ч)	[kolɛk'tiw], [ʃtat]
personnel	персонал (ч)	[pɛrso'nal]
career	кар'єра (ж)	[ka'rʲɛra]
prospects (chances)	перспектива (ж)	[pɛrspɛk'tiwa]
skills (mastery)	майстерність (ж)	[majs'tɛrnistʲ]
selection (screening)	підбір (ч)	[pid'bir]
employment agency	кадрове агентство (с)	['kadrowɛ a'ɦɛntstwo]
curriculum vitae, CV	резюме (с)	[rɛzʲu'mɛ]
job interview	співбесіда (ж)	[spiw'bɛsida]
vacancy	вакансія (ж)	[wa'kansiʲa]
salary, pay	зарплатня (ж)	[zarplat'nʲa]
fixed salary	оклад (ч)	[ok'lad]
pay, compensation	оплата (ж)	[op'lata]
position (job)	посада (ж)	[po'sada]
duty (of an employee)	обов'язок (ч)	[o'bɔwʲʲazok]
range of duties	коло (с)	['kɔlo]
busy (I'm ~)	зайнятий	['zajnʲatij]
to fire (dismiss)	звільнити	[zwilʲ'niti]
dismissal	звільнення (с)	['zwilʲnɛnʲa]
unemployment	безробіття (с)	[bɛzro'bittʲa]
unemployed (n)	безробітний (ч)	[bɛzro'bitnij]
retirement	пенсія (ж)	['pɛnsiʲa]
to retire (from job)	вийти на пенсію	['wijti na 'pɛnsiʲu]

124. Business people

director	директор (ч)	[di'rɛktor]
manager (director)	управляючий (ч)	[upraw'lʲaʲutʃij]
boss	керівник (ч)	[kɛriw'nik]
superior	начальник (ч)	[na'tʃalʲnik]
superiors	керівництво (с)	[kɛriw'nitstwo]
president	президент (ч)	[prɛzi'dɛnt]
chairman	голова (ч)	[ɦolo'wa]
deputy (substitute)	заступник (ч)	[za'stupnik]
assistant	помічник (ч)	[pomitʃ'nik]

| secretary | секретар (ч) | [sɛkrɛ'tar] |
| personal assistant | особистий секретар (ч) | [oso'bistij sɛkrɛ'tar] |

businessman	бізнесмен (ч)	[biznɛs'mɛn]
entrepreneur	підприємець (ч)	[pidpri'ɛmɛts]
founder	засновник (ч)	[zas'nɔwnik]
to found (vt)	заснувати	[zasnu'wati]

founding member	фундатор (ч)	[fun'dator]
partner	партнер (ч)	[part'nɛr]
shareholder	акціонер (ч)	[aktsio'nɛr]

millionaire	мільйонер (ч)	[milʲo'nɛr]
billionaire	мільярдер (ч)	[miljar'dɛr]
owner, proprietor	власник (ч)	['wlasnik]
landowner	землевласник (ч)	[zɛmlɛw'lasnik]

client	клієнт (ч)	[kli'ɛnt]
regular client	постійний клієнт (ч)	[pos'tijnij kli'ɛnt]
buyer (customer)	покупець (ч)	[poku'pɛts]
visitor	відвідувач (ч)	[wid'widuwatʃ]

professional (n)	професіонал (ч)	[profɛsio'nal]
expert	експерт (ч)	[ɛks'pɛrt]
specialist	фахівець (ч)	[fahi'wɛts]

| banker | банкір (ч) | [ba'nkir] |
| broker | брокер (ч) | ['brɔkɛr] |

cashier	касир (ч)	[ka'sir]
accountant	бухгалтер (ч)	[buh'haltɛr]
security guard	охоронник (ч)	[oho'rɔnik]

investor	інвестор (ч)	[in'wɛstor]
debtor	боржник (ч)	[borʒ'nik]
creditor	кредитор (ч)	[krɛdi'tɔr]
borrower	боржник (ч)	[borʒ'nik]

| importer | імпортер (ч) | [impor'tɛr] |
| exporter | експортер (ч) | [ɛkspor'tɛr] |

manufacturer	виробник (ч)	[wirob'nik]
distributor	дистриб'ютор (ч)	[distri'bʲutor]
middleman	посередник (ч)	[posɛ'rɛdnik]

consultant	консультант (ч)	[konsulʲ'tant]
sales representative	представник (ч)	[prɛdstaw'nik]
agent	агент (ч)	[a'ɦɛnt]
insurance agent	страховий агент (ч)	[straho'wij a'ɦɛnt]

125. Service professions

| cook | кухар (ч) | ['kuhar] |
| chef (kitchen chef) | шеф-кухар (ч) | [ʃɛf 'kuhar] |

baker	пекар (ч)	['pɛkar]
barman	бармен (ч)	[bar'mɛn]
waiter	офіціант (ч)	[ofiʦi'ant]
waitress	офіціантка (ж)	[ofiʦi'antka]

lawyer, barrister	адвокат (ч)	[adwo'kat]
lawyer (legal expert)	юрист (ч)	[ʲu'rist]
notary public	нотаріус (ч)	[no'tarius]

electrician	електрик (ч)	[ɛ'lɛktrik]
plumber	сантехнік (ч)	[san'tɛhnik]
carpenter	тесля (ч)	['tɛslʲa]

masseur	масажист (ч)	[masa'ʒist]
masseuse	масажистка (ж)	[masa'ʒistka]
doctor	лікар (ч)	['likar]

taxi driver	таксист (ч)	[tak'sist]
driver	шофер (ч)	[ʃo'fɛr]
delivery man	кур'єр (ч)	[ku'rʲɛr]

chambermaid	покоївка (ж)	[poko'jiwka]
security guard	охоронник (ч)	[oho'rɔnik]
flight attendant (fem.)	стюардеса (ж)	[stʲuar'dɛsa]

schoolteacher	вчитель (ч)	['wtʃitɛlʲ]
librarian	бібліотекар (ч)	[biblio'tɛkar]
translator	перекладач (ч)	[pɛrɛkla'datʃ]
interpreter	перекладач (ч)	[pɛrɛkla'datʃ]
guide	гід (ч)	[ɦid]

hairdresser	перукар (ч)	[pɛru'kar]
postman	листоноша (ч)	[listo'nɔʃa]
salesman (store staff)	продавець (ч)	[proda'wɛʦ]

gardener	садівник (ч)	[sadiw'nik]
domestic servant	слуга (ч)	[slu'ɦa]
maid (female servant)	служниця (ж)	[sluʒ'niʦʲa]
cleaner (cleaning lady)	прибиральниця (ж)	[pribiʲralʲniʦʲa]

126. Military professions and ranks

private	рядовий (ч)	[rʲado'wij]
sergeant	сержант (ч)	[sɛr'ʒant]
lieutenant	лейтенант (ч)	[lɛjtɛ'nant]
captain	капітан (ч)	[kapi'tan]

major	майор (ч)	[ma'jɔr]
colonel	полковник (ч)	[pol'kɔwnik]
general	генерал (ч)	[ɦɛnɛ'ral]
marshal	маршал (ч)	['marʃal]
admiral	адмірал (ч)	[admi'ral]
military (n)	військовий (ч)	[wijsʲʲkɔwij]
soldier	солдат (ч)	[sol'dat]

| officer | офіцер (ч) | [ofi'tsɛr] |
| commander | командир (ч) | [koman'dir] |

border guard	прикордонник (ч)	[prikor'dɔnik]
radio operator	радист (ч)	[ra'dist]
scout (searcher)	розвідник (ч)	[roz'widnik]
pioneer (sapper)	сапер (ч)	[sa'pɛr]
marksman	стрілок (ч)	[stri'lɔk]
navigator	штурман (ч)	['ʃturman]

127. Officials. Priests

| king | король (ч) | [ko'rɔlʲ] |
| queen | королева (ж) | [koro'lɛwa] |

| prince | принц (ч) | [prinʦ] |
| princess | принцеса (ж) | [prin'ʦɛsa] |

| czar | цар (ч) | [ʦar] |
| czarina | цариця (ж) | [ʦa'riʦʲa] |

president	президент (ч)	[prɛzi'dɛnt]
Secretary (minister)	міністр (ч)	[mi'nistr]
prime minister	прем'єр-міністр (ч)	[prɛ'm'ɛr mi'nistr]
senator	сенатор (ч)	[sɛ'nator]

diplomat	дипломат (ч)	[diplo'mat]
consul	консул (ч)	['kɔnsul]
ambassador	посол (ч)	[po'sɔl]
counselor (diplomatic officer)	радник (ч)	['radnik]

official, functionary (civil servant)	чиновник (ч)	[tʃi'nɔwnik]
prefect	префект (ч)	[prɛ'fɛkt]
mayor	мер (ч)	[mɛr]

| judge | суддя (ч) | [sud'dʲa] |
| prosecutor | прокурор (ч) | [proku'rɔr] |

missionary	місіонер (ч)	[misio'nɛr]
monk	чернець (ч)	[tʃɛr'nɛʦ]
abbot	абат (ч)	[a'bat]
rabbi	рабин (ч)	[ra'bin]

vizier	візир (ч)	[wi'zir]
shah	шах (ч)	[ʃah]
sheikh	шейх (ч)	[ʃɛjh]

128. Agricultural professions

| beekeeper | пасічник (ч) | ['pasitʃnik] |
| shepherd | пастух (ч) | [pas'tuh] |

agronomist	агроном (ч)	[afro'nɔm]
cattle breeder	тваринник (ч)	[twa'rinik]
veterinary surgeon	ветеринар (ч)	[wɛtɛri'nar]
farmer	фермер (ч)	['fɛrmɛr]
winemaker	винороб (ч)	[wino'rɔb]
zoologist	зоолог (ч)	[zo'ɔlofi]
cowboy	ковбой (ч)	[kow'bɔj]

129. Art professions

actor	актор (ч)	[ak'tɔr]
actress	акторка (ж)	[ak'tɔrka]
singer (masc.)	співак (ч)	[spi'wak]
singer (fem.)	співачка (ж)	[spi'watʃka]
dancer (masc.)	танцюрист (ч)	[tanʦu'rist]
dancer (fem.)	танцюристка (ж)	[tanʦu'ristka]
performer (masc.)	артист (ч)	[ar'tist]
performer (fem.)	артистка (ж)	[ar'tistka]
musician	музикант (ч)	[muzi'kant]
pianist	піаніст (ч)	[pia'nist]
guitar player	гітарист (ч)	[fita'rist]
conductor (orchestra ~)	диригент (ч)	[diri'fɛnt]
composer	композитор (ч)	[kompo'zitor]
impresario	імпресаріо (ч)	[imprɛ'sario]
film director	режисер (ч)	[rɛʒi'sɛr]
producer	продюсер (ч)	[pro'dʲusɛr]
scriptwriter	сценарист (ч)	[sʦɛna'rist]
critic	критик (ч)	['kritik]
writer	письменник (ч)	[pisʲ'mɛnik]
poet	поет (ч)	[po'ɛt]
sculptor	скульптор (ч)	['skulʲptor]
artist (painter)	художник (ч)	[hu'dɔʒnik]
juggler	жонглер (ч)	[ʒonfi'lɛr]
clown	клоун (ч)	['klɔun]
acrobat	акробат (ч)	[akro'bat]
magician	фокусник (ч)	['fɔkusnik]

130. Various professions

doctor	лікар (ч)	['likar]
nurse	медсестра (ж)	[mɛdsɛst'ra]
psychiatrist	психіатр (ч)	[psihi'atr]
dentist	стоматолог (ч)	[stoma'tɔlofi]

surgeon	хірург (ч)	[hi'rurɦ]
astronaut	астронавт (ч)	[astro'nawt]
astronomer	астроном (ч)	[astro'nɔm]
driver (of a taxi, etc.)	водій (ч)	[wo'dij]
train driver	машиніст (ч)	[maʃi'nist]
mechanic	механік (ч)	[mɛ'hanik]
miner	шахтар (ч)	[ʃah'tar]
worker	робочий (ч)	[ro'bɔtʃij]
locksmith	слюсар (ч)	['slʲusar]
joiner (carpenter)	столяр (ч)	['stɔlʲar]
turner (lathe operator)	токар (ч)	['tɔkar]
building worker	будівельник (ч)	[budi'wɛlʲnik]
welder	зварник (ч)	['zwarnik]
professor (title)	професор (ч)	[pro'fɛsor]
architect	архітектор (ч)	[arhi'tɛktor]
historian	історик (ч)	[is'tɔrik]
scientist	вчений (ч)	['wtʃɛnij]
physicist	фізик (ч)	['fizik]
chemist (scientist)	хімік (ч)	['himik]
archaeologist	археолог (ч)	[arhɛ'ɔloɦ]
geologist	геолог (ч)	[ɦɛ'ɔloɦ]
researcher (scientist)	дослідник (ч)	[do'slidnik]
babysitter	няня (ж)	['nʲanʲa]
teacher, educator	педагог (ч)	[pɛda'ɦɔɦ]
editor	редактор (ч)	[rɛ'daktor]
editor-in-chief	головний редактор (ч)	[ɦolow'nij rɛ'daktor]
correspondent	кореспондент (ч)	[korɛspon'dɛnt]
typist (fem.)	машиністка (ж)	[maʃi'nistka]
designer	дизайнер (ч)	[di'zajnɛr]
computer expert	комп'ютерник (ч)	[kom'pʲʲutɛrnik]
programmer	програміст (ч)	[proɦ'ramist]
engineer (designer)	інженер (ч)	[inʒɛ'nɛr]
sailor	моряк (ч)	[mo'rʲak]
seaman	матрос (ч)	[mat'rɔs]
rescuer	рятувальник (ч)	[rʲatu'walʲnik]
firefighter	пожежник (ч)	[po'ʒɛʒnik]
police officer	поліцейський (ч)	[poli'ʦɛjsʲkij]
watchman	сторож (ч)	['stɔroʒ]
detective	сищик (ч)	['siɕik]
customs officer	митник (ч)	['mitnik]
bodyguard	охоронець (ч)	[oho'rɔnɛʦ]
prison officer	доглядач (ч)	[doɦlʲa'datʃ]
inspector	інспектор (ч)	[ins'pɛktor]
sportsman	спортсмен (ч)	[sporʦ'mɛn]
trainer, coach	тренер (ч)	['trɛnɛr]

butcher	м'ясник (ч)	[mʲas'nik]
cobbler (shoe repairer)	чоботар (ч)	[ʧobo'tar]
merchant	комерсант (ч)	[komɛr'sant]
loader (person)	вантажник (ч)	[wan'taʒnik]

| fashion designer | модельєр (ч) | [modɛ'ljɛr] |
| model (fem.) | модель (ж) | [modɛlʲ] |

131. Occupations. Social status

| schoolboy | школяр (ч) | [ʃko'lʲar] |
| student (college ~) | студент (ч) | [stu'dɛnt] |

philosopher	філософ (ч)	[fi'lɔsof]
economist	економіст (ч)	[ɛkono'mist]
inventor	винахідник (ч)	[wina'hidnik]

unemployed (n)	безробітний (ч)	[bɛzro'bitnij]
retiree, pensioner	пенсіонер (ч)	[pɛnsio'nɛr]
spy, secret agent	шпигун (ч)	[ʃpi'hun]

prisoner	в'язень (ч)	['wʲazɛnʲ]
striker	страйкар (ч)	[straj'kar]
bureaucrat	бюрократ (ч)	[bʲuro'krat]
traveller (globetrotter)	мандрівник (ч)	[mandriw'nik]

| gay, homosexual (n) | гомосексуаліст (ч) | [ɦomosɛksua'list] |
| hacker | хакер (ч) | ['hakɛr] |

bandit	бандит (ч)	[ban'dit]
hit man, killer	найманий вбивця (ч)	['najmanij 'wbiwʦʲa]
drug addict	наркоман (ч)	[narko'man]
drug dealer	наркоторгівець (ч)	[narkotor'ɦiwɛʦ]
prostitute (fem.)	проститутка (ж)	[prosti'tutka]
pimp	сутенер (ч)	[sutɛ'nɛr]

sorcerer	чаклун (ч)	[ʧak'lun]
sorceress (evil ~)	чаклунка (ж)	[ʧak'lunka]
pirate	пірат (ч)	[pi'rat]
slave	раб (ч)	[rab]
samurai	самурай (ч)	[samu'raj]
savage (primitive)	дикун (ч)	[di'kun]

Sports

132. Kinds of sports. Sportspersons

sportsman	спортсмен (ч)	[sports'mɛn]
kind of sport	вид спорту (ч)	[wid 'spɔrtu]
basketball	баскетбол (ч)	[baskɛt'bɔl]
basketball player	баскетболіст (ч)	[baskɛtbo'list]
baseball	бейсбол (ч)	[bɛjs'bɔl]
baseball player	бейсболіст (ч)	[bɛjsbo'list]
football	футбол (ч)	[fut'bɔl]
football player	футболіст (ч)	[futbo'list]
goalkeeper	воротар (ч)	[woro'tar]
ice hockey	хокей (ч)	[ho'kɛj]
ice hockey player	хокеїст (ч)	[hokɛ'jist]
volleyball	волейбол (ч)	[wolɛj'bɔl]
volleyball player	волейболіст (ч)	[wolɛjbo'list]
boxing	бокс (ч)	[boks]
boxer	боксер (ч)	[bok'sɛr]
wrestling	боротьба (ж)	[borotʲ'ba]
wrestler	борець (ч)	[bo'rɛʦ]
karate	карате (с)	[kara'tɛ]
karate fighter	каратист (ч)	[kara'tist]
judo	дзюдо (с)	[dzʲu'dɔ]
judo athlete	дзюдоїст (ч)	[dzʲudo'jist]
tennis	теніс (ч)	['tɛnis]
tennis player	тенісист (ч)	[tɛni'sist]
swimming	плавання (с)	['plawanʲa]
swimmer	плавець (ч)	[pla'wɛʦ]
fencing	фехтування (с)	[fɛhtu'wanʲa]
fencer	фехтувальник (ч)	[fɛhtu'walʲnik]
chess	шахи (мн)	['ʃahi]
chess player	шахіст (ч)	[ʃa'hist]
alpinism	альпінізм (ч)	[alʲpi'nizm]
alpinist	альпініст (ч)	[alʲpi'nist]
running	біг (ч)	[biɦ]

runner	бігун (ч)	[bi'ɦun]
athletics	легка атлетика (ж)	[lɛɦ'ka at'lɛtika]
athlete	атлет (ч)	[at'lɛt]
horse riding	кінний спорт (ч)	['kinij 'spɔrt]
horse rider	наїзник (ч)	[na'jiznik]
figure skating	фігурне катання (с)	[fi'ɦurnɛ ka'tanʲa]
figure skater (masc.)	фігурист (ч)	[fiɦu'rist]
figure skater (fem.)	фігуристка (ж)	[fiɦu'ristka]
powerlifting	важка атлетика (ж)	[waʒ'ka at'lɛtika]
car racing	автогонки (мн)	[awto'ɦɔnki]
racer (driver)	гонщик (ч)	['ɦɔnɕik]
cycling	велоспорт (ч)	[wɛlo'spɔrt]
cyclist	велосипедист (ч)	[wɛlosipɛ'dist]
long jump	стрибки (мн) в довжину	[strib'ki w dowʒi'nu]
pole vaulting	стрибки (мн) з жердиною	[strib'ki z ʒɛr'dinoʲu]
jumper	стрибун (ч)	[stri'bun]

133. Kinds of sports. Miscellaneous

American football	американський футбол (ч)	[amɛri'kansʲkij fut'bɔl]
badminton	бадмінтон (ч)	[badmin'tɔn]
biathlon	біатлон (ч)	[biat'lɔn]
billiards	більярд (ч)	[bi'ljard]
bobsleigh	бобслей (ч)	[bob'slɛj]
bodybuilding	бодібілдинг (ч)	[bodi'bildinɦ]
water polo	водне поло (с)	['wɔdnɛ 'pɔlo]
handball	гандбол (ч)	[ɦand'bɔl]
golf	гольф (ч)	[ɦolʲf]
rowing	гребля (ч)	['ɦrɛblʲa]
scuba diving	дайвінг (ч)	['dajwinɦ]
cross-country skiing	лижні гонки (мн)	['lɨʒni 'ɦɔnkɨ]
table tennis (ping-pong)	настільний теніс (ч)	[na'stilʲnij 'tɛnis]
sailing	парусний спорт (ч)	['parusnij sport]
rally	ралі (с)	['rali]
rugby	регбі (с)	['rɛɦbi]
snowboarding	сноуборд (ч)	[snou'bɔrd]
archery	стрільба (ж) з луку	[strilʲ'ba z 'luku]

134. Gym

barbell	штанга (ж)	['ʃtanɦa]
dumbbells	гантелі (мн)	[ɦan'tɛli]
training machine	тренажер (ч)	[trɛna'ʒɛr]
exercise bicycle	велотренажер (ч)	[wɛlotrɛna'ʒɛr]

treadmill	бігова доріжка (ж)	[biɦo'wa do'riʒka]
horizontal bar	перекладина (ж)	[pɛrɛk'ladina]
parallel bars	бруси (мн)	['brusi]
vault (vaulting horse)	кінь (ч)	[kinʲ]
mat (exercise ~)	мат (ч)	[mat]

| aerobics | аеробіка (ж) | [aɛ'rɔbika] |
| yoga | йога (ж) | ['jɔɦa] |

135. Ice hockey

ice hockey	хокей (ч)	[ho'kɛj]
ice hockey player	хокеїст (ч)	[hokɛ'jist]
to play ice hockey	грати в хокей	['ɦrati w ho'kɛj]
ice	лід (ч)	[lid]

puck	шайба (ж)	['ʃajba]
ice hockey stick	ключка (ж)	['klʲuʧka]
ice skates	ковзани (мн)	[kowza'ni]

| board (ice hockey rink ~) | борт (ч) | [bort] |
| shot | кидок (ч) | [ki'dɔk] |

goaltender	воротар (ч)	[woro'tar]
goal (score)	гол (ч)	[ɦol]
to score a goal	забити гол	[za'biti ɦol]

| period | період (ч) | [pɛ'riod] |
| substitutes bench | лава (ж) запасних | ['lawa zapas'nih] |

136. Football

football	футбол (ч)	[fut'bɔl]
football player	футболіст (ч)	[futbo'list]
to play football	грати в футбол	['ɦrati w fut'bɔl]

major league	вища ліга (ж)	['wiɕa 'liɦa]
football club	футбольний клуб (ч)	[fut'bɔlʲnij klub]
coach	тренер (ч)	['trɛnɛr]
owner, proprietor	власник (ч)	['wlasnik]

team	команда (ж)	[ko'manda]
team captain	капітан (ч) команди	[kapi'tan ko'mandi]
player	гравець (ч)	[ɦra'wɛʦ]
substitute	запасний гравець (ч)	[zapas'nij ɦra'wɛʦ]

| forward | нападаючий (ч) | [napa'daʲuʧij] |
| centre forward | центральний нападаючий (ч) | [ʦɛn'tralʲnij napa'daʲuʧij] |

scorer	бомбардир (ч)	[bombar'dir]
defender, back	захисник (ч)	[zahis'nik]
midfielder, halfback	півзахисник (ч)	[piwzahis'nik]

match	матч (ч)	[matʃ]
to meet (vi, vt)	зустрічатися	[zustriˈtʃatisʲa]
final	фінал (ч)	[fiˈnal]
semi-final	напівфінал (ч)	[napiwfiˈnal]
championship	чемпіонат (ч)	[tʃɛmpioˈnat]
period, half	тайм (ч)	[tajm]
first period	перший тайм (ч)	[ˈpɛrʃij tajm]
half-time	перерва (ж)	[pɛˈrɛrwa]
goal	ворота (мн)	[woˈrɔta]
goalkeeper	воротар (ч)	[woroˈtar]
goalpost	штанга (ж)	[ˈʃtanɦa]
crossbar	перекладина (ж)	[pɛrɛkˈladina]
net	сітка (ж)	[ˈsitka]
to concede a goal	пропустити гол	[propusˈtiti ɦol]
ball	м'яч (ч)	[mʲʲatʃ]
pass	пас (ч)	[pas]
kick	удар (ч)	[uˈdar]
to kick (~ the ball)	нанести удар	[naˈnɛsti uˈdar]
free kick (direct ~)	штрафний удар (ч)	[ʃtrafˈnij uˈdar]
corner kick	кутовий удар (ч)	[kuˈtɔwij uˈdar]
attack	атака (ж)	[aˈtaka]
counterattack	контратака (ж)	[kontraˈtaka]
combination	комбінація (ж)	[kombiˈnatsʲʲa]
referee	арбітр (ч)	[arˈbitr]
to blow the whistle	свистіти	[swisˈtiti]
whistle (sound)	свисток (ч)	[swisˈtɔk]
foul, misconduct	порушення (с)	[poˈruʃɛnʲʲa]
to commit a foul	порушувати	[poˈruʃuwati]
to send off	видалити з поля	[ˈwidaliti z ˈpɔlʲa]
yellow card	жовта картка (ж)	[ˈʒɔwta ˈkartka]
red card	червона картка (ж)	[tʃɛrˈwɔna ˈkartka]
disqualification	дискваліфікація (ж)	[diskwalifiˈkatsʲa]
to disqualify (vt)	дискваліфікувати	[diskwalifikuˈwati]
penalty kick	пенальті (с)	[pɛˈnalʲti]
wall	стінка (ж)	[ˈstinka]
to score (vi, vt)	забити	[zaˈbiti]
goal (score)	гол (ч)	[ɦol]
to score a goal	забити гол	[zaˈbiti ɦol]
substitution	заміна (ж)	[zaˈmina]
to replace (a player)	замінити	[zamiˈniti]
rules	правила (мн)	[ˈprawila]
tactics	тактика (ж)	[ˈtaktika]
stadium	стадіон (ч)	[stadiˈɔn]
terrace	трибуна (ж)	[triˈbuna]
fan, supporter	болільник (ч)	[boˈlilʲnik]
to shout (vi)	кричати	[kriˈtʃati]
scoreboard	табло (с)	[tabˈlɔ]

score	рахунок (ч)	[ra'ɦunok]
defeat	поразка (ж)	[po'razka]
to lose (not win)	програти	[proɦ'rati]
draw	нічия (ж)	[nitʃi'ʲa]
to draw (vi)	зіграти внічию	[zi'ɦrati wnitʃi'ʲu]
victory	перемога (ж)	[pɛrɛ'mɔɦa]
to win (vi, vt)	перемогти	[pɛrɛmoɦ'ti]
champion	чемпіон (ч)	[tʃɛmpi'ɔn]
best (adj)	кращий	['kraɕij]
to congratulate (vt)	вітати	[wi'tati]
commentator	коментатор (ч)	[komɛn'tator]
to commentate (vt)	коментувати	[komɛntu'wati]
broadcast	трансляція (ж)	[trans'lʲatsiʲa]

137. Alpine skiing

skis	лижі (мн)	['liʒi]
to ski (vi)	кататися на лижах	[ka'tatisʲa na 'liʒah]
mountain-ski resort	гірськолижній курорт (ч)	[ɦirsʲko'liʒnij ku'rɔrt]
ski lift	підйомник (ч)	[pid'jɔmnik]
ski poles	палиці (мн)	['palitsi]
slope	схил (ч)	[shil]
slalom	слалом (ч)	['slalom]

138. Tennis. Golf

golf	гольф (ч)	[ɦolʲf]
golf club	гольф-клуб (ч)	[ɦolʲf klub]
golfer	гравець (ч) в гольф	[ɦra'wɛts w ɦolʲf]
hole	лунка (ж)	['lunka]
club	ключка (ж)	['klʲutʃka]
golf trolley	візок (ч) для ключок	[wi'zɔk dlʲa 'klʲutʃok]
tennis	теніс (ч)	['tɛnis]
tennis court	корт (ч)	[kort]
serve	подача (ж)	[po'datʃa]
to serve (vt)	подавати	[poda'wati]
racket	ракетка (ж)	[ra'kɛtka]
net	сітка (ж)	['sitka]
ball	м'яч (ч)	[mʲʲatʃ]

139. Chess

chess	шахи (мн)	['ʃahi]
chessmen	шахи (мн)	['ʃahi]
chess player	шахіст (ч)	[ʃa'hist]

chessboard	шахова дошка (ж)	['ʃahowa 'dɔʃka]
chessman	фігура (ж)	[fi'ɦura]
White (white pieces)	білі (мн)	['bili]
Black (black pieces)	чорні (мн)	['tʃɔrni]
pawn	пішак (ч)	[pi'ʃak]
bishop	слон (ч)	[slon]
knight	кінь (ч)	[kinʲ]
rook	тура (ж)	[tu'ra]
queen	ферзь (ч)	[fɛrzʲ]
king	король (ч)	[ko'rɔlʲ]
move	хід (ч)	[hid]
to move (vi, vt)	ходити	[ho'diti]
to sacrifice (vt)	пожертвувати	[po'ʒɛrtwuwati]
castling	рокірування (с)	[rokiru'wanʲa]
check	шах (ч)	[ʃah]
checkmate	мат (ч)	[mat]
chess tournament	шаховий турнір (ч)	['ʃahowij tur'nir]
Grand Master	гросмейстер (ч)	[ɦros'mɛjstɛr]
combination	комбінація (ж)	[kombi'natsiʲa]
game (in chess)	партія (ж)	['partiʲa]
draughts	шашки (мн)	['ʃaʃki]

140. Boxing

boxing	бокс (ч)	[boks]
fight (bout)	бій (ч)	[bij]
boxing match	двобій (ч)	[dwo'bij]
round (in boxing)	раунд (ч)	['raund]
ring	ринг (ч)	[rinɦ]
gong	гонг (ч)	[ɦonɦ]
punch	удар (ч)	[u'dar]
knockdown	нокдаун (ч)	[nok'daun]
knockout	нокаут (ч)	[no'kaut]
to knock out	нокаутувати	[nokautu'wati]
boxing glove	боксерська рукавичка (ж)	[bok'sɛrsʲka ruka'witʃka]
referee	рефері (ч)	['rɛfɛri]
lightweight	легка вага (ж)	['lɛɦka wa'ɦa]
middleweight	середня вага (ж)	[sɛ'rɛdnʲa wa'ɦa]
heavyweight	важка вага (ж)	[waʒ'ka wa'ɦa]

141. Sports. Miscellaneous

| Olympic Games | Олімпійські ігри (мн) | [olim'pijsʲki 'iɦri] |
| winner | переможець (ч) | [pɛrɛ'mɔʒɛts] |

to be winning	перемагати (ч)	[pɛrɛma'ɦati]
to win (vi)	виграти	['wiɦrati]
leader	лідер (ч)	['lidɛr]
to lead (vi)	лідирувати	[li'diruwati]
first place	перше місце (с)	['pɛrʃɛ 'mistsɛ]
second place	друге місце (с)	['druɦɛ 'mistsɛ]
third place	третє місце (с)	['trɛtɛ 'mistsɛ]
medal	медаль (ж)	[mɛ'dalʲ]
trophy	трофей (ч)	[tro'fɛj]
prize cup (trophy)	кубок (ч)	['kubok]
prize (in game)	приз (ч)	[priz]
main prize	головний приз (ч)	[ɦolow'nij priz]
record	рекорд (ч)	[rɛ'kɔrd]
to set a record	встановлювати рекорд	[wsta'nɔwlʲuwati rɛ'kɔrd]
final	фінал (ч)	[fi'nal]
final (adj)	фінальний	[fi'nalʲnij]
champion	чемпіон (ч)	[ʧɛmpi'ɔn]
championship	чемпіонат (ч)	[ʧɛmpio'nat]
stadium	стадіон (ч)	[stadi'ɔn]
terrace	трибуна (ж)	[tri'buna]
fan, supporter	уболівальник (ч)	[uboli'walʲnik]
opponent, rival	супротивник (ч)	[supro'tiwnik]
start (start line)	старт (ч)	[start]
finish line	фініш (ч)	['finiʃ]
defeat	поразка (ж)	[po'razka]
to lose (not win)	програти	[proɦ'rati]
referee	суддя (ч)	[sud'dʲa]
jury (judges)	журі (с)	[ʒu'ri]
score	рахунок (ч)	[ra'ɦunok]
draw	нічия (ж)	[niʧi'ʲa]
to draw (vi)	зіграти внічию	[zi'ɦrati wniʧiʲu]
point	очко (с)	[oʧ'kɔ]
result (final score)	результат (ч)	[rɛzulʲ'tat]
half-time	перерва (ж)	[pɛ'rɛrwa]
doping	допінг (ч)	['dɔpinɦ]
to penalise (vt)	штрафувати	[ʃtrafu'wati]
to disqualify (vt)	дискваліфікувати	[diskwalifiku'wati]
apparatus	снаряд (ч)	[sna'rʲad]
javelin	спис (ч)	[spis]
shot (metal ball)	ядро (с)	[jad'rɔ]
ball (snooker, etc.)	куля (ж)	['kulʲa]
aim (target)	ціль (ж)	[tsilʲ]
target	мішень (ж)	[mi'ʃɛnʲ]

to shoot (vi)	**стріляти**	[stri'lʲati]
accurate (~ shot)	**влучний**	['wlutʃnij]
trainer, coach	**тренер** (ч)	['trɛnɛr]
to train (sb)	**тренувати**	[trɛnu'wati]
to train (vi)	**тренуватися**	[trɛnu'watisʲa]
training	**тренування** (с)	[trɛnu'wanʲa]
gym	**спортзал** (ч)	[sport'zal]
exercise (physical)	**вправа** (ж)	['wprawa]
warm-up (athlete ~)	**розминка** (ж)	[roz'minka]

Education

142. School

school	школа (ж)	['ʃkɔla]
headmaster	директор (ч) школи	[di'rɛktor 'ʃkɔli]
student (m)	учень (ч)	['uʧɛnʲ]
student (f)	учениця (ж)	[uʧɛ'niʦʲa]
schoolboy	школяр (ч)	[ʃko'lʲar]
schoolgirl	школярка (ж)	[ʃko'lʲarka]
to teach (sb)	вчити	['wʧiti]
to learn (language, etc.)	вчити	['wʧiti]
to learn by heart	вчити напам'ять	['wʧiti na'pamʲatʲ]
to learn (~ to count, etc.)	вчитися	['wʧitisʲa]
to be at school	вчитися	['wʧitisʲa]
to go to school	йти до школи	[jti do ʃkoli]
alphabet	алфавіт (ч)	[alfa'wit]
subject (at school)	предмет (ч)	[prɛd'mɛt]
classroom	клас (ч)	[klas]
lesson	урок (ч)	[u'rɔk]
playtime, break	перерва (ж)	[pɛ'rɛrwa]
school bell	дзвінок (ч)	[dzwi'nɔk]
school desk	парта (ж)	['parta]
blackboard	дошка (ж)	['dɔʃka]
mark	відмітка (ж)	[wid'mitka]
good mark	добра оцінка (ж)	['dɔbra o'ʦinka]
bad mark	погана оцінка (ж)	[po'ɦana o'ʦinka]
to give a mark	ставити оцінку	['stawiti o'ʦinku]
mistake, error	помилка (ж)	[po'milka]
to make mistakes	робити помилки	[ro'biti 'pɔmilki]
to correct (an error)	виправляти	[wiprawʲ'lʲati]
crib	шпаргалка (ж)	[ʃpar'ɦalka]
homework	домашнє завдання (с)	[do'maʃnɛ zaw'danʲa]
exercise (in education)	вправа (ж)	['wprawa]
to be present	бути присутнім	['buti pri'sutnim]
to be absent	бути відсутнім	['buti wid'sutnim]
to punish (vt)	покарати	[poka'rati]
punishment	покарання (с)	[poka'ranʲa]
conduct (behaviour)	поведінка (ж)	[powɛ'dinka]
school report	щоденник (ч)	[ɕo'dɛnik]

pencil	олівець (ч)	[oli'wɛʦ]
rubber	гумка (ж)	['ɦumka]
chalk	крейда (ж)	['krɛjda]
pencil case	пенал (ч)	[pɛ'nal]

schoolbag	портфель (ч)	[port'fɛlʲ]
pen	ручка (ж)	['ruʧka]
exercise book	зошит (ч)	['zɔʃit]
textbook	підручник (ч)	[pid'ruʧnik]
compasses	циркуль (ч)	['ʦirkulʲ]

| to make technical drawings | креслити | ['krɛsliti] |
| technical drawing | креслення (с) | ['krɛslɛnʲa] |

poem	вірш (ч)	[wirʃ]
by heart (adv)	напам'ять	[na'pamʲʲatʲ]
to learn by heart	вчити напам'ять	['wʧiti na'pamʲʲatʲ]

| school holidays | канікули (мн) | [ka'nikuli] |
| to be on holiday | бути на канікулах | ['buti na ka'nikulah] |

test (at school)	контрольна робота (ж)	[kon'trɔlʲna ro'bɔta]
essay (composition)	твір (ч)	[twir]
dictation	диктант (ч)	[dik'tant]

exam (examination)	іспит (ч)	['ispit]
to do an exam	складати іспити	[skla'dati 'ispiti]
experiment (e.g., chemistry ~)	досвід (ч)	['dɔswid]

143. College. University

academy	академія (ж)	[aka'dɛmiʲa]
university	університет (ч)	[uniwɛrsi'tɛt]
faculty (e.g., ~ of Medicine)	факультет (ч)	[fakulʲ'tɛt]

student (masc.)	студент (ч)	[stu'dɛnt]
student (fem.)	студентка (ж)	[stu'dɛntka]
lecturer (teacher)	викладач (ч)	[wikla'daʧ]

| lecture hall, room | аудиторія (ж) | [audi'tɔriʲa] |
| graduate | випускник (ч) | [wipusk'nik] |

| diploma | диплом (ч) | [dip'lɔm] |
| dissertation | дисертація (ж) | [disɛr'taʦiʲa] |

| study (report) | дослідження (с) | [do'slidʒɛnʲa] |
| laboratory | лабораторія (ж) | [labora'tɔriʲa] |

| lecture | лекція (ж) | ['lɛkʦiʲa] |
| coursemate | однокурсник (ч) | [odno'kursnik] |

| scholarship, bursary | стипендія (ж) | [sti'pɛndiʲa] |
| academic degree | вчений ступінь (ч) | ['wʧɛnij 'stupinʲ] |

144. Sciences. Disciplines

mathematics	математика (ж)	[matɛ'matika]
algebra	алгебра (ж)	['alhɛbra]
geometry	геометрія (ж)	[ɦɛo'mɛtriʲa]
astronomy	астрономія (ж)	[astro'nɔmiʲa]
biology	біологія (ж)	[bio'lɔɦiʲa]
geography	географія (ж)	[ɦɛo'ɦrafiʲa]
geology	геологія (ж)	[ɦɛo'lɔɦiʲa]
history	історія (ж)	[is'tɔriʲa]
medicine	медицина (ж)	[mɛdi'ʦina]
pedagogy	педагогіка (ж)	[pɛda'ɦɔɦika]
law	право (с)	['prawo]
physics	фізика (ж)	['fizika]
chemistry	хімія (ж)	['himiʲa]
philosophy	філософія (ж)	[filo'sɔfiʲa]
psychology	психологія (ж)	[psiho'lɔɦiʲa]

145. Writing system. Orthography

grammar	граматика (ж)	[ɦra'matika]
vocabulary	лексика (ж)	['lɛksika]
phonetics	фонетика (ж)	[fo'nɛtika]
noun	іменник (ч)	[i'mɛnik]
adjective	прикметник (ч)	[prik'mɛtnik]
verb	дієслово (с)	[diɛ'slɔwo]
adverb	прислівник (ч)	[pris'liwnik]
pronoun	займенник (ч)	[zaj'mɛnik]
interjection	вигук (ч)	['wiɦuk]
preposition	прийменник (ч)	[prij'mɛnik]
root	корінь (ч) слова	['kɔriɲ 'slɔwa]
ending	закінчення (с)	[za'kinʧɛnʲa]
prefix	префікс (ч)	['prɛfiks]
syllable	склад (ч)	['sklad]
suffix	суфікс (ч)	['sufiks]
stress mark	наголос (ч)	['naɦolos]
apostrophe	апостроф (ч)	[a'pɔstrof]
full stop	крапка (ж)	['krapka]
comma	кома (ж)	['kɔma]
semicolon	крапка (ж) з комою	['krapka z 'kɔmoʲu]
colon	двокрапка (ж)	[dwo'krapka]
ellipsis	крапки (мн)	[krap'ki]
question mark	знак (ч) питання	[znak pi'tanʲa]
exclamation mark	знак (ч) оклику	[znak 'ɔkliku]

inverted commas	лапки (мн)	[lap'ki]
in inverted commas	в лапках	[w lap'kah]
parenthesis	дужки (мн)	[duʒ'ki]
in parenthesis	в дужках	[w duʒ'kah]

hyphen	дефіс (ч)	[dɛ'fis]
dash	тире (с)	[ti'rɛ]
space (between words)	пробіл (ч)	[pro'bil]

letter	літера (ж)	['litɛra]
capital letter	велика літера (ж)	[wɛ'lika 'litɛra]

vowel (n)	голосний звук (ч)	[ɦolos'nij zwuk]
consonant (n)	приголосний (ч)	['priɦolosnij]

sentence	речення (с)	['rɛtʃɛnʲa]
subject	підмет (ч)	['pidmɛt]
predicate	присудок (ч)	['prisudok]

line	рядок (ч)	[rʲa'dɔk]
on a new line	с нової стрічки (ж)	[s no'wɔjі 'stritʃki]
paragraph	абзац (ч)	[ab'zats]

word	слово (с)	['slɔwo]
group of words	словосполучення (с)	[slowospo'lutʃɛnʲa]
expression	вислів (ч)	['wisliw]
synonym	синонім (ч)	[si'nɔnim]
antonym	антонім (ч)	[an'tɔnim]

rule	правило (с)	['prawilo]
exception	виняток (ч)	['winʲatok]
correct (adj)	вірний	['wirnij]

conjugation	дієвідміна (ж)	[diɛwid'mina]
declension	відміна (ж)	[wid'mina]
nominal case	відмінок (ч)	[wid'minok]
question	питання (с)	[pi'tanʲa]
to underline (vt)	підкреслити	[pid'krɛsliti]
dotted line	пунктир (ч)	[punk'tir]

146. Foreign languages

language	мова (ж)	['mɔwa]
foreign language	іноземна мова (ж)	[ino'zɛmna 'mɔwa]
to study (vt)	вивчати	[wiw'tʃati]
to learn (language, etc.)	вчити	['wtʃiti]

to read (vi, vt)	читати	[tʃi'tati]
to speak (vi, vt)	розмовляти	[rozmow'lʲati]
to understand (vt)	розуміти	[rozu'miti]
to write (vt)	писати	[pi'sati]

fast (adv)	швидко	['ʃwidko]
slowly (adv)	повільно	[po'wilʲno]

fluently (adv)	вільно	['wilʲno]
rules	правила (мн)	['prawila]
grammar	граматика (ж)	[ɦra'matika]
vocabulary	лексика (ж)	['lɛksika]
phonetics	фонетика (ж)	[fo'nɛtika]
textbook	підручник (ч)	[pid'rutʃnik]
dictionary	словник (ч)	[slow'nik]
teach-yourself book	самовчитель (ч)	[samow'tʃitɛlʲ]
phrasebook	розмовник (ч)	[roz'mownik]
cassette, tape	касета (ж)	[ka'sɛta]
videotape	відеокасета (ж)	['widɛo ka'sɛta]
CD, compact disc	CD-диск (ч)	[si'di disk]
DVD	DVD (ч)	[diwi'di]
alphabet	алфавіт (ч)	[alfa'wit]
to spell (vt)	говорити по буквах	[ɦowo'riti po 'bukwah]
pronunciation	вимова (ж)	[wi'mɔwa]
accent	акцент (ч)	[ak'tsɛnt]
with an accent	з акцентом	[z ak'tsɛntom]
without an accent	без акценту (ч)	[bɛz ak'tsɛntu]
word	слово (с)	['slɔwo]
meaning	сенс (ч)	[sɛns]
course (e.g. a French ~)	курси (мн)	['kursi]
to sign up	записатися	[zapi'satisʲa]
teacher	викладач (ч)	[wikla'datʃ]
translation (process)	переклад (ч)	[pɛ'rɛklad]
translation (text, etc.)	переклад (ч)	[pɛ'rɛklad]
translator	перекладач (ч)	[pɛrɛkla'datʃ]
interpreter	перекладач (ч)	[pɛrɛkla'datʃ]
polyglot	поліглот (ч)	[poliɦ'lɔt]
memory	пам'ять (ж)	['pamʲʲatʲ]

147. Fairy tale characters

Father Christmas	Санта Клаус (ч)	['santa 'klaus]
mermaid	русалка (ж)	[ru'salka]
magician, wizard	чарівник (ч)	[tʃariw'nik]
fairy	чарівниця (ж)	[tʃariw'nitsʲa]
magic (adj)	чарівний	[tʃariw'nij]
magic wand	чарівна паличка (ж)	[tʃa'riwna 'palitʃka]
fairy tale	казка (ж)	['kazka]
miracle	диво (с)	['diwo]
dwarf	гном (ч)	[ɦnom]
to turn into ...	перетворитися на	[pɛrɛtwo'ritisʲa na]
ghost	привид (ч)	['priwid]

phantom	**примара** (ж)	[pri'mara]
monster	**чудовисько** (с)	[ʧu'dɔwisko]
dragon	**дракон** (ч)	[dra'kɔn]
giant	**велетень** (ч)	['wɛlɛtɛnʲ]

148. Zodiac Signs

Aries	**Овен** (ч)	['ɔwɛn]
Taurus	**Тілець** (ч)	[ti'lɛʦ]
Gemini	**Близнюки** (мн)	[bliznʲu'ki]
Cancer	**Рак** (ч)	[rak]
Leo	**Лев** (ч)	[lɛw]
Virgo	**Діва** (ж)	['diwa]
Libra	**Терези** (мн)	[tɛrɛ'zi]
Scorpio	**Скорпіон** (ч)	[skorpi'ɔn]
Sagittarius	**Стрілець** (ч)	[stri'lɛʦ]
Capricorn	**Козеріг** (ч)	[kozɛ'rɔɦ]
Aquarius	**Водолій** (ч)	[wodo'lij]
Pisces	**Риби** (мн)	['ribi]
character	**характер** (ч)	[ha'raktɛr]
character traits	**риси** (мн) **характеру**	['risi ha'raktɛru]
behaviour	**поведінка** (ж)	[powɛ'dinka]
to tell fortunes	**ворожити**	[woro'ʒiti]
fortune-teller	**гадалка** (ж)	[ɦa'dalka]
horoscope	**гороскоп** (ч)	[ɦoro'skɔp]

Arts

theatre	театр (ч)	[tɛ'atr]
opera	опера (ж)	['ɔpɛra]
operetta	оперета (ж)	[opɛ'rɛta]
ballet	балет (ч)	[ba'lɛt]
theatre poster	афіша (ж)	[a'fiʃa]
theatre company	трупа (ж)	['trupa]
tour	гастролі (мн)	[ɦa'strɔli]
to be on tour	гастролювати	[ɦastrolʲu'wati]
to rehearse (vi, vt)	репетирувати	[rɛpɛ'tiruwati]
rehearsal	репетиція (ж)	[rɛpɛ'titsiʲa]
repertoire	репертуар (ч)	[rɛpɛrtu'ar]
performance	вистава (ж)	[wis'tawa]
theatrical show	спектакль (ч)	[spɛk'taklʲ]
play	п'єса (ж)	['pʲɛsa]
ticket	квиток (ч)	[kwi'tɔk]
booking office	квиткова каса (ж)	[kwit'kɔwa 'kasa]
lobby, foyer	хол (ч)	[hol]
coat check (cloakroom)	гардероб (ж)	[ɦardɛ'rɔb]
cloakroom ticket	номерок (ч)	[nomɛ'rɔk]
binoculars	бінокль (ч)	[bi'nɔklʲ]
usher	контролер (ч)	[kontro'lɛr]
stalls (orchestra seats)	партер (ч)	[par'tɛr]
balcony	балкон (ч)	[bal'kɔn]
dress circle	бельетаж (ч)	[bɛlʲʲɛ'taʒ]
box	ложа (ж)	['lɔʒa]
row	ряд (ч)	[rʲad]
seat	місце (с)	['mistsɛ]
audience	публіка (ж)	['publika]
spectator	глядач (ч)	[ɦlʲa'datʃ]
to clap (vi, vt)	плескати	[plɛs'kati]
applause	аплодисменти (мн)	[aplodis'mɛnti]
ovation	овації (мн)	[o'watsiji]
stage	сцена (ж)	['stsɛna]
curtain	завіса (ж)	[za'wisa]
scenery	декорація (ж)	[dɛko'ratsiʲa]
backstage	куліси (мн)	[ku'lisi]
scene (e.g. the last ~)	дія (ж)	['diʲa]
act	акт (ч)	[akt]
interval	антракт (ч)	[an'trakt]

150. Cinema

actor	актор (ч)	[ak'tɔr]
actress	акторка (ж)	[ak'tɔrka]
film	кіно (с)	[ki'nɔ]
episode	серія (ж)	['sɛriʲa]
detective film	детектив (ч)	[dɛtɛk'tiw]
action film	бойовик (ч)	[boʲo'wik]
adventure film	пригодницький фільм (ч)	[pri'ɦɔdnitskij filʲm]
science fiction film	фантастичний фільм (ч)	[fantas'titʃnij filʲm]
horror film	фільм (ч) жахів	[filʲm 'ʒahiw]
comedy film	кінокомедія (ж)	[kinoko'mɛdiʲa]
melodrama	мелодрама (ж)	[mɛlod'rama]
drama	драма (ж)	['drama]
fictional film	художній фільм (ч)	[hu'dɔʒnij filʲm]
documentary	документальний фільм (ч)	[dokumɛn'talʲnij filʲm]
cartoon	мультфільм (ч)	[mulʲt'filʲm]
silent films	німе кіно (с)	[ni'mɛ ki'nɔ]
role (part)	роль (ж)	[rolʲ]
leading role	головна роль (ж)	[ɦolow'na rolʲ]
to play (vi, vt)	грати	['ɦrati]
film star	кінозірка (ж)	[kino'zirka]
well-known (adj)	відомий	[wi'dɔmij]
famous (adj)	відомий	[wi'dɔmij]
popular (adj)	популярний	[popu'lʲarnij]
script (screenplay)	сценарій (ч)	[stsɛ'narij]
scriptwriter	сценарист (ч)	[stsɛna'rist]
film director	режисер (ч)	[rɛʒi'sɛr]
producer	продюсер (ч)	[pro'dʲusɛr]
assistant	асистент (ч)	[asis'tɛnt]
cameraman	оператор (ч)	[opɛ'rator]
stuntman	каскадер (ч)	[kaska'dɛr]
to shoot a film	знімати фільм	[zni'mati filʲm]
audition, screen test	проби (мн)	['prɔbi]
shooting	зйомки (мн)	['zʲʲomki]
film crew	знімальна група (ж)	[zni'malʲna 'ɦrupa]
film set	знімальний майданчик (ч)	[zni'malʲnij maj'dantʃik]
camera	кінокамера (ж)	[kino'kamɛra]
cinema	кінотеатр (ч)	[kinotɛ'atr]
screen (e.g. big ~)	екран (ч)	[ɛk'ran]
to show a film	показувати фільм	[po'kazuwati filʲm]
soundtrack	звукова доріжка (ж)	[zwuko'wa do'riʒka]
special effects	спеціальні ефекти (мн)	[spɛtsi'alʲni ɛ'fɛkti]
subtitles	субтитри (мн)	[sub'titri]
credits	титри (мн)	['titri]
translation	переклад (ч)	[pɛ'rɛklad]

151. Painting

art	мистецтво (с)	[mis'tɛtstwo]
fine arts	образотворчі мистецтва (мн)	[obrazot'wortʃi mis'tɛtstwa]
art gallery	галерея (ж)	[ɦalɛ'rɛʲa]
art exhibition	виставка (ж) картин	['wistawka kar'tin]
painting (art)	живопис (ч)	[ʒi'wɔpis]
graphic art	графіка (ж)	['ɦrafika]
abstract art	абстракціонізм (ч)	[abstraktsio'nizm]
impressionism	імпресіонізм (ч)	[imprɛsio'nizm]
picture (painting)	картина (ж)	[kar'tina]
drawing	малюнок (ч)	[ma'lʲunok]
poster	плакат (ч)	[pla'kat]
illustration (picture)	ілюстрація (ж)	[ilʲust'ratsiʲa]
miniature	мініатюра (ж)	[minia'tʲura]
copy (of painting, etc.)	копія (ж)	['kɔpiʲa]
reproduction	репродукція (ж)	[rɛpro'duktsiʲa]
mosaic	мозаїка (ж)	[mo'zajika]
stained glass window	вітраж (ч)	[wit'raʒ]
fresco	фреска (ж)	['frɛska]
engraving	гравюра (ж)	[ɦra'wʲura]
bust (sculpture)	бюст (ч)	[bʲust]
sculpture	скульптура (ж)	[skulʲp'tura]
statue	статуя (ж)	['statuʲa]
plaster of Paris	гіпс (ч)	[ɦips]
plaster (as adj)	з гіпсу	[z 'ɦipsu]
portrait	портрет (ч)	[port'rɛt]
self-portrait	автопортрет (ч)	[awtopor'trɛt]
landscape painting	пейзаж (ч)	[pɛj'zaʒ]
still life	натюрморт (ч)	[natʲur'mɔrt]
caricature	карикатура (ж)	[karika'tura]
sketch	нарис (ч)	['naris]
paint	фарба (ж)	['farba]
watercolor paint	акварель (ж)	[akwa'rɛlʲ]
oil (paint)	масло (с)	['maslo]
pencil	олівець (ч)	[oli'wɛts]
Indian ink	туш (ж)	[tuʃ]
charcoal	вугілля (с)	[wu'ɦilʲa]
to draw (vi, vt)	малювати	[malʲu'wati]
to paint (vi, vt)	малювати	[malʲu'wati]
to pose (vi)	позувати	[pozu'wati]
artist's model (masc.)	натурник (ч)	[na'turnik]
artist's model (fem.)	натурниця (ж)	[na'turnitsʲa]
artist (painter)	художник (ч)	[hu'dɔʒnik]
work of art	витвір (ч)	['witwir]

masterpiece	шедевр (ч)	[ʃɛˈdɛwr]
studio (artist's workroom)	майстерня (ж)	[majsˈtɛrnʲa]
canvas (cloth)	полотно (с)	[polotˈnɔ]
easel	мольберт (ч)	[molʲˈbɛrt]
palette	палітра (ж)	[paˈlitra]
frame (picture ~, etc.)	рама (ж)	[ˈrama]
restoration	реставрація (ж)	[rɛstawˈraʦiʲa]
to restore (vt)	реставрувати	[rɛstawruˈwati]

152. Literature & Poetry

literature	література (ж)	[litɛraˈtura]
author (writer)	автор (ч)	[ˈawtor]
pseudonym	псевдонім (ч)	[psɛwdoˈnim]
book	книга (ж)	[ˈkniɦa]
volume	видання (с)	[widaˈnʲa]
table of contents	зміст (ч)	[zmist]
page	сторінка (ж)	[stoˈrinka]
main character	головний герой (ч)	[ɦolowˈnij ɦɛˈrɔj]
autograph	автограф (ч)	[awˈtɔɦraf]
short story	оповідання (с)	[opowiˈdanʲa]
story (novella)	повість (ж)	[ˈpɔwistʲ]
novel	роман (ч)	[roˈman]
work (writing)	твір (ч)	[twir]
fable	байка (ж)	[ˈbajka]
detective novel	детектив (ч)	[dɛtɛkˈtiw]
poem (verse)	вірш (ч)	[wirʃ]
poetry	поезія (ж)	[poˈɛziʲa]
poem (epic, ballad)	поема (ж)	[poˈɛma]
poet	поет (ч)	[poˈɛt]
fiction	белетристика (ж)	[bɛlɛtˈristika]
science fiction	наукова фантастика (ж)	[nauˈkɔwa fanˈtastika]
adventures	пригоди (мн)	[priˈɦɔdi]
educational literature	учбова література (ж)	[uʧˈbɔwa litɛraˈtura]
children's literature	дитяча література (ж)	[diˈtʲaʧa litɛraˈtura]

153. Circus

circus	цирк (ч)	[ʦirk]
travelling circus	цирк-шапіто (ч)	[ʦirk ʃapiˈtɔ]
programme	програма (ж)	[proɦˈrama]
performance	вистава (ж)	[wisˈtawa]
act (circus ~)	номер (ч)	[ˈnɔmɛr]
circus ring	арена (ж)	[aˈrɛna]
pantomime (act)	пантоміма (ж)	[pantoˈmima]

clown	клоун (ч)	['kloun]
acrobat	акробат (ч)	[akro'bat]
acrobatics	акробатика (ж)	[akro'batika]
gymnast	гімнаст (ч)	[ɦim'nast]
acrobatic gymnastics	гімнастика (ж)	[ɦim'nastika]
somersault	сальто (с)	['salʲto]

strongman	атлет (ч)	[at'lɛt]
tamer (e.g., lion ~)	приборкувач (ч)	[pri'borkuwatʃ]
rider (circus horse ~)	наїзник (ч)	[na'jiznik]
assistant	асистент (ч)	[asis'tɛnt]

stunt	трюк (ч)	[trʲuk]
magic trick	фокус (ч)	['fokus]
conjurer, magician	фокусник (ч)	['fokusnik]

juggler	жонглер (ч)	[ʒonɦ'lɛr]
to juggle (vi, vt)	жонглювати	[ʒonɦlʲu'wati]
animal trainer	дресирувальник (ч)	[drɛsiru'walʲnik]
animal training	дресура (ж)	[drɛ'sura]
to train (animals)	дресирувати	[drɛsiru'wati]

154. Music. Pop music

music	музика (ж)	['muzika]
musician	музикант (ч)	[muzi'kant]
musical instrument	музичний інструмент (ч)	[mu'zitʃnij instru'mɛnt]
to play …	грати на …	['ɦrati na]

guitar	гітара (ж)	[ɦi'tara]
violin	скрипка (ж)	['skripka]
cello	віолончель (ж)	[wiolon'tʃɛlʲ]
double bass	контрабас (ч)	[kontra'bas]
harp	арфа (ж)	['arfa]

piano	піаніно (с)	[pia'nino]
grand piano	рояль (ч)	[ro'ʲalʲ]
organ	орган (ч)	[or'ɦan]

wind instruments	духові інструменти (мн)	[duho'wi instru'mɛnti]
oboe	гобой (ч)	[ɦo'boj]
saxophone	саксофон (ч)	[sakso'fon]
clarinet	кларнет (ч)	[klar'nɛt]
flute	флейта (ж)	['flɛjta]
trumpet	труба (ж)	[tru'ba]

| accordion | акордеон (ч) | [akordɛ'ɔn] |
| drum | барабан (ч) | [bara'ban] |

duo	дует (ч)	[du'ɛt]
trio	тріо (с)	['trio]
quartet	квартет (ч)	[kwar'tɛt]
choir	хор (ч)	[hor]
orchestra	оркестр (ч)	[or'kɛstr]

pop music	**поп-музика** (ж)	[pop 'muzika]
rock music	**рок-музика** (ж)	[rok 'muzika]
rock group	**рок-група** (ж)	[rok 'ɦrupa]
jazz	**джаз** (ч)	[dʒaz]
idol	**кумир** (ч)	[ku'mir]
admirer, fan	**шанувальник** (ч)	[ʃanu'walʲnik]
concert	**концерт** (ч)	[kon'tsɛrt]
symphony	**симфонія** (ж)	[sim'fɔniʲa]
composition	**твір** (ч)	[twir]
to compose (write)	**створити**	[stwo'riti]
singing (n)	**спів** (ч)	[spiw]
song	**пісня** (ж)	['pisnʲa]
tune (melody)	**мелодія** (ж)	[mɛ'lɔdiʲa]
rhythm	**ритм** (ч)	[ritm]
blues	**блюз** (ч)	[blʲuz]
sheet music	**ноти** (мн)	['nɔti]
baton	**паличка** (ж)	['palitʃka]
bow	**смичок** (ч)	[smi'tʃɔk]
string	**струна** (ж)	[stru'na]
case (e.g. guitar ~)	**футляр** (ч)	[fut'lʲar]

Rest. Entertainment. Travel

tourism, travel	**туризм** (ч)	[tu'rizm]
tourist	**турист** (ч)	[tu'rist]
trip, voyage	**мандрівка** (ж)	[mand'riwka]
adventure	**пригода** (ж)	[pri'ɦɔda]
trip, journey	**поїздка** (ж)	[po'jizdka]
holiday	**відпустка** (ж)	[wid'pustka]
to be on holiday	**бути у відпустці**	['buti u wid'pusttsi]
rest	**відпочинок** (ч)	[widpo'tʃinok]
train	**поїзд** (ч)	['pɔjizd]
by train	**поїздом**	['pɔjizdom]
aeroplane	**літак** (ч)	[li'tak]
by aeroplane	**літаком**	[lita'kɔm]
by car	**автомобілем**	[awtomo'bilɛm]
by ship	**кораблем**	[korab'lɛm]
luggage	**багаж** (ч)	[ba'ɦaʒ]
suitcase	**валіза** (ж)	[wa'liza]
luggage trolley	**візок** (ч) **для багажу**	[wi'zɔk dlʲa baɦa'ʒu]
passport	**паспорт** (ч)	['pasport]
visa	**віза** (ж)	['wiza]
ticket	**квиток** (ч)	[kwi'tɔk]
air ticket	**авіаквиток** (ч)	[awiakwi'tɔk]
guidebook	**путівник** (ч)	[putiw'nik]
map (tourist ~)	**карта** (ж)	['karta]
area (rural ~)	**місцевість** (ж)	[mis'tsɛwistʲ]
place, site	**місце** (с)	['mistsɛ]
exotica (n)	**екзотика** (ж)	[ɛk'zɔtika]
exotic (adj)	**екзотичний**	[ɛkzo'titʃnij]
amazing (adj)	**дивовижний**	['diwowiʒnij]
group	**група** (ж)	['ɦrupa]
excursion, sightseeing tour	**екскурсія** (ж)	[ɛks'kursiʲa]
guide (person)	**екскурсовод** (ч)	[ɛkskurso'wɔd]

hotel	**готель** (ч)	[ɦo'tɛlʲ]
motel	**мотель** (ч)	[mo'tɛlʲ]
three-star (~ hotel)	**три зірки**	[tri 'zirki]

| five-star | п'ять зірок | [pʲˈatʲ ziˈrɔk] |
| to stay (in a hotel, etc.) | зупинитися | [zupiˈnitisʲa] |

room	номер (ч)	[ˈnɔmɛr]
single room	одномісний номер (ч)	[odnoˈmisnij nomɛr]
double room	двомісний номер (ч)	[dwoˈmisnij ˈnɔmɛr]
to book a room	резервувати номер	[rɛzɛrwuˈwati ˈnɔmɛr]

| half board | напівпансіон (ч) | [napiwpansiˈɔn] |
| full board | повний пансіон (ч) | [ˈpɔwnij pansiˈɔn] |

with bath	з ванною	[z ˈwanoʲu]
with shower	з душем	[z ˈduʃɛm]
satellite television	супутникове телебачення (с)	[suˈputnikowɛ tɛlɛˈbatʃɛnʲa]

air-conditioner	кондиціонер (ч)	[konditsioˈnɛr]
towel	рушник (ч)	[ruʃˈnik]
key	ключ (ч)	[klʲutʃ]

administrator	адміністратор (ч)	[adminiˈstrator]
chambermaid	покоївка (ж)	[pokoˈjiwka]
porter	носильник (ч)	[noˈsilʲnik]
doorman	портьє (ч)	[porˈtʲɛ]

restaurant	ресторан (ч)	[rɛstoˈran]
pub, bar	бар (ч)	[bar]
breakfast	сніданок (ч)	[sniˈdanok]
dinner	вечеря (ж)	[wɛˈtʃɛrʲa]
buffet	шведський стіл (ч)	[ˈʃwɛdsʲkij stil]

| lobby | вестибюль (ч) | [wɛstiˈbʲulʲ] |
| lift | ліфт (ч) | [lift] |

| DO NOT DISTURB | НЕ ТУРБУВАТИ | [nɛ turbuˈwati] |
| NO SMOKING | ПАЛИТИ ЗАБОРОНЕНО | [paˈliti zaboˈrɔnɛno] |

157. Books. Reading

book	книга (ж)	[ˈkniɦa]
author	автор (ч)	[ˈawtor]
writer	письменник (ч)	[pisʲˈmɛnik]
to write (~ a book)	написати	[napiˈsati]

reader	читач (ч)	[tʃiˈtatʃ]
to read (vi, vt)	читати	[tʃiˈtati]
reading (activity)	читання (с)	[tʃiˈtanʲa]

| silently (to oneself) | про себе | [pro ˈsɛbɛ] |
| aloud (adv) | вголос | [ˈwɦɔlos] |

to publish (vt)	видавати	[widaˈwati]
publishing (process)	примірник (ч)	[priˈmirnik]
publisher	видавець (ч)	[widaˈwɛts]
publishing house	видавництво (с)	[widawˈnitstwo]

to come out (be released)	вийти	['wijti]
release (of a book)	вихід (ч)	['wihid]
print run	наклад (ч)	['naklad]
bookshop	книгарня (ж)	[kni'harnʲa]
library	бібліотека (ж)	[biblio'tɛka]
story (novella)	повість (ж)	['powistʲ]
short story	оповідання (с)	[opowi'danʲa]
novel	роман (ч)	[ro'man]
detective novel	детектив (ч)	[dɛtɛk'tiw]
memoirs	мемуари (мн)	[mɛmu'ari]
legend	легенда (ж)	[lɛ'hɛnda]
myth	міф (ч)	[mif]
poetry, poems	вірші (мн)	['wirʃi]
autobiography	автобіографія (ж)	[awtobio'hrafʲia]
selected works	вибране (с)	['wibranɛ]
science fiction	фантастика (ж)	[fan'tastika]
title	назва (ж)	['nazwa]
introduction	вступ (ч)	[wstup]
title page	титульна сторінка (ж)	['titulʲna sto'rinka]
chapter	розділ (ч)	['rozdil]
extract	уривок (ч)	[u'riwok]
episode	епізод (ч)	[ɛpi'zɔd]
plot (storyline)	сюжет (ч)	[sʲu'ʒɛt]
contents	зміст (ч)	[zmist]
table of contents	зміст (ч)	[zmist]
main character	головний герой (ч)	[holow'nij hɛ'rɔj]
volume	том (ч)	[tom]
cover	обкладинка (ж)	[ob'kladinka]
binding	палітура (ж)	[pali'tura]
bookmark	закладка (ж)	[za'kladka]
page	сторінка (ж)	[sto'rinka]
to page through	гортати	[hor'tati]
margins	поля (мн)	[po'lʲa]
annotation	позначка (ж)	['pɔznatʃka]
(marginal note, etc.)		
footnote	примітка (ж)	[pri'mitka]
text	текст (ч)	[tɛkst]
type, fount	шрифт (ч)	[ʃrift]
misprint, typo	помилка (ж)	[po'milka]
translation	переклад (ч)	[pɛ'rɛklad]
to translate (vt)	перекладати	[pɛrɛkla'dati]
original (n)	оригінал (ч)	[orihi'nal]
famous (adj)	відомий	[wi'dɔmij]
unknown (not famous)	невідомий	[nɛwi'dɔmij]

| interesting (adj) | цікавий | [tsi'kawij] |
| bestseller | бестселер (ч) | [bɛst'sɛlɛr] |

dictionary	словник (ч)	[slow'nik]
textbook	підручник (ч)	[pid'rutʃnik]
encyclopedia	енциклопедія (ж)	[ɛntsiklo'pɛdiʲa]

158. Hunting. Fishing

hunting	полювання (с)	[polʲu'wanʲa]
to hunt (vi, vt)	полювати	[polʲu'wati]
hunter	мисливець (ч)	[mis'liwɛts]

to shoot (vi)	стріляти	[stri'lʲati]
rifle	рушниця (ж)	[ruʃ'nitsʲa]
bullet (shell)	патрон (ч)	[pat'rɔn]
shot (lead balls)	шріт (ч)	[ʃrit]

steel trap	капкан (ч)	[kap'kan]
snare (for birds, etc.)	пастка (ж)	['pastka]
to lay a steel trap	ставити пастку	['stawiti 'pastku]

poacher	браконьєр (ч)	[brako'nʲɛr]
game (in hunting)	дичина (ж)	[ditʃi'na]
hound dog	мисливський пес (ч)	[mis'liwsʲkij pɛs]
safari	сафарі (с)	[sa'fari]
mounted animal	опудало (с)	[o'pudalo]

fisherman	рибалка (ч)	[ri'balka]
fishing (angling)	риболовля (ж)	[ribo'lɔwlʲa]
to fish (vi)	ловити рибу	[lo'witi 'ribu]

fishing rod	вудочка (ж)	['wudotʃka]
fishing line	волосінь (ж)	[wolo'sinʲ]
hook	гачок (ч)	[ɦa'tʃɔk]
float	поплавець (ч)	[popla'wɛts]
bait	наживка (ж)	[na'ʒiwka]

| to cast a line | закинути вудочку | [za'kinuti 'wudotʃku] |
| to bite (ab. fish) | клювати | [klʲu'wati] |

| catch (of fish) | улов (ч) | [u'lɔw] |
| ice-hole | ополонка (ж) | [opo'lɔnka] |

fishing net	сітка (ж)	['sitka]
boat	човен (ч)	['tʃɔwɛn]
to net (to fish with a net)	ловити	[lo'witi]

| to cast[throw] the net | закидати сіті | [zaki'dati 'siti] |
| to haul the net in | витягати сіті | [witʲa'ɦati 'siti] |

whaler (person)	китобій (ч)	[kito'bij]
whaleboat	китобійне судно (с)	[kito'bijnɛ 'sudno]
harpoon	гарпун (ч)	[ɦar'pun]

159. Games. Billiards

billiards	більярд (ч)	[bi'ljard]
billiard room, hall	більярдна (ж)	[bi'ljardna]
ball (snooker, etc.)	більярдна куля (ж)	[bi'ljardna 'kulʲa]
to pocket a ball	загнати кулю	[za'ɦnati 'kulʲu]
cue	кий (ч)	[kij]
pocket	луза (ж)	['luza]

160. Games. Playing cards

diamonds	бубни (мн)	['bubni]
spades	піки (мн)	['piki]
hearts	черви (мн)	['t͡ʃɛrwi]
clubs	трефи (мн)	['trɛfi]
ace	туз (ч)	[tuz]
king	король (ч)	[ko'rɔlʲ]
queen	дама (ж)	['dama]
jack, knave	валет (ч)	[wa'lɛt]
playing card	карта (ж)	['karta]
cards	карти (мн)	['karti]
trump	козир (ч)	['kɔzir]
pack of cards	колода (ж)	[ko'lɔda]
to deal (vi, vt)	здавати	[zda'wati]
to shuffle (cards)	тасувати	[tasu'wati]
lead, turn (n)	хід (ч)	[hid]
cardsharp	шулер (ч)	['ʃulɛr]

161. Casino. Roulette

casino	казино (с)	[kazi'nɔ]
roulette (game)	рулетка (ж)	[ru'lɛtka]
bet	ставка (ж)	['stawka]
to place bets	робити ставки	[ro'biti 'stawki]
red	червоне (с)	[t͡ʃɛr'wɔnɛ]
black	чорне (с)	['t͡ʃɔrnɛ]
to bet on red	ставити на червоне	['stawiti na t͡ʃɛr'wɔnɛ]
to bet on black	ставити на чорне	['stawiti na 't͡ʃɔrnɛ]
croupier (dealer)	круп'є (ч)	[kru'pʲɛ]
to spin the wheel	крутити барабан	[kru'titi bara'ban]
rules (~ of the game)	правила (мн) гри	['prawila ɦri]
chip	фішка (ж)	['fiʃka]
to win (vi, vt)	виграти	['wiɦrati]
win (winnings)	виграш (ч)	['wiɦraʃ]

to lose (~ 100 dollars)	програти	[proɦ'rati]
loss (losses)	програш (ч)	['prɔɦraʃ]
player	гравець (ч)	[ɦra'wɛʧ]
blackjack (card game)	блек джек (ч)	[blɛk 'dʒɛk]
craps (dice game)	гра (ж) в кості	[ɦra w 'kɔsti]
fruit machine	гральний автомат (ч)	['ɦralʲnij awto'mat]

162. Rest. Games. Miscellaneous

to stroll (vi, vt)	прогулюватися	[pro'ɦulʲuwatisʲa]
stroll (leisurely walk)	прогулянка (ж)	[pro'ɦulʲanka]
car ride	поїздка (ж)	[po'jizdka]
adventure	пригода (ж)	[pri'ɦɔda]
picnic	пікнік (ч)	[pik'nik]
game (chess, etc.)	гра (ж)	[ɦra]
player	гравець (ч)	[ɦra'wɛʧ]
game (one ~ of chess)	партія (ж)	['partiʲa]
collector (e.g. philatelist)	колекціонер (ч)	[kolɛkʦio'nɛr]
to collect (stamps, etc.)	колекціонувати	[kolɛkʦionu'wati]
collection	колекція (ж)	[ko'lɛkʦiʲa]
crossword puzzle	кросворд (ч)	[kros'wɔrd]
racecourse (hippodrome)	іподром (ч)	[ipod'rɔm]
disco (discotheque)	дискотека (ж)	[disko'tɛka]
sauna	сауна (ж)	['sauna]
lottery	лотерея (ж)	[lotɛ'rɛʲa]
camping trip	похід (ч)	[po'hid]
camp	табір (ч)	['tabir]
tent (for camping)	намет (ч)	[na'mɛt]
compass	компас (ч)	['kɔmpas]
camper	турист (ч)	[tu'rist]
to watch (film, etc.)	дивитися	[di'witisʲa]
viewer	телеглядач (ч)	[tɛlɛɦlʲa'daʧ]
TV show (TV program)	телепередача (ж)	['tɛlɛ pɛrɛ'daʧa]

163. Photography

camera (photo)	фотоапарат (ч)	[fotoapa'rat]
photo, picture	фото (с)	['fɔto]
photographer	фотограф (ч)	[fo'tɔɦraf]
photo studio	фотостудія (ж)	[foto'studiʲa]
photo album	фотоальбом (ч)	[fotoalʲ'bɔm]
camera lens	об'єктив (ч)	[obʲɛk'tiw]
telephoto lens	телеоб'єктив (ч)	[tɛlɛobʲɛk'tiw]

| filter | фільтр (ч) | ['filʲtr] |
| lens | лінза (ж) | ['linza] |

optics (high-quality ~)	оптика (ж)	['ɔptika]
diaphragm (aperture)	діафрагма (ж)	[dia'fraɦma]
exposure time (shutter speed)	витримка (ж)	['witrimka]
viewfinder	видошукач (ч)	[widoʃu'katʃ]

digital camera	цифрова камера (ж)	[tsifro'wa 'kamɛra]
tripod	штатив (ч)	[ʃta'tiw]
flash	спалах (ч)	['spalah]

to photograph (vt)	фотографувати	[fotoɦrafu'wati]
to take pictures	знімати	[zni'mati]
to have one's picture taken	фотографуватися	[fotoɦrafu'watisʲa]

focus	різкість (ж)	['rizkistʲ]
to focus	наводити різкість	[na'wɔditi 'rizkistʲ]
sharp, in focus (adj)	різкий	[riz'kij]
sharpness	різкість (ж)	['rizkistʲ]

| contrast | контраст (ч) | [kon'trast] |
| contrast (as adj) | контрастний | [kon'trastnij] |

picture (photo)	знімок (ч)	['znimok]
negative (n)	негатив (ч)	[nɛɦa'tiw]
film (a roll of ~)	фотоплівка (ж)	[foto'pliwka]
frame (still)	кадр (ч)	[kadr]
to print (photos)	друкувати	[druku'wati]

164. Beach. Swimming

beach	пляж (ч)	[plʲaʒ]
sand	пісок (ч)	[pi'sɔk]
deserted (beach)	пустельний	[pus'tɛlʲnij]

suntan	засмага (ж)	[zas'maɦa]
to get a tan	засмагати	[zasma'ɦati]
tanned (adj)	засмаглий	[zas'maɦlij]
sunscreen	крем (ч) для засмаги	[krɛm dlʲa zas'maɦi]

bikini	бікіні (мн)	[bi'kini]
swimsuit, bikini	купальник (ч)	[ku'palʲnik]
swim trunks	плавки (мн)	['plawki]

swimming pool	басейн (ч)	[ba'sɛjn]
to swim (vi)	плавати	['plawati]
shower	душ (ч)	[duʃ]
to change (one's clothes)	перевдягатися	[pɛrɛwdʲa'ɦatisʲa]
towel	рушник (ч)	[ruʃ'nik]

| boat | човен (ч) | ['tʃɔwɛn] |
| motorboat | катер (ч) | ['katɛr] |

water ski	водяні лижі (мн)	[wodʲaˈni ˈliʒi]
pedalo	водяний велосипед (ч)	[wodʲaˈnij wɛlosiˈpɛd]
surfing	серфінг (ч)	[ˈsɛrfinɦ]
surfer	серфінгіст (ч)	[sɛrfiˈnɦist]

scuba set	акваланг (ч)	[akwaˈlanɦ]
flippers (swim fins)	ласти (мн)	[ˈlasti]
mask (diving ~)	маска (ж)	[ˈmaska]
diver	нирець (ч)	[niˈrɛts]
to dive (vi)	пірнати	[pirˈnati]
underwater (adv)	під водою	[pid woˈdɔʲu]

beach umbrella	парасолька (ж)	[paraˈsɔlʲka]
beach chair (sun lounger)	шезлонг (ч)	[ʃɛzˈlɔnɦ]
sunglasses	окуляри (мн)	[okuˈlʲari]
air mattress	плавальний матрац (ч)	[ˈplawalʲnij matˈrats]

| to play (amuse oneself) | грати | [ˈɦrati] |
| to go for a swim | купатися | [kuˈpatisʲa] |

beach ball	м'яч (ч)	[mʲɑtʃ]
to inflate (vt)	надувати	[naduˈwati]
inflatable, air (adj)	надувний	[naduwˈnij]

wave	хвиля (ж)	[ˈhwilʲa]
buoy (line of ~s)	буй (ч)	[buj]
to drown (ab. person)	тонути	[toˈnuti]

to save, to rescue	рятувати	[rʲatuˈwati]
life jacket	рятувальний жилет (ч)	[rʲatuˈwalʲnij ʒiˈlɛt]
to observe, to watch	спостерігати	[spostɛriˈɦati]
lifeguard	рятувальник (ч)	[rʲatuˈwalʲnik]

TECHNICAL EQUIPMENT. TRANSPORT

Technical equipment

165. Computer

computer	комп'ютер (ч)	[kom'pʲutɛr]
notebook, laptop	ноутбук (ч)	[nout'buk]
to turn on	увімкнути	[uwimk'nuti]
to turn off	вимкнути	['wimknuti]
keyboard	клавіатура (ж)	[klawia'tura]
key	клавіша (ж)	['klawiʃa]
mouse	миша (ж)	['miʃa]
mouse mat	килимок (ч)	[kili'mɔk]
button	кнопка (ж)	['knɔpka]
cursor	курсор (ч)	[kur'sɔr]
monitor	монітор (ч)	[moni'tɔr]
screen	екран (ч)	[ɛk'ran]
hard disk	жорсткий диск (ч)	[ʒor'stkij disk]
hard disk capacity	об'єм (ч)	[o'bʲɛm]
memory	пам'ять (ж)	['pamʲatʲ]
random access memory	оперативна пам'ять (ж)	[opɛra'tiwna 'pamʲatʲ]
file	файл (ч)	[fajl]
folder	папка (ж)	['papka]
to open (vt)	відкрити файл	[wid'kriti 'fajl]
to close (vt)	закрити файл	[za'kriti 'fajl]
to save (vt)	зберегти	[zbɛrɛɦ'ti]
to delete (vt)	видалити	['widaliti]
to copy (vt)	скопіювати	[skopiʲu'wati]
to sort (vt)	сортувати	[sortu'wati]
to transfer (copy)	переписати	[pɛrɛpi'sati]
programme	програма (ж)	[proɦ'rama]
software	програмне забезпечення (с)	[proɦ'ramnɛ zabɛz'pɛtʃɛnʲa]
programmer	програміст (ч)	[proɦ'ramist]
to program (vt)	програмувати	[proɦramu'wati]
hacker	хакер (ч)	['hakɛr]
password	пароль (ч)	[pa'rɔlʲ]
virus	вірус (ч)	['wirus]
to find, to detect	виявити	['wijawiti]

byte	байт (ч)	[bajt]
megabyte	мегабайт (ч)	[mɛɦa'bajt]
data	дані (мн)	['dani]
database	база (ж) даних	['baza 'danih]
cable (USB, etc.)	кабель (ч)	['kabɛlʲ]
to disconnect (vt)	від'єднати	[wid'ɛd'nati]
to connect (sth to sth)	під'єднати	[pid'ɛd'nati]

166. Internet. E-mail

Internet	інтернет (ч)	[intɛr'nɛt]
browser	браузер (ч)	['brauzɛr]
search engine	пошуковий ресурс (ч)	[poʃu'kɔwij rɛ'surs]
provider	провайдер (ч)	[pro'wajdɛr]
webmaster	веб-майстер (ч)	[wɛb 'majstɛr]
website	веб-сайт (ч)	[wɛb 'sajt]
web page	веб-сторінка (ж)	[wɛb sto'rinka]
address (e-mail ~)	адреса (ж)	[ad'rɛsa]
address book	адресна книга (ж)	['adrɛsna 'kniɦa]
postbox	поштова скринька (ж)	[poʃ'tɔwa sk'rinʲka]
post	пошта (ж)	['pɔʃta]
message	повідомлення (с)	[powi'dɔmlɛnʲa]
sender	відправник (ч)	[wid'prawnik]
to send (vt)	відправити	[wid'prawiti]
sending (of mail)	відправлення (с)	[wid'prawlɛnʲa]
receiver	одержувач (ч)	[o'dɛrʒuwatʃ]
to receive (vt)	отримати	[ot'rimati]
correspondence	листування (с)	[listu'wanʲa]
to correspond (vi)	листуватися	[listu'watisʲa]
file	файл (ч)	[fajl]
to download (vt)	скачати	[ska'tʃati]
to create (vt)	створити	[stwo'riti]
to delete (vt)	видалити	['widaliti]
deleted (adj)	видалений	['widalɛnij]
connection (ADSL, etc.)	зв'язок (ч)	[zwʲa'zɔk]
speed	швидкість (ж)	['ʃwidkistʲ]
modem	модем (ч)	[mo'dɛm]
access	доступ (ч)	['dɔstup]
port (e.g. input ~)	порт (ч)	[port]
connection (make a ~)	підключення (с)	[pid'klʲutʃɛnʲa]
to connect to ... (vi)	підключитися	[pidklʲu'tʃitisʲa]
to select (vt)	вибрати	['wibrati]
to search (for ...)	шукати	[ʃu'kati]

167. Electricity

electricity	електрика (ж)	[ɛ'lɛktrika]
electric, electrical (adj)	електричний	[ɛlɛkt'ritʃnij]
electric power station	електростанція (ж)	[ɛlɛktro'stantsiʲa]
energy	енергія (ж)	[ɛ'nɛrɦiʲa]
electric power	електроенергія (ж)	[ɛlɛktroɛ'nɛrɦiʲa]
light bulb	лампочка (ж)	['lampotʃka]
torch	ліхтар (ч)	[lih'tar]
street light	ліхтар (ч)	[lih'tar]
light	світло (с)	['switlo]
to turn on	вмикати	[wmi'kati]
to turn off	вимикати	[wimi'kati]
to turn off the light	погасити світло	[poɦa'siti 'switlo]
to burn out (vi)	перегоріти	[pɛrɛɦo'riti]
short circuit	коротке замикання (с)	[ko'rɔtkɛ zami'kanʲa]
broken wire	обрив (ч)	[ob'riw]
contact (electrical ~)	контакт (ч)	[kon'takt]
light switch	вимикач (ч)	[wimi'katʃ]
socket outlet	розетка (ж)	[ro'zɛtka]
plug	штепсель (ч)	['ʃtɛpsɛlʲ]
extension lead	подовжувач (ч)	[po'dɔwʒuwatʃ]
fuse	запобіжник (ч)	[zapo'biʒnik]
cable, wire	провід (ч)	['prɔwid]
wiring	проводка (ж)	[pro'wɔdka]
ampere	ампер (ч)	[am'pɛr]
amperage	сила (ж) струму	['sila st'rumu]
volt	вольт (ч)	[wolʲt]
voltage	напруга (ж)	[na'pruɦa]
electrical device	електроприлад (ч)	[ɛlɛktro'prilad]
indicator	індикатор (ч)	[indi'kator]
electrician	електрик (ч)	[ɛ'lɛktrik]
to solder (vt)	паяти	[pa'ʲati]
soldering iron	паяльник (ч)	[pa'ʲalʲnik]
electric current	струм (ч)	[strum]

168. Tools

tool, instrument	інструмент (ч)	[instru'mɛnt]
tools	інструменти (мн)	[instru'mɛnti]
equipment (factory ~)	обладнання (с)	[ob'ladnanʲa]
hammer	молоток (ч)	[molo'tɔk]
screwdriver	викрутка (ж)	['wikrutka]
axe	сокира (ж)	[so'kira]

saw	пила (ж)	['pila]
to saw (vt)	пиляти	[pi'lʲati]
plane (tool)	рубанок (ч)	[ru'banok]
to plane (vt)	стругати	[stru'ɦati]
soldering iron	паяльник (ч)	[pa'ʲalʲnik]
to solder (vt)	паяти	[pa'ʲati]
file (tool)	терпуг (ч)	[tɛr'puɦ]
carpenter pincers	обценьки (мн)	[ob'tsɛnʲki]
combination pliers	плоскогубці (мн)	[plosko'ɦubtsi]
chisel	стамеска (ж)	[sta'mɛska]
drill bit	свердло (с)	[swɛr'lɔ]
electric drill	дриль (ч)	[drilʲ]
to drill (vi, vt)	свердлити	[swɛr'liti]
knife	ніж (ч)	[niʒ]
blade	лезо (с)	['lɛzo]
sharp (blade, etc.)	гострий	['ɦostrij]
dull, blunt (adj)	тупий	[tu'pij]
to get blunt (dull)	затупитися	[zatu'pitisʲa]
to sharpen (vt)	точити	[to'tʃiti]
bolt	болт (ч)	[bolt]
nut	гайка (ж)	['ɦajka]
thread (of a screw)	різьба (ж)	[rizʲ'ba]
wood screw	шуруп (ч)	[ʃu'rup]
nail	цвях (ч)	[tswʲah]
nailhead	головка (ж)	[ɦo'lɔwka]
ruler (for measuring)	лінійка (ж)	[li'nijka]
tape measure	рулетка (ж)	[ru'lɛtka]
spirit level	рівень (ч)	['riwɛnʲ]
magnifying glass	лупа (ж)	['lupa]
measuring instrument	вимірювальний прилад (ч)	[wi'mirʲuwalʲnij 'prilad]
to measure (vt)	вимірювати	[wi'mirʲuwati]
scale (temperature ~, etc.)	шкала (ж)	[ʃka'la]
readings	показання (с)	[poka'zanʲa]
compressor	компресор (ч)	[kom'prɛsor]
microscope	мікроскоп (ч)	[mikro'skɔp]
pump (e.g. water ~)	помпа (ж)	['pɔmpa]
robot	робот (ч)	['rɔbot]
laser	лазер (ч)	['lazɛr]
spanner	гайковий ключ (ч)	['ɦajkowij klʲutʃ]
adhesive tape	стрічка-скотч (ч)	['stritʃka skotʃ]
glue	клей (ч)	[klɛj]
sandpaper	наждачний папір (ч)	[naʒ'datʃnij pa'pir]
spring	пружина (ж)	[pru'ʒina]

magnet	магніт (ч)	[maɦ'nit]
gloves	рукавички (мн)	[ruka'witʃki]
rope	мотузка (ж)	[mo'tuzka]
cord	шнур (ч)	[ʃnur]
wire (e.g. telephone ~)	провід (ч)	['prɔwid]
cable	кабель (ч)	['kabɛlʲ]
sledgehammer	кувалда (ж)	[ku'walda]
prybar	лом (ч)	[lom]
ladder	драбина (ж)	[dra'bina]
stepladder	стрем'янка (ж)	[strɛ'mʲanka]
to screw (tighten)	закручувати	[za'krutʃuwati]
to unscrew (lid, filter, etc.)	відкручувати	[wid'krutʃuwati]
to tighten (e.g. with a clamp)	затискати	[zatis'kati]
to glue, to stick	приклеїти	[prik'lɛjiti]
to cut (vt)	різати	['rizati]
malfunction (fault)	несправність (ж)	[nɛ'sprawnistʲ]
repair (mending)	ремонт (ч)	[rɛ'mɔnt]
to repair, to fix (vt)	ремонтувати	[rɛmontu'wati]
to adjust (machine, etc.)	регулювати	[rɛɦulʲu'wati]
to check (to examine)	перевіряти	[pɛrɛwi'rʲati]
checking	перевірка (ж)	[pɛrɛ'wirka]
readings	показання (с)	[poka'zanʲa]
reliable, solid (machine)	надійний	[na'dijnij]
complex (adj)	складний	[sklad'nij]
to rust (get rusted)	іржавіти	[irʒa'witi]
rusty (adj)	іржавий	[ir'ʒawij]
rust	іржа (ж)	[ir'ʒa]

Transport

169. Aeroplane

aeroplane	**літак** (ч)	[li'tak]
air ticket	**авіаквиток** (ч)	[awiakwɨ'tɔk]
airline	**авіакомпанія** (ж)	[awiakom'paniʲa]
airport	**аеропорт** (ч)	[aɛro'pɔrt]
supersonic (adj)	**надзвуковий**	[nadʣwuko'wɨj]
captain	**командир** (ч) **корабля**	[koman'dɨr korab'lʲa]
crew	**екіпаж** (ч)	[ɛki'paʒ]
pilot	**пілот** (ч)	[pi'lɔt]
stewardess	**стюардеса** (ж)	[stʲuar'dɛsa]
navigator	**штурман** (ч)	['ʃturman]
wings	**крила** (мн)	['krɨla]
tail	**хвіст** (ч)	[hwist]
cockpit	**кабіна** (ж)	[ka'bina]
engine	**двигун** (ч)	[dwɨ'ɦun]
undercarriage (landing gear)	**шасі** (с)	[ʃa'si]
turbine	**турбіна** (ж)	[tur'bina]
propeller	**пропелер** (ч)	[pro'pɛlɛr]
black box	**чорна скринька** (ж)	['ʧɔrna 'skrɨnʲka]
yoke (control column)	**штурвал** (ч)	[ʃtur'wal]
fuel	**пальне** (с)	[palʲ'nɛ]
safety card	**інструкція** (ж)	[inst'ruktsiʲa]
oxygen mask	**киснева маска** (ж)	['kɨsnɛwa 'maska]
uniform	**уніформа** (ж)	[uni'fɔrma]
lifejacket	**рятувальний жилет** (ч)	[rʲatu'walʲnɨj ʒɨ'lɛt]
parachute	**парашут** (ч)	[para'ʃut]
takeoff	**зліт** (ч)	[zlit]
to take off (vi)	**злітати**	[zli'tatɨ]
runway	**злітна смуга** (ж)	['zlitna 'smuɦa]
visibility	**видимість** (ж)	['wɨdɨmistʲ]
flight (act of flying)	**політ** (ч)	[po'lit]
altitude	**висота** (ж)	[wɨso'ta]
air pocket	**повітряна яма** (ж)	[po'witrʲana 'jama]
seat	**місце** (с)	['misʦɛ]
headphones	**навушники** (мн)	[na'wuʃnɨkɨ]
folding tray (tray table)	**відкидний столик** (ч)	[widkɨd'nɨj 'stɔlɨk]
airplane window	**ілюмінатор** (ч)	[ilʲumi'nator]
aisle	**прохід** (ч)	[pro'hid]

170. Train

train	поїзд (ч)	['pɔjizd]
commuter train	електропоїзд (ч)	[ɛlɛktro'pɔjizd]
express train	швидкий поїзд (ч)	[ʃwid'kij 'pɔjizd]
diesel locomotive	тепловоз (ч)	[tɛplo'wɔz]
steam locomotive	паровоз (ч)	[paro'wɔz]
coach, carriage	вагон (ч)	[wa'ɦon]
buffet car	вагон-ресторан (ч)	[wa'ɦon rɛsto'ran]
rails	рейки (мн)	['rɛjki]
railway	залізниця (ж)	[zaliz'nitsʲa]
sleeper (track support)	шпала (ж)	['ʃpala]
platform (railway ~)	платформа (ж)	[plat'fɔrma]
platform (~ 1, 2, etc.)	колія (ж)	['kɔliʲa]
semaphore	семафор (ч)	[sɛma'fɔr]
station	станція (ж)	['stantsiʲa]
train driver	машиніст (ч)	[maʃi'nist]
porter (of luggage)	носильник (ч)	[no'silʲnik]
carriage attendant	провідник (ч)	[prowid'nik]
passenger	пасажир (ч)	[pasa'ʒir]
ticket inspector	контролер (ч)	[kontro'lɛr]
corridor (in train)	коридор (ч)	[kori'dɔr]
emergency brake	стоп-кран (ч)	[stop kran]
compartment	купе (с)	[ku'pɛ]
berth	полиця (ж)	[po'litsʲa]
upper berth	полиця (ж) верхня	[po'litsʲa 'wɛrhnʲa]
lower berth	полиця (ж) нижня	[po'litsʲa 'niʒnʲa]
bed linen, bedding	білизна (ж)	[bi'lizna]
ticket	квиток (ч)	[kwi'tɔk]
timetable	розклад (ч)	['rɔzklad]
information display	табло (с)	[tab'lɔ]
to leave, to depart	відходити	[wid'ɦoditi]
departure (of a train)	відправлення (с)	[wid'prawlɛnʲa]
to arrive (ab. train)	прибувати	[pribu'wati]
arrival	прибуття (с)	[pribut'tʲa]
to arrive by train	приїхати поїздом	[pri'jihati 'pɔjizdom]
to get on the train	сісти на поїзд	['sisti na 'pɔjizd]
to get off the train	зійти з поїзду	[zij'ti z 'pɔjizdu]
train crash	катастрофа (ж)	[kata'strɔfa]
steam locomotive	паровоз (ч)	[paro'wɔz]
stoker, fireman	кочегар (ч)	[kotʃɛ'har]
firebox	топка (ж)	['tɔpka]
coal	вугілля (с)	[wu'ɦilʲa]

171. Ship

ship	корабель (ч)	[kora'bɛlʲ]
vessel	судно (с)	['sudno]
steamship	пароплав (ч)	[paro'plaw]
riverboat	теплохід (ч)	[tɛplo'hid]
cruise ship	лайнер (ч)	['lajnɛr]
cruiser	крейсер (ч)	['krɛjsɛr]
yacht	яхта (ж)	['ʲahta]
tugboat	буксир (ч)	[buk'sir]
barge	баржа (ж)	['barʒa]
ferry	паром (ч)	[pa'rɔm]
sailing ship	вітрильник (ч)	[wi'trilʲnik]
brigantine	бригантина (ж)	[briĥan'tina]
ice breaker	криголам (ч)	[kriĥo'lam]
submarine	човен (ч) підводний	['ʧɔwɛn pid'wɔdnij]
boat (flat-bottomed ~)	човен (ч)	['ʧɔwɛn]
dinghy (lifeboat)	шлюпка (ж)	['ʃlʲupka]
lifeboat	шлюпка (ж) рятувальна	['ʃlʲupka rʲatu'walʲna]
motorboat	катер (ч)	['katɛr]
captain	капітан (ч)	[kapi'tan]
seaman	матрос (ч)	[mat'rɔs]
sailor	моряк (ч)	[mo'rʲak]
crew	екіпаж (ч)	[ɛki'paʒ]
boatswain	боцман (ч)	['bɔʦman]
ship's boy	юнга (ч)	['ʲunĥa]
cook	кок (ч)	[kok]
ship's doctor	судновий лікар (ч)	['sudnowij 'likar]
deck	палуба (ж)	['paluba]
mast	щогла (ж)	['ɕoĥla]
sail	вітрило (с)	[wi'trilo]
hold	трюм (ч)	[trʲum]
bow (prow)	ніс (ч)	[nis]
stern	корма (ж)	[kor'ma]
oar	весло (с)	[wɛs'lɔ]
screw propeller	гвинт (ч)	[ĥwint]
cabin	каюта (ж)	[ka'ʲuta]
wardroom	кают-компанія (ж)	[ka'ʲut kom'paniʲa]
engine room	машинне відділення (с)	[ma'ʃinɛ wid'dilɛnʲa]
bridge	капітанський місток (ч)	[kapi'tansʲkij mis'tɔk]
radio room	радіорубка (ж)	[radio'rubka]
wave (radio)	хвиля (ж)	['hwilʲa]
logbook	судновий журнал (ч)	['sudnowij ʒur'nal]
spyglass	підзорна труба (ж)	[pi'dzorna tru'ba]
bell	дзвін (ч)	[dzwin]

flag	прапор (ч)	['prapor]
hawser (mooring ~)	канат (ч)	[ka'nat]
knot (bowline, etc.)	вузол (ч)	['wuzol]

| deckrails | поручень (ч) | ['pɔrutʃɛnʲ] |
| gangway | трап (ч) | [trap] |

anchor	якір (ч)	['ʲakir]
to weigh anchor	підняти якір	[pid'nʲati 'jakir]
to drop anchor	кинути якір	['kinuti 'jakir]
anchor chain	якірний ланцюг (ч)	['ʲakirnij lan'tsʲuɦ]

port (harbour)	порт (ч)	[port]
quay, wharf	причал (ч)	[pri'tʃal]
to berth (moor)	причалювати	[pri'tʃalʲuwati]
to cast off	відчалювати	[wid'tʃalʲuwati]

trip, voyage	подорож (ж)	['pɔdorɔʒ]
cruise (sea trip)	круїз (ч)	[kru'jiz]
course (route)	курс (ч)	[kurs]
route (itinerary)	маршрут (ч)	[marʃ'rut]

fairway (safe water channel)	фарватер (ч)	[far'watɛr]
shallows	мілина (ж)	[mili'na]
to run aground	сісти на мілину	['sisti na mili'nu]

storm	буря (ж)	['burʲa]
signal	сигнал (ч)	[siɦ'nal]
to sink (vi)	тонути	[to'nuti]
SOS (distress signal)	SOS	[sos]
ring buoy	рятувальний круг (ч)	[rʲatu'walʲnij 'kruɦ]

172. Airport

airport	аеропорт (ч)	[aɛro'pɔrt]
aeroplane	літак (ч)	[li'tak]
airline	авіакомпанія (ж)	[awiakom'paniʲa]
air traffic controller	диспетчер (ч)	[dis'pɛtʃɛr]

departure	виліт (ч)	['wilit]
arrival	приліт (ч)	[pri'lit]
to arrive (by plane)	прилетіти	[pri'lɛtiti]

| departure time | час (ч) вильоту | [tʃas 'wilʲotu] |
| arrival time | час (ч) прильоту | [tʃas prilʲotu] |

| to be delayed | затримуватися | [za'trimuwatisʲa] |
| flight delay | затримка (ж) вильоту | [za'trimka 'wilʲotu] |

information board	інформаційне табло (с)	[informa'tsijnɛ tab'lɔ]
information	інформація (ж)	[infor'matsiʲa]
to announce (vt)	оголошувати	[oɦo'lɔʃuwati]
flight (e.g. next ~)	рейс (ч)	[rɛjs]
customs	митниця (ж)	['mitnitsʲa]

customs officer	митник (ч)	['mitnik]
customs declaration	декларація (ж)	[dɛkla'ratsi/a]
to fill in (vt)	заповнити	[za'pɔwniti]
to fill in the declaration	заповнити декларацію	[za'pɔwniti dɛkla'ratsi/u]
passport control	паспортний контроль (ч)	['pasportnij kon'trɔl/]

luggage	багаж (ч)	[ba'ɦaʒ]
hand luggage	ручний вантаж (ж)	[rutʃ'nij wan'taʒ]
luggage trolley	візок (ч) для багажу	[wi'zɔk dl/a baɦa'ʒu]

landing	посадка (ж)	[po'sadka]
landing strip	посадкова смуга (ж)	[po'sadkowa 'smuɦa]
to land (vi)	сідати	[si'dati]
airstair (passenger stair)	трап (ч)	[trap]

check-in	реєстрація (ж)	[reɛ'stratsi/a]
check-in counter	реєстрація (ж)	[reɛ'stratsi/a]
to check-in (vi)	зареєструватися	[zarɛestru'watis/a]
boarding card	посадковий талон (ч)	[po'sadkowij ta'lɔn]
departure gate	вихід (ч)	['wihid]

transit	транзит (ч)	[tran'zit]
to wait (vt)	чекати	[tʃɛ'kati]
departure lounge	зал (ч) очікування	['zal o'tʃikuwan/a]
to see off	проводжати	[prowo'dʒati]
to say goodbye	прощатися	[pro'ɕatis/a]

173. Bicycle. Motorcycle

bicycle	велосипед (ч)	[wɛlosi'pɛd]
scooter	моторолер (ч)	[moto'rɔlɛr]
motorbike	мотоцикл (ч)	[moto'tsikl]

to go by bicycle	їхати на велосипеді	['jihati na wɛlosi'pɛdi]
handlebars	кермо (с)	[kɛr'mɔ]
pedal	педаль (ж)	[pɛ'dal/]
brakes	гальма (мн)	['ɦal/ma]
bicycle seat (saddle)	сідло (с)	[sid'lɔ]

pump	помпа (ж)	['pɔmpa]
pannier rack	багажник (ч)	[ba'ɦaʒnik]
front lamp	ліхтар (ч)	[lih'tar]
helmet	шолом (ч)	[ʃo'lɔm]

wheel	колесо (с)	['kɔlɛso]
mudguard	крило (с)	[kri'lɔ]
rim	обвід (ч)	['ɔbwid]
spoke	спиця (ж)	['spits/a]

Cars

| car | автомобіль (ч) | [awtomo'bilʲ] |
| sports car | спортивний автомобіль (ч) | [spor'tiwnij awtomo'bilʲ] |

limousine	лімузин (ч)	[limu'zin]
off-road vehicle	позадорожник (ч)	[pozado'rɔʒnik]
drophead coupé (convertible)	кабріолет (ч)	[kabrio'lɛt]
minibus	мікроавтобус (ч)	[mikroaw'tɔbus]

| ambulance | швидка допомога (ж) | [ʃwid'ka dopo'mɔɦa] |
| snowplough | снігоприбиральна машина (ж) | [sniɦopribi'ralʲna ma'ʃina] |

lorry	вантажівка (ж)	[wanta'ʒiwka]
road tanker	бензовоз (ч)	[bɛnzo'wɔz]
van (small truck)	фургон (ч)	[fur'ɦɔn]
tractor unit	тягач (ч)	[tʲa'ɦatʃ]
trailer	причіп (ч)	[pri'tʃip]

| comfortable (adj) | комфортабельний | [komfor'tabɛlʲnij] |
| used (adj) | вживаний | ['wʒiwanij] |

bonnet	капот (ч)	[ka'pɔt]
wing	крило (с)	[kri'lɔ]
roof	дах (ч)	[dah]

windscreen	вітрове скло (с)	[witro'wɛ 'sklo]
rear-view mirror	дзеркало (с) заднього виду	['dzɛrkalo 'zadnʲoɦo 'widu]
windscreen washer	омивач (ч)	[omi'watʃ]
windscreen wipers	склоочисники (мн)	[skloo'tʃisniki]

side window	бічне скло (с)	['bitʃnɛ 'sklo]
electric window	склопідіймач (ч)	[sklopidij'matʃ]
aerial	антена (ж)	[an'tɛna]
sunroof	люк (ч)	[lʲuk]

bumper	бампер (ч)	['bampɛr]
boot	багажник (ч)	[ba'ɦaʒnik]
door	дверцята (мн)	[dwɛr'tsʲata]
door handle	ручка (ж)	['rutʃka]
door lock	замок (ч)	[za'mɔk]

number plate	номер (ч)	['nɔmɛr]
silencer	глушник (ч)	[ɦluʃˈnik]
petrol tank	бензобак (ч)	[bɛnzoˈbak]
exhaust pipe	вихлопна труба (ж)	[wihlopˈna truˈba]
accelerator	газ (ч)	[ɦaz]
pedal	педаль (ж)	[pɛˈdalʲ]
accelerator pedal	педаль (ж) газу	[pɛˈdalʲ ˈɦazu]
brake	гальмо (с)	[ɦalʲˈmɔ]
brake pedal	педаль (ж) гальма	[pɛˈdalʲ ɦalʲˈma]
to brake (use the brake)	гальмувати	[ɦalʲmuˈwati]
handbrake	стоянкове гальмо (с)	[stoˈʲankowɛ ɦalʲˈmɔ]
clutch	зчеплення (с)	[ˈztʃɛplɛnʲa]
clutch pedal	педаль (ж) зчеплення	[pɛˈdalʲ ˈztʃɛplɛnʲa]
clutch disc	диск (ч) зчеплення	[ˈdisk ˈztʃiplɛnʲa]
shock absorber	амортизатор (ч)	[amortiˈzator]
wheel	колесо (с)	[ˈkɔlɛso]
spare tyre	запасне колесо (с)	[zapasˈnɛ ˈkɔlɛso]
wheel cover (hubcap)	ковпак (ч)	[kowˈpak]
driving wheels	ведучі колеса (мн)	[wɛˈdutʃi koˈlɛsa]
front-wheel drive (as adj)	передньопривідний	[pɛrɛdnʲopˈriwidnij]
rear-wheel drive (as adj)	задньопривідний	[zadnʲopriwidˈnij]
all-wheel drive (as adj)	повнопривідний	[pownopˈriwidnij]
gearbox	коробка (ж) передач	[koˈrɔbka pɛrɛˈdatʃ]
automatic (adj)	автоматичний	[awtomaˈtitʃnij]
mechanical (adj)	механічний	[mɛhaˈnitʃnij]
gear lever	важіль (ч) коробки передач	[ˈwaʒilʲ koˈrɔbki pɛrɛˈdatʃ]
headlamp	фара (ж)	[ˈfara]
headlights	фари (мн)	[ˈfari]
dipped headlights	ближнє світло (с)	[ˈbliʒnɛ ˈswitlo]
full headlights	дальнє світло (с)	[ˈdalʲnɛ ˈswitlo]
brake light	стоп-сигнал (ч)	[stop siɦˈnal]
sidelights	габаритні вогні (мн)	[ɦabaˈritni woɦˈni]
hazard lights	аварійні вогні (мн)	[awaˈrijni woɦˈni]
fog lights	протитуманні фари (мн)	[protituˈmani ˈfari]
turn indicator	поворотник (ч)	[powoˈrɔtnik]
reversing light	задній хід (ч)	[ˈzadnij hid]

176. Cars. Passenger compartment

car interior	салон (ч)	[saˈlɔn]
leather (as adj)	шкіряний	[ʃkirʲaˈnij]
velour (as adj)	велюровий	[wɛˈlʲurowij]
upholstery	оббивка (ж)	[obˈbiwka]
instrument (gage)	прилад (ч)	[ˈprilad]

dashboard	приладовий щиток (ч)	['priladowij çi'tɔk]
speedometer	спідометр (ч)	[spi'dɔmɛtr]
needle (pointer)	стрілка (ж)	['strilka]

mileometer	лічильник (ч)	[li'tʃilʲnik]
indicator (sensor)	датчик (ч)	['datʃik]
level	рівень (ч)	['riwɛnʲ]
warning light	лампочка (ж)	['lampotʃka]

steering wheel	кермо (с)	[kɛr'mɔ]
horn	сигнал (ч)	[siɦ'nal]
button	кнопка (ж)	['knɔpka]
switch	перемикач (ч)	[pɛrɛmi'katʃ]

seat	сидіння (с)	[si'dinʲa]
backrest	спинка (ж)	['spinka]
headrest	підголівник (ч)	[pidɦo'liwnik]
seat belt	ремінь (ч) безпеки	['rɛminʲ bɛz'pɛki]
to fasten the belt	пристебнути ремінь	[pristɛb'nuti 'rɛminʲ]
adjustment (of seats)	регулювання (с)	[rɛɦulʲu'wanʲa]

| airbag | повітряна подушка (ж) | [po'witrʲana po'duʃka] |
| air-conditioner | кондиціонер (ч) | [konditsio'nɛr] |

radio	радіо (с)	['radio]
CD player	CD-програвач (ч)	[si'di proɦra'watʃ]
to turn on	увімкнути	[uwimk'nuti]
aerial	антена (ж)	[an'tɛna]
glove box	бардачок (ч)	[barda'tʃɔk]
ashtray	попільниця (ж)	[popilʲ'nitsʲa]

177. Cars. Engine

engine	двигун (ч)	[dwi'ɦun]
motor	мотор (ч)	[mo'tɔr]
diesel (as adj)	дизельний	['dizɛlʲnij]
petrol (as adj)	бензиновий	[bɛn'zinowij]

engine volume	об'єм (ч) двигуна	[o'bʲɛm dwiɦu'na]
power	потужність (ж)	[po'tuʒnistʲ]
horsepower	кінська сила (ж)	['kinsʲka 'sila]
piston	поршень (ч)	['porʃɛnʲ]
cylinder	циліндр (ч)	[tsi'lindr]
valve	клапан (ч)	['klapan]

injector	інжектор (ч)	[in'ʒɛktor]
generator (alternator)	генератор (ч)	[ɦɛnɛ'rator]
carburettor	карбюратор (ч)	[karbʲu'rator]
motor oil	масло (с) моторне	['maslo mo'tɔrnɛ]

radiator	радіатор (ч)	[radi'ator]
coolant	охолоджувальна рідина (ж)	[oɦo'lɔdʒuwalʲna ridi'na]
cooling fan	вентилятор (ч)	[wɛnti'lʲator]

battery (accumulator)	акумулятор (ч)	[akumu'lʲator]
starter	стартер (ч)	['startɛr]
ignition	запалювання (с)	[za'palʲuwanʲa]
sparking plug	свічка (ж) запалювання	['switʃka za'palʲuwanʲa]

terminal (battery ~)	клема (ж)	['klɛma]
positive terminal	плюс (ч)	[plʲus]
negative terminal	мінус (ч)	['minus]
fuse	запобіжник (ч)	[zapo'biʒnik]

air filter	повітряний фільтр (ч)	[po'witrʲanij 'filʲtr]
oil filter	масляний фільтр (ч)	['maslʲanij 'filʲtr]
fuel filter	паливний фільтр (ч)	['paliwnij 'filʲtr]

178. Cars. Crash. Repair

car crash	аварія (ж)	[a'wariʲa]
traffic accident	дорожня пригода (ж)	[do'roʒnʲa pri'ɦoda]
to crash (into the wall, etc.)	врізатися	['wrizatisʲa]
to get smashed up	розбитися	[roz'bitisʲa]
damage	пошкодження (с)	[poʃ'koʤɛnʲa]
intact (unscathed)	цілий	[tsi'lij]

| to break down (vi) | зламатися | [zla'matisʲa] |
| towrope | буксирний трос (ч) | [buk'sirnij tros] |

puncture	прокол (ч)	[pro'kɔl]
to have a puncture	спустити	[spus'titi]
to pump up	накачати	[naka'tʃati]
pressure	тиск (ч)	[tisk]
to check (to examine)	перевірити	[pɛrɛ'wiriti]

repair	ремонт (ч)	[rɛ'mɔnt]
garage (auto service shop)	ремонтна майстерня (ж)	[rɛ'mɔntna majs'tɛrnʲa]
spare part	запчастина (ж)	[zaptʃas'tina]
part	деталь (ж)	[dɛ'talʲ]

bolt (with nut)	болт (ч)	[bolt]
screw (fastener)	гвинт (ч)	[ɦwint]
nut	гайка (ж)	['ɦajka]
washer	шайба (ж)	['ʃajba]
bearing (e.g. ball ~)	підшипник (ч)	[pid'ʃipnik]

tube	трубка (ж)	['trubka]
gasket (head ~)	прокладка (ж)	[prok'ladka]
cable, wire	провід (ч)	['prɔwid]

jack	домкрат (ч)	[domk'rat]
spanner	ключ (ч)	[klʲutʃ]
hammer	молоток (ч)	[molo'tɔk]
pump	помпа (ж)	['pɔmpa]
screwdriver	викрутка (ж)	['wikrutka]
fire extinguisher	вогнегасник (ч)	[woɦnɛ'ɦasnik]
warning triangle	аварійний трикутник (ч)	[awa'rijnij tri'kutnik]

to stall (vi)	глохнути	['ɦlɔhnuti]
stall (n)	зупинка (ж)	[zu'pinka]
to be broken	бути зламаним	['buti 'zlamanim]
to overheat (vi)	перегрітися	[pɛrɛɦ'ritisʲa]
to freeze up (pipes, etc.)	замерзнути	[za'mɛrznuti]
to burst (vi, ab. tube)	лопнути	['lɔpnuti]
pressure	тиск (ч)	[tisk]
level	рівень (ч)	['riwɛnʲ]
slack (~ belt)	слабкий	[slab'kij]
dent	вм'ятина (ж)	['wmʲʲatina]
knocking noise (engine)	стукіт (ч)	['stukit]
crack	тріщина (ж)	['triɕina]
scratch	подряпина (ж)	[pod'rʲapina]

179. Cars. Road

road	дорога (ж)	[do'rɔɦa]
motorway	автомагістраль (ж)	[awtomaɦi'stralʲ]
highway	шосе (с)	[ʃo'sɛ]
direction (way)	напрямок (ч)	['naprʲamok]
distance	відстань (ж)	['widstanʲ]
bridge	міст (ч)	[mist]
car park	паркінг (ч)	['parkinɦ]
square	площа (ж)	['plɔɕa]
road junction	розв'язка (ж)	[roz'wʲʲazka]
tunnel	тунель (ч)	[tu'nɛlʲ]
petrol station	автозаправка (ж)	[awtoza'prawka]
car park	автостоянка (ж)	[awtosto'ʲanka]
petrol pump	бензоколонка (ж)	[bɛnzoko'lɔnka]
auto repair shop	гараж (ч)	[ɦa'raʒ]
to fill up	заправити	[za'prawiti]
fuel	паливо (с)	['paliwo]
jerrycan	каністра (ж)	[ka'nistra]
asphalt, tarmac	асфальт (ч)	[as'falʲt]
road markings	розмітка (ж)	[roz'mitka]
kerb	бордюр (ч)	[bor'dʲur]
crash barrier	огорожа (ж)	[oɦo'rɔʒa]
ditch	кювет (ч)	[kʲu'wɛt]
roadside (shoulder)	узбіччя (с)	[uz'bitʃʲa]
lamppost	стовп (ч)	[stowp]
to drive (a car)	вести	['wɛsti]
to turn (e.g., ~ left)	повертати	[powɛr'tati]
to make a U-turn	розвертатися	[rozwɛr'tatisʲa]
reverse (~ gear)	задній хід (ч)	['zadnij hid]
to honk (vi)	сигналити	[siɦ'naliti]
honk (sound)	звуковий сигнал (ч)	[zwuko'wij siɦ'nal]

to get stuck (in the mud, etc.)	застрягти	[za'strʲaɦti]
to spin the wheels	буксувати	[buksu'wati]
to cut, to turn off (vt)	глушити	[ɦlu'ʃiti]

speed	швидкість (ж)	['ʃwidkistʲ]
to exceed the speed limit	перевищити швидкість	[pɛrɛ'wiɕiti 'ʃwidkistʲ]
to give a ticket	штрафувати	[ʃtrafu'wati]
traffic lights	світлофор (ч)	[switlo'fɔr]
driving licence	посвідчення (с) водія	[pos'widtʃɛnja wodiʲa]

level crossing	переїзд (ч)	[pɛrɛ'jizd]
crossroads	перехрестя (с)	[pɛrɛh'rɛstʲa]
zebra crossing	пішохідний перехід (ч)	[piʃo'hidnij pɛrɛ'hid]
bend, curve	поворот (ч)	[powo'rɔt]
pedestrian precinct	пішохідна зона (ж)	[piʃo'hidna 'zɔna]

180. Signs

Highway Code	правила (мн) дорожнього руху	['prawila do'rɔʒnʲoɦo 'ruhu]
road sign (traffic sign)	знак (ч)	[znak]
overtaking	обгін (ч)	[ob'ɦin]
curve	поворот (ч)	[powo'rɔt]
U-turn	розворот (ч)	[rozwo'rɔt]
roundabout	круговий рух (ч)	[kruɦo'wij ruh]

No entry	в'їзд заборонено	[wʲj'izd zabo'rɔnɛno]
All vehicles prohibited	рух (ч) заборонено	[ruh zabo'rɔnɛno]
No overtaking	обгін заборонено	[ob'ɦin zabo'rɔnɛno]
No parking	стоянку заборонено	[sto'ʲanku zabo'rɔnɛno]
No stopping	зупинку заборонено	[zu'pinku zabo'rɔnɛno]

dangerous curve	небезпечний поворот (ч)	[nɛbɛz'pɛtʃnij powo'rɔt]
steep descent	крутий спуск (ч)	[kru'tij 'spusk]
one-way traffic	односторонній рух (ч)	[odnosto'rɔnij ruh]
zebra crossing	пішохідний перехід (ч)	[piʃo'hidnij pɛrɛ'hid]
slippery road	слизька дорога (ж)	[sliz'ʲka do'rɔɦa]
GIVE WAY	дати дорогу	['dati do'rɔɦu]

PEOPLE. LIFE EVENTS

181. Holidays. Event

celebration, holiday	свято (с)	['swіato]
national day	національне свято (с)	[natsio'nalіnɛ 'swіato]
public holiday	святковий день (ч)	[swіat'kɔwij dɛnі]
to commemorate (vt)	святкувати	[swіatku'wati]
event (happening)	подія (ж)	[po'diіa]
event (organized activity)	захід (ч)	['zahid]
banquet (party)	бенкет (ч)	[bɛ'nkɛt]
reception (formal party)	прийом (ч)	[pri'jɔm]
feast	бенкет (ч)	[bɛ'nkɛt]
anniversary	річниця (ж)	[ritʃ'nitsіa]
jubilee	ювілей (ч)	[іuwi'lɛj]
to celebrate (vt)	відмітити	[wid'mititi]
New Year	Новий рік (ч)	[no'wij rik]
Happy New Year!	З Новим Роком!	[z no'wim 'rɔkom]
Christmas	Різдво (с)	[rizd'wɔ]
Merry Christmas!	Щасливого Різдва!	[ɕas'liwoɦo rizd'wa]
Christmas tree	Новорічна ялинка (ж)	[nowo'ritʃna ja'linka]
fireworks (fireworks show)	салют (ч)	[sa'lіut]
wedding	весілля (с)	[wɛ'silіa]
groom	наречений (ч)	[narɛ'tʃɛnij]
bride	наречена (ж)	[narɛ'tʃɛna]
to invite (vt)	запрошувати	[za'prɔʃuwati]
invitation card	запрошення (с)	[za'prɔʃɛnіa]
guest	гість (ч)	[ɦistі]
to visit (~ your parents, etc.)	йти в гості	[jti w 'ɦosti]
to meet the guests	зустрічати гостей	[zustri'tʃati ɦos'tɛj]
gift, present	подарунок (ч)	[poda'runok]
to give (sth as present)	дарувати	[daru'wati]
to receive gifts	отримувати подарунки	[ot'rimuwati poda'runkі]
bouquet (of flowers)	букет (ч)	[bu'kɛt]
congratulations	привітання (с)	[priwi'tanіa]
to congratulate (vt)	вітати	[wi'tati]
greetings card	вітальна листівка (ж)	[wi'talіna lis'tiwka]
to send a postcard	надіслати листівку	[nadi'slati lis'tiwku]
to get a postcard	отримати листівку	[ot'rimati lis'tiwku]
toast	тост (ч)	[tost]

| to offer (a drink, etc.) | пригощати | [priɦo'ɕati] |
| champagne | шампанське (с) | [ʃam'pansʲkɛ] |

to enjoy oneself	веселитися	[wɛsɛ'litisʲa]
merriment (gaiety)	веселощі (мн)	[wɛ'sɛloɕi]
joy (emotion)	радість (ж)	['radistʲ]

| dance | танець (ч) | ['tanɛʦ] |
| to dance (vi, vt) | танцювати | [tanʦʲu'wati] |

| waltz | вальс (ч) | [walʲs] |
| tango | танго (с) | ['tanɦo] |

182. Funerals. Burial

cemetery	цвинтар (ч)	['ʦwintar]
grave, tomb	могила (ж)	[mo'ɦila]
cross	хрест (ч)	[hrɛst]
gravestone	нагробок (ч)	[na'ɦrɔbok]
fence	огорожа (ж)	[oɦo'rɔʒa]
chapel	каплиця (ж)	[kap'liʦʲa]

death	смерть (ж)	[smɛrtʲ]
to die (vi)	померти	[po'mɛrti]
the deceased	покійник (ч)	[po'kijnik]
mourning	траур (ч)	['traur]

to bury (vt)	ховати	[ho'wati]
undertakers	похоронне бюро (с)	[poho'rɔnɛ bʲuro]
funeral	похорон (ч)	['pɔhoron]

wreath	вінок (ч)	[wi'nɔk]
coffin	труна (ж)	[tru'na]
hearse	катафалк (ч)	[kata'falk]
shroud	саван (ч)	[sa'wan]

| funerary urn | урна (ж) | ['urna] |
| crematorium | крематорій (ч) | [krɛma'tɔrij] |

obituary	некролог (ч)	[nɛkro'lɔɦ]
to cry (weep)	плакати	['plakati]
to sob (vi)	ридати	[ri'dati]

183. War. Soldiers

platoon	взвод (ч)	[wzwod]
company	рота (ж)	['rɔta]
regiment	полк (ч)	[polk]
army	армія (ж)	['armiʲa]
division	дивізія (ж)	[di'wiziʲa]
section, squad	загін (ч)	[za'ɦin]
host (army)	військо (с)	['wijsʲko]

| soldier | солдат (ч) | [sol'dat] |
| officer | офіцер (ч) | [ofi'tsɛr] |

private	рядовий (ч)	[rʲado'wij]
sergeant	сержант (ч)	[sɛr'ʒant]
lieutenant	лейтенант (ч)	[lɛjtɛ'nant]
captain	капітан (ч)	[kapi'tan]
major	майор (ч)	[ma'jɔr]
colonel	полковник (ч)	[pol'kɔwnik]
general	генерал (ч)	[ɦɛnɛ'ral]

sailor	моряк (ч)	[mo'rʲak]
captain	капітан (ч)	[kapi'tan]
boatswain	боцман (ч)	['bɔtsman]

artilleryman	артилерист (ч)	[artiɫɛ'rist]
paratrooper	десантник (ч)	[dɛ'santnik]
pilot	льотчик (ч)	[lʲotʃik]
navigator	штурман (ч)	['ʃturman]
mechanic	механік (ч)	[mɛ'hanik]

pioneer (sapper)	сапер (ч)	[sa'pɛr]
parachutist	парашутист (ч)	[paraʃu'tist]
reconnaissance scout	розвідник (ч)	[roz'widnik]
sniper	снайпер (ч)	['snajpɛr]

patrol (group)	патруль (ч)	[pat'rulʲ]
to patrol (vt)	патрулювати	[patrulʲu'wati]
sentry, guard	вартовий (ч)	[warto'wij]

warrior	воїн (ч)	['wojin]
patriot	патріот (ч)	[patri'ɔt]
hero	герой (ч)	[ɦɛ'rɔj]
heroine	героїня (ж)	[ɦɛro'jinʲa]

traitor	зрадник (ч)	['zradnik]
deserter	дезертир (ч)	[dɛzɛr'tir]
to desert (vi)	дезертирувати	[dɛzɛr'tiruwati]

mercenary	найманець (ч)	['najmanɛts]
recruit	новобранець (ч)	[nowo'branɛts]
volunteer	доброволець (ч)	[dobro'wɔlɛts]

dead (n)	убитий (ч)	[u'bitij]
wounded (n)	поранений (ч)	[po'ranɛnij]
prisoner of war	полонений (ч)	[polo'nɛnij]

184. War. Military actions. Part 1

war	війна (ж)	[wij'na]
to be at war	воювати	[wo'u'wati]
civil war	громадянська війна (ж)	[ɦroma'dʲansʲka wij'na]
treacherously (adv)	віроломно	[wiro'lɔmno]
declaration of war	оголошення (с)	[oɦo'lɔʃɛnʲa]

to declare (~ war)	оголосити	[oɦolo'siti]
aggression	агресія (ж)	[aɦ'rɛsi̯a]
to attack (invade)	нападати	[napa'dati]
to invade (vt)	захоплювати	[za'ɦopl'uwati]
invader	загарбник (ч)	[za'ɦarbnik]
conqueror	завойовник (ч)	[zawo'i̯ownik]
defence	оборона (ж)	[obo'rɔna]
to defend (a country, etc.)	обороняти	[oboro'n'ati]
to defend (against …)	оборонятися	[oboro'n'atis'a]
enemy	ворог (ч)	['wɔroɦ]
foe, adversary	супротивник (ч)	[supro'tiwnik]
enemy (as adj)	ворожий	[wo'rɔʒij]
strategy	стратегія (ж)	[stra'tɛɦi̯a]
tactics	тактика (ж)	['taktika]
order	наказ (ч)	[na'kaz]
command (order)	команда (ж)	[ko'manda]
to order (vt)	наказувати	[na'kazuwati]
mission	завдання (с)	[zaw'dan'a]
secret (adj)	таємний	[ta'ɛmnij]
battle	битва (ж)	['bitwa]
combat	бій (ч)	[bij]
attack	атака (ж)	[a'taka]
charge (assault)	штурм (ч)	[ʃturm]
to storm (vt)	штурмувати	[ʃturmu'wati]
siege (to be under ~)	облога (ж)	[ob'lɔɦa]
offensive (n)	наступ (ч)	['nastup]
to go on the offensive	наступати	[nastu'pati]
retreat	відступ (ч)	['widstup]
to retreat (vi)	відступати	[widstu'pati]
encirclement	оточення (с)	[o'tɔtʃɛn'a]
to encircle (vt)	оточувати	[o'tɔtʃuwati]
bombing (by aircraft)	бомбардування (с)	[bombardu'wan'a]
to drop a bomb	скинути бомбу	['skinuti 'bɔmbu]
to bomb (vt)	бомбардувати	[bombardu'wati]
explosion	вибух (ч)	['wibuh]
shot	постріл (ч)	['pɔstril]
to fire (~ a shot)	вистрілити	['wistriliti]
firing (burst of ~)	стрілянина (ж)	[stril'a'nina]
to aim (to point a weapon)	цілитися	['tsilitis'a]
to point (a gun)	навести	[na'wɛsti]
to hit (the target)	влучити	['wlutʃiti]
to sink (~ a ship)	потопити	[poto'piti]
hole (in a ship)	пробоїна (ж)	[pro'bɔjina]

to founder, to sink (vi)	йти на дно	[jti na dno]
front (war ~)	фронт (ч)	[front]
evacuation	евакуація (ж)	[ɛwaku'atsiʲa]
to evacuate (vt)	евакуювати	[ɛwakuʲu'wati]

barbed wire	колючий дріт (ч)	[ko'lʲutʃij drit]
barrier (anti tank ~)	загородження (с)	[zaɦo'rɔdʒɛnʲa]
watchtower	вишка (ж)	['wiʃka]

military hospital	госпіталь (ч)	['ɦɔspitalʲ]
to wound (vt)	поранити	[po'raniti]
wound	рана (ж)	['rana]
wounded (n)	поранений (ч)	[po'ranɛnij]
to be wounded	одержати поранення	[o'dɛrʒati po'ranɛnʲa]
serious (wound)	важкий	[waʒ'kij]

185. War. Military actions. Part 2

captivity	полон (ч)	[po'lɔn]
to take captive	взяти в полон	['wzʲati w po'lɔn]
to be held captive	бути в полоні	['buti w po'lɔni]
to be taken captive	потрапити в полон	[pot'rapiti w po'lɔn]

concentration camp	концтабір (ч)	[konts'tabir]
prisoner of war	полонений (ч)	[polo'nɛnij]
to escape (vi)	тікати	[ti'kati]

to betray (vt)	зрадити	['zraditi]
betrayer	зрадник (ч)	['zradnik]
betrayal	зрада (ж)	['zrada]

| to execute (by firing squad) | розстріляти | [rozstri'lʲati] |
| execution (by firing squad) | розстріл (ч) | ['rɔzstril] |

equipment (military gear)	обмундирування (с)	[obmundiru'wanʲa]
shoulder board	погон (ч)	[po'ɦɔn]
gas mask	протигаз (ч)	[proti'ɦaz]

field radio	рація (ж)	['ratsiʲa]
cipher, code	шифр (ч)	[ʃifr]
secrecy	конспірація (ж)	[konspi'ratsiʲa]
password	пароль (ч)	[pa'rɔlʲ]

land mine	міна (ж)	['mina]
to mine (road, etc.)	мінувати	[minu'wati]
minefield	мінне поле (с)	['minɛ 'pɔlɛ]

air-raid warning	повітряна тривога (ж)	[po'witrʲana tri'wɔɦa]
alarm (alert signal)	тривога (ж)	[tri'wɔɦa]
signal	сигнал (ч)	[siɦ'nal]
signal flare	сигнальна ракета (ж)	[siɦ'nalʲna ra'kɛta]

| headquarters | штаб (ч) | [ʃtab] |
| reconnaissance | розвідка (ж) | ['rɔzwidka] |

situation	обстановка (ж)	[obsta'nɔwka]
report	рапорт (ч)	['raport]
ambush	засідка (ж)	['zasidka]
reinforcement (army)	підкріплення (с)	[pid'kriplɛnʲa]

target	мішень (ж)	[mi'ʃɛnʲ]
training area	полігон (ч)	[poli'ɦɔn]
military exercise	маневри (мн)	[ma'nɛwri]

panic	паніка (ж)	['panika]
devastation	розруха (ж)	[roz'ruha]
destruction, ruins	руйнування (мн)	[rujnu'wanʲa]
to destroy (vt)	зруйнувати	[zrujnu'wati]

to survive (vi, vt)	вижити	['wiʒiti]
to disarm (vt)	обеззброїти	[obɛz'zbrɔjiti]
to handle (~ a gun)	поводитися	[po'wɔditisʲa]

| Attention! | Струнко! | ['strunko] |
| At ease! | Вільно! | ['wilʲno] |

feat, act of courage	подвиг (ч)	['pɔdwiɦ]
oath (vow)	клятва (ж)	['klʲatwa]
to swear (an oath)	клястися	['klʲastisʲa]

decoration (medal, etc.)	нагорода (ж)	[naɦo'rɔda]
to award (give a medal to)	нагороджувати	[naɦo'rɔdʒuwati]
medal	медаль (ж)	[mɛ'dalʲ]
order (e.g. ~ of Merit)	орден (ч)	['ɔrdɛn]

victory	перемога (ж)	[pɛrɛ'mɔɦa]
defeat	поразка (ж)	[po'razka]
armistice	перемир'я (с)	[pɛrɛ'mirʲʲa]

standard (battle flag)	прапор (ч)	['prapor]
glory (honour, fame)	слава (ж)	['slawa]
parade	парад (ч)	[pa'rad]
to march (on parade)	марширувати	[marʃiru'wati]

186. Weapons

weapons	зброя (ж)	['zbrɔʲa]
firearms	вогнепальна зброя	[woɦnɛ'palʲna 'zbrɔʲa]
cold weapons (knives, etc.)	холодна зброя (ж)	[ho'lɔdna 'zbrɔʲa]

chemical weapons	хімічна зброя (ж)	[hi'miʧna 'zbrɔʲa]
nuclear (adj)	ядерний	['ʲadɛrnij]
nuclear weapons	ядерна зброя (ж)	['ʲadɛrna 'zbrɔʲa]

| bomb | бомба (ж) | ['bɔmba] |
| atomic bomb | атомна бомба (ж) | ['atomna 'bɔmba] |

| pistol (gun) | пістолет (ч) | [pisto'lɛt] |
| rifle | рушниця (ж) | [ruʃ'nitsʲa] |

| submachine gun | автомат (ч) | [awto'mat] |
| machine gun | кулемет (ч) | [kulɛ'mɛt] |

muzzle	дуло (с)	['dulo]
barrel	ствол (ч)	[stwol]
calibre	калібр (ч)	[ka'libr]

trigger	курок (ч)	[ku'rɔk]
sight (aiming device)	приціл (ч)	[pri'ʦil]
magazine	магазин (ч)	[maɦa'zin]
butt (shoulder stock)	приклад (ч)	[prik'lad]

| hand grenade | граната (ж) | [ɦra'nata] |
| explosive | вибухівка (ж) | [wibu'ɦiwka] |

| bullet | куля (ж) | ['kulʲa] |
| cartridge | патрон (ч) | [pat'rɔn] |

| charge | заряд (ч) | [za'rʲad] |
| ammunition | боєприпаси (мн) | [boɛpri'pasi] |

bomber (aircraft)	бомбардувальник (ч)	[bombardu'walʲnik]
fighter	винищувач (ч)	[wi'niɕuwatʃ]
helicopter	вертоліт (ч)	[wɛrto'lit]

anti-aircraft gun	зенітка (ж)	[zɛ'nitka]
tank	танк (ч)	[tank]
tank gun	гармата (ж)	[ɦar'mata]

artillery	артилерія (ж)	[arti'lɛrʲiʲa]
gun (cannon, howitzer)	гармата (ж)	[ɦar'mata]
to lay (a gun)	навести	[na'wɛsti]

| shell (projectile) | снаряд (ч) | [sna'rʲad] |
| mortar bomb | міна (ж) | ['mina] |

| mortar | міномет (ч) | [mino'mɛt] |
| splinter (shell fragment) | осколок (ч) | [os'kɔlok] |

submarine	підводний човен (ч)	[pid'wɔdnij 'ʧɔwɛn]
torpedo	торпеда (ж)	[tor'pɛda]
missile	ракета (ж)	[ra'kɛta]

| to load (gun) | заряджати | [zarʲa'ʤati] |
| to shoot (vi) | стріляти | [stri'lʲati] |

| to point at (the cannon) | цілитися | ['ʦilitisʲa] |
| bayonet | багнет (ч) | [baɦ'nɛt] |

rapier	шпага (ж)	['ʃpaɦa]
sabre (e.g. cavalry ~)	шабля (ж)	['ʃablʲa]
spear (weapon)	спис (ч)	[spis]
bow	лук (ч)	[luk]
arrow	стріла (ж)	[stri'la]
musket	мушкет (ч)	[muʃ'kɛt]
crossbow	арбалет (ч)	[arba'lɛt]

187. Ancient people

primitive (prehistoric)	первісний	[pɛr'wisnij]
prehistoric (adj)	доісторичний	[doisto'ritʃnij]
ancient (~ civilization)	стародавній	[staro'dawnij]

Stone Age	Кам'яний вік (ч)	[kamʲa'nij wik]
Bronze Age	Бронзовий вік (ч)	['brɔnzowij wik]
Ice Age	льодовиковий період (ч)	[lʲodowi'kɔwij pɛ'riod]

tribe	плем'я (с)	['plɛmʲa]
cannibal	людоїд (ч)	[lʲudo'jid]
hunter	мисливець (ч)	[mis'liwɛʦ]
to hunt (vi, vt)	полювати	[polʲu'wati]
mammoth	мамонт (ч)	['mamont]

cave	печера (ж)	[pɛ'ʧɛra]
fire	вогонь (ч)	[wo'hɔnʲ]
campfire	багаття (с)	[ba'hattʲa]
cave painting	наскальний малюнок (ч)	[na'skalʲnij ma'lʲunok]

tool (e.g. stone axe)	знаряддя (с) праці	[zna'rʲaddʲa 'praʦi]
spear	спис (ч)	[spis]
stone axe	кам'яна сокира (ж)	[kamʲa'na so'kira]
to be at war	воювати	[woʲu'wati]
to domesticate (vt)	приручати	[priru'ʧati]

idol	ідол (ч)	['idol]
to worship (vt)	поклонятися	[poklo'nʲatisʲa]
superstition	забобони (мн)	[zabo'boni]

evolution	еволюція (ж)	[ɛwo'lʲuʦiʲa]
development	розвиток (ч)	['rɔzwitok]
disappearance (extinction)	зникнення (с)	['zniknɛnʲa]
to adapt oneself	пристосовуватися	[pristosowu'watisʲa]

archaeology	археологія (ж)	[arhɛo'lɔhiʲa]
archaeologist	археолог (ч)	[arhɛ'ɔloh]
archaeological (adj)	археологічний	[arhɛolo'hitʃnij]

excavation site	розкопки (мн)	[roz'kɔpki]
excavations	розкопки (мн)	[roz'kɔpki]
find (object)	знахідка (ж)	[zna'hidka]
fragment	фрагмент (ч)	[frah'mɛnt]

188. Middle Ages

people (ethnic group)	народ (ч)	[na'rɔd]
peoples	народи (мн)	[na'rɔdi]
tribe	плем'я (с)	['plɛmʲa]
tribes	племена (мн)	[plɛmɛ'na]
barbarians	варвари (мн)	['warwari]
Gauls	гали (ч)	['hali]

Goths	готи (мн)	['hɔti]
Slavs	слов'яни (мн)	[slo'wʲani]
Vikings	вікінги (мн)	['wikinɦi]

| Romans | римляни (мн) | [rim'lʲani] |
| Roman (adj) | Римський Папа | ['rimsʲkij 'papa] |

Byzantines	візантійці (мн)	[wizan'tijʦi]
Byzantium	Візантія (ж)	[wizan'tiʲa]
Byzantine (adj)	візантійський	[wizan'tijsʲkij]

emperor	імператор (ч)	[impɛ'rator]
leader, chief (tribal ~)	вождь (ч)	[woʒdʲ]
powerful (~ king)	могутній	[mo'ɦutnij]
king	король (ч)	[ko'rɔlʲ]
ruler (sovereign)	правитель (ч)	[pra'witɛlʲ]

knight	лицар (ч)	['liʦar]
feudal lord	феодал (ч)	[fɛo'dal]
feudal (adj)	феодальний	[fɛo'dalʲnij]
vassal	васал (ч)	[wa'sal]

duke	герцог (ч)	['ɦɛrʦoɦ]
earl	граф (ч)	[ɦraf]
baron	барон (ч)	[ba'rɔn]
bishop	єпископ (ч)	[ɛ'piskop]

armour	лати (мн)	['lati]
shield	щит (ч)	[ɕit]
sword	меч (ч)	[mɛʧ]
visor	забрало (с)	[za'bralo]
chainmail	кольчуга (ж)	[kolʲ'ʧuɦa]

| Crusade | хрестовий похід (ч) | [hrɛs'tɔwij po'hid] |
| crusader | хрестоносець (ч) | [hrɛsto'nɔsɛʦ] |

territory	територія (ж)	[tɛri'tɔriʲa]
to attack (invade)	нападати	[napa'dati]
to conquer (vt)	завоювати	[zawoʲu'wati]
to occupy (invade)	захватити	[zahwa'titi]

siege (to be under ~)	облога (ж)	[ob'lɔɦa]
besieged (adj)	обложений	[ob'lɔʒenij]
to besiege (vt)	облягати	[oblʲa'ɦati]

inquisition	інквізиція (ж)	[inkwi'ziʦiʲa]
inquisitor	інквізитор (ч)	[inkwi'zitor]
torture	катування (с)	[katu'wanʲa]
cruel (adj)	жорстокий	[ʒor'stɔkij]
heretic	єретик (ч)	[ɛ'rɛtik]
heresy	єресь (ж)	['ɛrɛsʲ]

seafaring	мореплавання (с)	[morɛ'plawanʲa]
pirate	пірат (ч)	[pi'rat]
piracy	піратство (с)	[pi'raʦtwo]
boarding (attack)	абордаж (ч)	[abor'daʒ]

| loot, booty | здобич (ж) | ['zdɔbitʃ] |
| treasure | скарби (мн) | [skar'bi] |

discovery	відкриття (с)	[widkrit'tʲa]
to discover (new land, etc.)	відкрити	[wid'kriti]
expedition	експедиція (ж)	[ɛkspɛ'ditsiʲa]

musketeer	мушкетер (ч)	[muʃkɛ'tɛr]
cardinal	кардинал (ч)	[kardi'nal]
heraldry	геральдика (ж)	[ɦɛ'ralʲdika]
heraldic (adj)	геральдичний	[ɦɛralʲ'ditʃnij]

189. Leader. Chief. Authorities

king	король (ч)	[ko'rɔlʲ]
queen	королева (ж)	[koro'lɛwa]
royal (adj)	королівський	[koro'liwsʲkij]
kingdom	королівство (с)	[koro'liwstwo]

| prince | принц (ч) | [prinʦ] |
| princess | принцеса (ж) | [prin'ʦɛsa] |

president	президент (ч)	[prɛzi'dɛnt]
vice-president	віце-президент (ч)	['witsɛ prɛzi'dɛnt]
senator	сенатор (ч)	[sɛ'nator]

monarch	монарх (ч)	[mo'narh]
ruler (sovereign)	правитель (ч)	[pra'witɛlʲ]
dictator	диктатор (ч)	[dik'tator]
tyrant	тиран (ч)	[ti'ran]
magnate	магнат (ч)	[maɦ'nat]

director	директор (ч)	[di'rɛktor]
chief	шеф (ч)	[ʃɛf]
manager (director)	управляючий (ч)	[upraw'lʲaʲutʃij]

| boss | бос (ч) | [bos] |
| owner | господар (ч) | [ɦos'pɔdar] |

head (~ of delegation)	голова (ж)	[ɦolo'wa]
authorities	влада (ж)	['wlada]
superiors	керівництво (с)	[kɛriw'niʦtwo]

governor	губернатор (ч)	[ɦubɛr'nator]
consul	консул (ч)	['kɔnsul]
diplomat	дипломат (ч)	[diplo'mat]

| mayor | мер (ч) | [mɛr] |
| sheriff | шериф (ч) | [ʃɛ'rif] |

emperor	імператор (ч)	[impɛ'rator]
tsar, czar	цар (ч)	[ʦar]
pharaoh	фараон (ч)	[fara'ɔn]
khan	хан (ч)	[han]

190. Road. Way. Directions

road	дорога (ж)	[do'rɔɦa]
way (direction)	шлях (ч)	[ʃlʲah]
highway	шосе (с)	[ʃo'sɛ]
motorway	автомагістраль (ж)	[awtomaɦi'stralʲ]
trunk road	національна дорога (ж)	[natsio'nalʲna do'rɔɦa]
main road	головна дорога (ж)	[ɦolow'na do'rɔɦa]
dirt road	польова дорога (ж)	[polʲo'wa do'rɔɦa]
pathway	стежка (ж)	['stɛʒka]
footpath (troddenpath)	стежина (ж)	[stɛ'ʒina]
Where?	Де?	[dɛ]
Where (to)?	Куди?	[ku'di]
From where?	Звідки?	['zwidki]
direction (way)	напрямок (ч)	['naprʲamok]
to point (~ the way)	вказати	[wka'zati]
to the left	ліворуч	[li'wɔrutʃ]
to the right	праворуч	[pra'wɔrutʃ]
straight ahead (adv)	прямо	['prʲamo]
back (e.g. to turn ~)	назад	[na'zad]
bend, curve	поворот (ч)	[powo'rɔt]
to turn (e.g., ~ left)	повертати	[powɛr'tati]
to make a U-turn	розвертатися	[rozwɛr'tatisʲa]
to be visible	виднітися	[wid'nitisʲa]
(mountains, castle, etc.)		
to appear (come into view)	з'явитися	[zʲʲa'witisʲa]
stop, halt (e.g., during a trip)	зупинка (ж)	[zu'pinka]
to rest, to pause (vi)	відпочити	[widpo'tʃiti]
rest (pause)	відпочинок (ч)	[widpo'tʃinok]
to lose one's way	заблукати	[zablu'kati]
to lead to ... (ab. road)	вести до	['wɛsti do]
to came out	вийти до ...	['wijti do]
(e.g., on the highway)		
stretch (of the road)	відрізок (ч)	[wid'rizok]
asphalt	асфальт (ч)	[as'falʲt]
kerb	бордюр (ч)	[bor'dʲur]
ditch	канава (ж)	[ka'nawa]
manhole	люк (ч)	[lʲuk]
roadside (shoulder)	узбіччя (с)	[uz'bitʃʲa]
pit, pothole	яма (ж)	['ʲama]
to go (on foot)	йти	[jti]
to overtake (vt)	обігнати	[obiɦ'nati]
step (footstep)	крок (ч)	[krok]

on foot (adv)	пішки	['piʃki]
to block (road)	перегородити	[pɛrɛɦoro'diti]
boom gate	шлагбаум (ч)	[ʃlaɦ'baum]
dead end	глухий кут (ч)	[ɦlu'hij kut]

191. Breaking the law. Criminals. Part 1

bandit	бандит (ч)	[ban'dit]
crime	злочин (ч)	['zlɔtʃin]
criminal (person)	злочинець (ч)	[zlo'tʃinɛts]

thief	злодій (ч)	['zlɔdij]
to steal (vi, vt)	красти	['krasti]
stealing (larceny)	крадеж (ч)	['kradɛʃ]
theft	крадіжка (ж)	[kra'diʒka]

to kidnap (vt)	викрадення	['wikradɛnʲa]
kidnapping	викрадення (с)	['wikradɛnʲa]
kidnapper	викрадач (ч)	[wikra'datʃ]

| ransom | викуп (ч) | ['wikup] |
| to demand ransom | вимагати викуп | [wima'ɦati 'wikup] |

| to rob (vt) | грабувати | [ɦrabu'wati] |
| robber | грабіжник (ч) | [ɦra'biʒnik] |

to extort (vt)	вимагати	[wima'ɦati]
extortionist	вимагач (ч)	[wima'ɦatʃ]
extortion	вимагання (с)	[wima'ɦanʲa]

to murder, to kill	вбити	['wbiti]
murder	вбивство (с)	['wbiwstwo]
murderer	вбивця (ч)	['wbiwtsʲa]

gunshot	постріл (ч)	['pɔstril]
to fire (~ a shot)	вистрілити	['wistriliti]
to shoot to death	застрелити	[za'strɛliti]
to shoot (vi)	стріляти	[stri'lʲati]
shooting	стрілянина (ж)	[strilʲa'nina]

incident (fight, etc.)	подія (ж)	[po'diʲa]
fight, brawl	бійка (ж)	['bijka]
victim	жертва (ж)	['ʒɛrtwa]

to damage (vt)	пошкодити	[poʃ'kɔditi]
damage	шкода (ж)	['ʃkɔda]
dead body, corpse	труп (ч)	[trup]
grave (~ crime)	важкий	[waʒ'kij]

to attack (vt)	напасти	[na'pasti]
to beat (to hit)	бити	['biti]
to beat up	побити	[po'biti]
to take (rob of sth)	забрати	[za'brati]
to stab to death	зарізати	[za'rizati]

| to maim (vt) | покалічити | [poka'litʃiti] |
| to wound (vt) | поранити | [po'raniti] |

blackmail	шантаж (ч)	[ʃan'taʒ]
to blackmail (vt)	шантажувати	[ʃantaʒu'wati]
blackmailer	шантажист (ч)	[ʃanta'ʒist]

protection racket	рекет (ч)	['rɛkɛt]
racketeer	рекетир (ч)	[rɛkɛ'tir]
gangster	гангстер (ч)	['ɦanɦstɛr]
mafia	мафія (ж)	['mafiʲa]

pickpocket	кишеньковий злодій (ч)	[kiʃɛnʲ'kɔwij 'zlɔdij]
burglar	зломщик (ч)	['zlɔmɕik]
smuggling	контрабанда (ж)	[kontra'banda]
smuggler	контрабандист (ч)	[kontraban'dist]

forgery	підробка (ж)	[pid'rɔbka]
to forge (counterfeit)	підробляти	[pidrob'lʲati]
fake (forged)	фальшивий	[falʲ'ʃiwij]

192. Breaking the law. Criminals. Part 2

rape	зґвалтування (с)	[zgwaltu'wanʲa]
to rape (vt)	зґвалтувати	[zgwaltu'wati]
rapist	ґвалтівник (ч)	[gwaltiw'nik]
maniac	маніяк (ч)	[maniʲak]

prostitute (fem.)	проститутка (ж)	[prosti'tutka]
prostitution	проституція (ж)	[prosti'tutsiʲa]
pimp	сутенер (ч)	[sutɛ'nɛr]

| drug addict | наркоман (ч) | [narko'man] |
| drug dealer | наркоторгівець (ч) | [narkotor'ɦiwɛts] |

to blow up (bomb)	підірвати	[pidir'wati]
explosion	вибух (ч)	['wibuh]
to set fire	підпалити	[pidpa'liti]
arsonist	підпалювач (ч)	[pid'palʲuwatʃ]

terrorism	тероризм (ч)	[tɛro'rizm]
terrorist	терорист (ч)	[tɛro'rist]
hostage	заручник (ч)	[za'rutʃnik]

to swindle (deceive)	обманути	[obma'nuti]
swindle, deception	обман (ч)	[ob'man]
swindler	шахрай (ч)	[ʃah'raj]

to bribe (vt)	підкупити	[pidku'piti]
bribery	підкуп (ч)	['pidkup]
bribe	хабар (ч)	[ha'bar]

| poison | отрута (ж) | [ot'ruta] |
| to poison (vt) | отруїти | [otru'jiti] |

to poison oneself	отруїтись	[otru'jitis^j]
suicide (act)	самогубство (с)	[samo'hubstwo]
suicide (person)	самовбивця (ч)	[samow'biwts^ja]
to threaten (vt)	погрожувати	[poɦ'rɔʒuwati]
threat	погроза (ж)	[poɦ'rɔza]
to make an attempt	вчинити замах	[wtʃi'niti 'zamah]
attempt (attack)	замах (ч)	['zamah]
to steal (a car)	украсти	[uk'rasti]
to hijack (a plane)	викрасти	['wikrasti]
revenge	помста (ж)	['pɔmsta]
to avenge (get revenge)	мстити	['mstiti]
to torture (vt)	катувати	[katu'wati]
torture	катування (с)	[katu'wan^ja]
to torment (vt)	мучити	['mutʃiti]
pirate	пірат (ч)	[pi'rat]
hooligan	хуліган (ч)	[huli'ɦan]
armed (adj)	озброєний	[oz'brɔɛnij]
violence	насильство (с)	[na'sil^jstwo]
spying (espionage)	шпигунство (с)	[ʃpi'ɦunstwo]
to spy (vi)	шпигувати	[ʃpiɦu'wati]

193. Police. Law. Part 1

justice	правосуддя (с)	[prawo'sudd^ja]
court (see you in ~)	суд (ч)	[sud]
judge	суддя (ч)	[sud'd^ja]
jurors	присяжні (мн)	[pri's^jaʒni]
jury trial	суд (ч) присяжних	[sud pri's^jaʒnih]
to judge, to try (vt)	судити	[su'diti]
lawyer, barrister	адвокат (ч)	[adwo'kat]
defendant	підсудний (ч)	[pid'sudnij]
dock	лава (ж) підсудних	['lawa pid'sudnih]
charge	обвинувачення (с)	[obwinu'watʃɛn^ja]
accused	обвинувачений (ч)	[obwinu'watʃɛnij]
sentence	вирок (ч)	['wirok]
to sentence (vt)	присудити	[prisu'diti]
guilty (culprit)	винуватець (ч)	[winu'watɛts]
to punish (vt)	покарати	[poka'rati]
punishment	покарання (с)	[poka'ran^ja]
fine (penalty)	штраф (ч)	[ʃtraf]
life imprisonment	довічне ув'язнення (с)	[do'witʃnɛ u'w^jaznɛn^ja]
death penalty	смертна кара (ж)	['smɛrtna 'kara]

| electric chair | електричний стілець (ч) | [ɛlɛkt'ritʃnij sti'lɛts] |
| gallows | шибениця (ж) | ['ʃibɛnitsʲa] |

| to execute (vt) | стратити | ['stratiti] |
| execution | страта (ж) | ['strata] |

| prison | в'язниця (ж) | [wʲaz'nitsʲa] |
| cell | камера (ж) | ['kamɛra] |

escort (convoy)	конвой (ч)	[kon'wɔj]
prison officer	наглядач (ч)	[naɦlʲa'datʃ]
prisoner	в'язень (ч)	['wʲazɛnʲ]

| handcuffs | наручники (мн) | [na'rutʃniki] |
| to handcuff (vt) | надіти наручники | [na'diti na'rutʃniki] |

prison break	втеча (ч)	['wtɛtʃa]
to break out (vi)	утекти	[utɛk'ti]
to disappear (vi)	зникнути	['zniknuti]
to release (from prison)	звільнити	[zwilʲ'niti]
amnesty	амністія (ж)	[am'nistiʲa]

police	поліція (ж)	[po'litsiʲa]
police officer	поліцейський (ч)	[poli'tsɛjsʲkij]
police station	поліцейський відділок (ч)	[poli'tsɛjsʲkij 'widdilok]
truncheon	гумовий кийок (ч)	['ɦumowij ki'jɔk]
megaphone (loudhailer)	рупор (ч)	['rupor]

patrol car	патрульна машина (ж)	[pat'rulʲna ma'ʃina]
siren	сирена (ж)	[si'rɛna]
to turn on the siren	увімкнути сирену	[uwimk'nuti si'rɛnu]
siren call	виття (с) сирени	[wit'tʲa si'rɛni]

crime scene	місце (с) події	['mistsɛ po'diji]
witness	свідок (ч)	['swidok]
freedom	воля (ж)	['wolʲa]
accomplice	спільник (ч)	['spilʲnik]
to flee (vi)	зникнути	['zniknuti]
trace (to leave a ~)	слід (ч)	[slid]

194. Police. Law. Part 2

search (investigation)	розшук (ч)	['rɔzʃuk]
to look for ...	розшукувати	[roz'ʃukuwati]
suspicion	підозра (ж)	[pi'dozra]
suspicious (e.g., ~ vehicle)	підозрілий	[pido'zrilij]
to stop (cause to halt)	зупинити	[zupi'niti]
to detain (keep in custody)	затримати	[za'trimati]

case (lawsuit)	справа (ж)	['sprawa]
investigation	слідство (с)	['slidstwo]
detective	детектив (ч)	[dɛtɛk'tiw]
investigator	слідчий (ч)	['slidtʃij]
hypothesis	версія (ж)	['wɛrsiʲa]

motive	мотив (ч)	[mo'tiw]
interrogation	допит (ч)	['dɔpit]
to interrogate (vt)	допитувати	[do'pituwati]
to question	опитувати	[o'pituwati]
(~ neighbors, etc.)		
check (identity ~)	перевірка (ж)	[pɛrɛ'wirka]
round-up (raid)	облава (ж)	[ob'lawa]
search (~ warrant)	обшук (ч)	['ɔbʃuk]
chase (pursuit)	погоня (ж)	[po'ɦɔnʲa]
to pursue, to chase	переслідувати	[pɛrɛs'liduwati]
to track (a criminal)	слідкувати	[slidku'wati]
arrest	арешт (ч)	[a'rɛʃt]
to arrest (sb)	заарештувати	[zaarɛʃtu'wati]
to catch (thief, etc.)	зловити	[zlo'witi]
capture	затримання (с)	[za'trimanʲa]
document	документ (ч)	[doku'mɛnt]
proof (evidence)	доказ (ч)	['dɔkaz]
to prove (vt)	доводити	[do'wɔditi]
footprint	слід (ч)	[slid]
fingerprints	відбитки (мн) пальців	[wid'bitki 'palʲtsiw]
piece of evidence	доказ (ч)	['dɔkaz]
alibi	алібі (с)	['alibi]
innocent (not guilty)	невинний	[nɛ'winij]
injustice	несправедливість (ж)	[nɛsprawɛd'liwistʲ]
unjust, unfair (adj)	несправедливий	[nɛsprawɛd'liwij]
criminal (adj)	кримінальний	[krimi'nalʲnij]
to confiscate (vt)	конфіскувати	[konfisku'wati]
drug (illegal substance)	наркотик (ч)	[nar'kɔtik]
weapon, gun	зброя (ж)	['zbrɔʲa]
to disarm (vt)	обеззброїти	[obɛz'zbrɔjiti]
to order (command)	наказувати	[na'kazuwati]
to disappear (vi)	зникнути	['zniknuti]
law	закон (ч)	[za'kɔn]
legal, lawful (adj)	законний	[za'kɔnij]
illegal, illicit (adj)	незаконний	[nɛza'kɔnij]
responsibility (blame)	відповідальність (ж)	[widpowi'dalʲnistʲ]
responsible (adj)	відповідальний	[widpowi'dalʲnij]

NATURE

The Earth. Part 1

195. Outer space

space	космос (ч)	['kɔsmos]
space (as adj)	космічний	[kos'mitʃnij]
outer space	космічний простір (ч)	[kos'mitʃnij 'prɔstir]
world, universe	всесвіт (ч)	['wsɛswit]
galaxy	галактика (ж)	[ħa'laktika]
star	зірка (ж)	['zirka]
constellation	сузір'я (с)	[su'zirʲ|a]
planet	планета (ж)	[pla'nɛta]
satellite	супутник (ч)	[su'putnik]
meteorite	метеорит (ч)	[mɛtɛo'rit]
comet	комета (ж)	[ko'mɛta]
asteroid	астероїд (ч)	[astɛ'rɔjid]
orbit	орбіта (ж)	[or'bita]
to revolve	обертатися	[obɛr'tatisʲa]
(~ around the Earth)		
atmosphere	атмосфера (ж)	[atmos'fɛra]
the Sun	Сонце (с)	['sɔntsɛ]
solar system	Сонячна система (ж)	['sɔnʲatʃna sis'tɛma]
solar eclipse	сонячне затемнення (с)	['sɔnʲatʃnɛ za'tɛmnɛnʲa]
the Earth	Земля (ж)	[zɛm'lʲa]
the Moon	Місяць (ж)	['misʲats]
Mars	Марс (ч)	[mars]
Venus	Венера (ж)	[wɛ'nɛra]
Jupiter	Юпітер (ч)	[ʲu'pitɛr]
Saturn	Сатурн (ч)	[sa'turn]
Mercury	Меркурій (ч)	[mɛr'kurij]
Uranus	Уран (ч)	[u'ran]
Neptune	Нептун (ч)	[nɛp'tun]
Pluto	Плутон (ч)	[plu'tɔn]
Milky Way	Чумацький Шлях (ч)	[tʃu'matskij ʃlʲah]
Great Bear (Ursa Major)	Велика Ведмедиця (ж)	[wɛ'lika wɛd'mɛditsʲa]
North Star	Полярна Зірка (ж)	[po'lʲarna 'zirka]
Martian	марсіанин (ч)	[marsi'anin]
extraterrestrial (n)	інопланетянин (ч)	[inoplanɛ'tʲanin]

| alien | прибулець (ч) | [pri'bulɛʦ] |
| flying saucer | літальна тарілка (ж) | [li'talʲna ta'rilka] |

spaceship	космічний корабель (ч)	[kos'miʧnij kora'bɛlʲ]
space station	орбітальна станція (ж)	[orbi'talʲna 'stanʦiʲa]
blast-off	старт (ч)	[start]

engine	двигун (ч)	[dwi'ɦun]
nozzle	сопло (с)	['sɔplo]
fuel	паливо (с)	['paliwo]

cockpit, flight deck	кабіна (ж)	[ka'bina]
aerial	антена (ж)	[an'tɛna]
porthole	ілюмінатор (ч)	[ilʲumi'nator]
solar panel	сонячна батарея (ж)	['sɔnʲatʃna bata'rɛʲa]
spacesuit	скафандр (ч)	[ska'fandr]

| weightlessness | невагомість (ж) | [nɛwa'ɦɔmistʲ] |
| oxygen | кисень (ч) | ['kisɛnʲ] |

| docking (in space) | стикування (с) | [stiku'wanʲa] |
| to dock (vi, vt) | здійснювати стикування | ['zdijsnʲuwati stiku'wanʲa] |

observatory	обсерваторія (ж)	[obsɛrwa'tɔriʲa]
telescope	телескоп (ч)	[tɛlɛ'skɔp]
to observe (vt)	спостерігати	[spostɛri'ɦati]
to explore (vt)	досліджувати	[do'sliʤuwati]

196. The Earth

the Earth	Земля (ж)	[zɛm'lʲa]
the globe (the Earth)	земна куля (ж)	[zɛm'na 'kulʲa]
planet	планета (ж)	[pla'nɛta]

atmosphere	атмосфера (ж)	[atmos'fɛra]
geography	географія (ж)	[ɦɛo'ɦrafiʲa]
nature	природа (ж)	[pri'rɔda]

globe (table ~)	глобус (ч)	['ɦlɔbus]
map	карта (ж)	['karta]
atlas	атлас (ч)	['atlas]

| Europe | Європа (ж) | [ɛw'rɔpa] |
| Asia | Азія (ж) | ['aziʲa] |

| Africa | Африка (ж) | ['afrika] |
| Australia | Австралія (ж) | [aw'straliʲa] |

America	Америка (ж)	[a'mɛrika]
North America	Північна Америка (ж)	[piw'niʧna a'mɛrika]
South America	Південна Америка (ж)	[piw'dɛna a'mɛrika]

| Antarctica | Антарктида (ж) | [antark'tida] |
| the Arctic | Арктика (ж) | ['arktika] |

197. Cardinal directions

north	північ (ж)	['piwnitʃ]
to the north	на північ	[na 'piwnitʃ]
in the north	на півночі	[na 'piwnotʃi]
northern (adj)	північний	[piw'nitʃnij]

south	південь (ч)	['piwdɛnʲ]
to the south	на південь	[na 'piwdɛnʲ]
in the south	на півдні	[na 'piwdni]
southern (adj)	південний	[piw'dɛnij]

west	захід (ч)	['zahid]
to the west	на захід	[na 'zahid]
in the west	на заході	[na 'zahodi]
western (adj)	західний	['zahidnij]

east	схід (ч)	[shid]
to the east	на схід	[na 'shid]
in the east	на сході	[na 'shodi]
eastern (adj)	східний	['shidnij]

198. Sea. Ocean

sea	море (с)	['mɔrɛ]
ocean	океан (ч)	[okɛ'an]
gulf (bay)	затока (ж)	[za'tɔka]
straits	протока (ж)	[pro'tɔka]

continent (mainland)	материк (ч)	[matɛ'rik]
island	острів (ч)	['ɔstriw]
peninsula	півострів (ч)	[pi'wɔstriw]
archipelago	архіпелаг (ч)	[arhipɛ'laɦ]

bay, cove	бухта (ж)	['buhta]
harbour	гавань (ж)	['ɦawanʲ]
lagoon	лагуна (ж)	[la'ɦuna]
cape	мис (ч)	[mis]

atoll	атол (ч)	[a'tɔl]
reef	риф (ч)	[rif]
coral	корал (ч)	[ko'ral]
coral reef	кораловий риф (ч)	[ko'ralowij rif]

deep (adj)	глибокий	[ɦli'bokij]
depth (deep water)	глибина (ж)	[ɦlibi'na]
abyss	безодня (ж)	['bɛzdna]
trench (e.g. Mariana ~)	западина (ж)	[za'padina]

current (Ocean ~)	течія (ж)	['tɛtʃiʲa]
to surround (bathe)	омивати	[omi'wati]
shore	берег (ч)	['bɛrɛɦ]
coast	узбережжя (с)	[uzbɛ'rɛzʲa]

flow (flood tide)	приплив (ч)	[prip'liw]
ebb (ebb tide)	відплив (ч)	[wid'pliw]
shoal	обмілина (ж)	[ob'milina]
bottom (~ of the sea)	дно (с)	[dno]

wave	хвиля (ж)	['hwilʲa]
crest (~ of a wave)	гребінь (ч) хвилі	['ɦrɛbinʲ 'hwili]
spume (sea foam)	піна (ж)	[pi'na]

storm (sea storm)	буря (ж)	['burʲa]
hurricane	ураган (ч)	[uraɦan]
tsunami	цунамі (с)	[ʦu'nami]
calm (dead ~)	штиль (ч)	[ʃtilʲ]
quiet, calm (adj)	спокійний	[spo'kijnij]

| pole | полюс (ч) | ['polʲus] |
| polar (adj) | полярний | [po'lʲarnij] |

latitude	широта (ж)	[ʃiro'ta]
longitude	довгота (ж)	[dowɦo'ta]
parallel	паралель (ж)	[para'lɛlʲ]
equator	екватор (ч)	[ɛk'wator]

sky	небо (с)	['nɛbo]
horizon	горизонт (ч)	[ɦori'zɔnt]
air	повітря (с)	[po'witrʲa]

lighthouse	маяк (ч)	[ma'ʲak]
to dive (vi)	пірнати	[pir'nati]
to sink (ab. boat)	затонути	[zato'nuti]
treasure	скарби (мн)	[skar'bi]

199. Seas & Oceans names

Atlantic Ocean	Атлантичний океан (ч)	[atlan'tiʧnij okɛ'an]
Indian Ocean	Індійський океан (ч)	[in'dijsʲkij okɛ'an]
Pacific Ocean	Тихий океан (ч)	['tihij okɛ'an]
Arctic Ocean	Північний Льодовитий океан (ч)	[piw'niʧnij lʲodo'witij okɛ'an]

Black Sea	Чорне море (с)	['ʧɔrnɛ 'mɔrɛ]
Red Sea	Червоне море (с)	[ʧɛr'wɔnɛ 'mɔrɛ]
Yellow Sea	Жовте море (с)	['ʒɔwtɛ 'mɔrɛ]
White Sea	Біле море (с)	['bilɛ 'mɔrɛ]

Caspian Sea	Каспійське море (с)	[kas'pijsʲkɛ 'mɔrɛ]
Dead Sea	Мертве море (с)	['mɛrtwɛ 'mɔrɛ]
Mediterranean Sea	Середземне море (с)	[sɛrɛ'dzɛmnɛ 'mɔrɛ]

| Aegean Sea | Егейське море (с) | [ɛ'ɦɛjsʲkɛ 'mɔrɛ] |
| Adriatic Sea | Адріатичне море (с) | [adria'tiʧnɛ 'mɔrɛ] |

| Arabian Sea | Аравійське море (с) | [ara'wijsʲkɛ 'mɔrɛ] |
| Sea of Japan | Японське море (с) | [ja'pɔnsʲkɛ 'mɔrɛ] |

Bering Sea	Берингове море (c)	['bɛrinɦowɛ 'mɔrɛ]
South China Sea	Південно-Китайське море (c)	[piw'dɛno ki'tajsʲkɛ 'mɔrɛ]
Coral Sea	Коралове море (c)	[ko'ralowɛ 'mɔrɛ]
Tasman Sea	Тасманове море (c)	[tas'manowɛ 'mɔrɛ]
Caribbean Sea	Карибське море (c)	[ka'ribsʲkɛ 'mɔrɛ]
Barents Sea	Баренцове море (c)	['barɛntsowɛ 'mɔrɛ]
Kara Sea	Карське море (c)	['karsʲkɛ 'mɔrɛ]
North Sea	Північне море (c)	[piw'nitʃnɛ 'mɔrɛ]
Baltic Sea	Балтійське море (c)	[bal'tijsʲkɛ 'mɔrɛ]
Norwegian Sea	Норвезьке море (c)	[nor'wɛzʲkɛ 'mɔrɛ]

200. Mountains

mountain	гора (ж)	[ɦo'ra]
mountain range	гірське пасмо (c)	[ɦirsʲ'kɛ 'pasmo]
mountain ridge	гірський хребет (ч)	[ɦirsʲ'kij hrɛ'bɛt]
summit, top	вершина (ж)	[wɛr'ʃina]
peak	шпиль (ч)	[ʃpilʲ]
foot (~ of the mountain)	підніжжя (c)	[pid'nizʲa]
slope (mountainside)	схил (ч)	[shil]
volcano	вулкан (ч)	[wul'kan]
active volcano	діючий вулкан (ч)	['diʲutʃij wul'kan]
dormant volcano	згаслий вулкан (ч)	['zɦaslij wul'kan]
eruption	виверження (c)	['wiwɛrʒɛnʲa]
crater	кратер (ч)	['kratɛr]
magma	магма (ж)	['maɦma]
lava	лава (ж)	['lawa]
molten (~ lava)	розжарений	[roz'ʒarɛnij]
canyon	каньйон (ч)	[kanʲ'jon]
gorge	ущелина (ж)	[u'ɕɛlina]
crevice	ущелина (c)	[u'ɕɛlina]
pass, col	перевал (ч)	[pɛrɛ'wal]
plateau	плато (c)	['plato]
cliff	скеля (ж)	['skɛlʲa]
hill	горб (ч)	[ɦorb]
glacier	льодовик (ч)	[lʲodo'wik]
waterfall	водоспад (ч)	[wodos'pad]
geyser	гейзер (ч)	['ɦejzɛr]
lake	озеро (c)	['ɔzɛro]
plain	рівнина (ж)	[riw'nina]
landscape	краєвид (ч)	[kraɛ'wid]
echo	луна (ж)	[lu'na]
alpinist	альпініст (ч)	[alʲpi'nist]

rock climber	скелелаз (ч)	[skɛlɛ'laz]
to conquer (in climbing)	підкоряти	[pidko'rʲati]
climb (an easy ~)	піднімання (с)	[pidni'manʲa]

201. Mountains names

The Alps	Альпи (мн)	['alʲpi]
Mont Blanc	Монблан (ч)	[mon'blan]
The Pyrenees	Піренеї (мн)	[pirɛ'nɛji]

The Carpathians	Карпати (мн)	[kar'pati]
The Ural Mountains	Уральські гори (мн)	[u'ralʲsʲki 'ɦori]
The Caucasus Mountains	Кавказ (ч)	[kaw'kaz]
Mount Elbrus	Ельбрус (ч)	[ɛlʲb'rus]

The Altai Mountains	Алтай (ч)	[al'taj]
The Tian Shan	Тянь-Шань (мн)	[tʲanʲ 'ʃanʲ]
The Pamirs	Памір (ч)	[pa'mir]
The Himalayas	Гімалаї (мн)	[ɦima'laji]
Mount Everest	Еверест (ч)	[ɛwɛ'rɛst]

| The Andes | Анди (мн) | ['andi] |
| Mount Kilimanjaro | Кіліманджаро (ж) | [kiliman'dʒaro] |

202. Rivers

river	ріка (ж)	['rika]
spring (natural source)	джерело (с)	[dʒɛrɛ'lɔ]
riverbed (river channel)	річище (с)	['ritʃiɕɛ]
basin (river valley)	басейн (ч)	[ba'sɛjn]
to flow into …	упадати	[upa'dati]

| tributary | притока (ж) | [pri'tɔka] |
| bank (river ~) | берег (ч) | ['bɛrɛɦ] |

current (stream)	течія (ж)	['tɛtʃiʲa]
downstream (adv)	вниз за течією (ж)	[wniz za 'tɛtʃiɛʲu]
upstream (adv)	уверх по течії	[u'wɛrɦ po 'tɛtʃiji]

inundation	повінь (ж)	['pɔwinʲ]
flooding	повінь (ж)	['pɔwinʲ]
to overflow (vi)	розливатися	[rozli'watisʲa]
to flood (vt)	затоплювати	[za'tɔplʲuwati]

| shallow (shoal) | мілина (ж) | [mili'na] |
| rapids | поріг (ч) | [po'riɦ] |

dam	гребля (ж)	['ɦrɛblʲa]
canal	канал (ч)	[ka'nal]
reservoir (artificial lake)	водосховище (с)	[wodo'sɦowiɕɛ]
sluice, lock	шлюз (ч)	[ʃlʲuz]
water body (pond, etc.)	водоймище (с)	[wo'dɔjmiɕɛ]

swamp (marshland)	болото (c)	[bo'lɔto]
bog, marsh	трясовина (ж)	[trʲasowi'na]
whirlpool	вир (ч)	[wir]

stream (brook)	струмок (ч)	[stru'mɔk]
drinking (ab. water)	питний	['pitnij]
fresh (~ water)	прісний	['prisnij]

| ice | крига (ж) | ['kriɦa] |
| to freeze over (ab. river, etc.) | замерзнути | [za'mɛrznuti] |

203. Rivers names

| Seine | Сена (ж) | ['sɛna] |
| Loire | Луара (ж) | [lu'ara] |

Thames	Темза (ж)	['tɛmza]
Rhine	Рейн (ч)	[rɛjn]
Danube	Дунай (ч)	[du'naj]

Volga	Волга (ж)	['wɔlɦa]
Don	Дон (ч)	[don]
Lena	Лена (ж)	['lɛna]

Yellow River	Хуанхе (ж)	[huan'hɛ]
Yangtze	Янцзи (ж)	[jantsʲzi]
Mekong	Меконг (ч)	[mɛ'kɔnɦ]
Ganges	Ганг (ч)	[ɦanɦ]

Nile River	Ніл (ч)	[nil]
Congo River	Конго (ж)	['kɔnɦo]
Okavango River	Окаванго (ж)	[oka'wanɦo]
Zambezi River	Замбезі (ж)	[zam'bɛzi]
Limpopo River	Лімпопо (ж)	[limpo'pɔ]
Mississippi River	Міссісіпі (ж)	[misi'sipi]

204. Forest

| forest, wood | ліс (ч) | [lis] |
| forest (as adj) | лісовий | [liso'wij] |

thick forest	хаща (ж)	['haɕa]
grove	гай (ч)	[ɦaj]
forest clearing	галявина (ж)	[ɦa'lʲawina]

| thicket | хащі (мн) | ['haɕi] |
| scrubland | чагарник (ч) | [ʧa'ɦarnik] |

footpath (troddenpath)	стежина (ж)	[stɛ'ʒina]
gully	яр (ч)	[jar]
tree	дерево (c)	['dɛrɛwo]
leaf	листок (ч)	[lis'tɔk]

leaves (foliage)	листя (c)	['listʲa]
fall of leaves	листопад (ч)	[listo'pad]
to fall (ab. leaves)	опадати	[opa'dati]
top (of the tree)	верхівка (ж)	[wɛr'hiwka]
branch	гілка (ж)	['hilka]
bough	сук (ч)	[suk]
bud (on shrub, tree)	брунька (ж)	['brunʲka]
needle (of the pine tree)	голка (ж)	['holka]
fir cone	шишка (ж)	['ʃiʃka]
tree hollow	дупло (c)	[dup'lɔ]
nest	гніздо (c)	[hniz'dɔ]
burrow (animal hole)	нора (ж)	[no'ra]
trunk	стовбур (ч)	['stɔwbur]
root	корінь (ч)	['kɔrinʲ]
bark	кора (ж)	[ko'ra]
moss	мох (ч)	[moh]
to uproot (remove trees or tree stumps)	корчувати	[kortʃu'wati]
to chop down	рубати	[ru'bati]
to deforest (vt)	вирубувати	[wi'rubuwati]
tree stump	пень (ч)	[pɛnʲ]
campfire	багаття (c)	[ba'hattʲa]
forest fire	пожежа (ж)	[po'ʒɛʒa]
to extinguish (vt)	тушити	[tu'ʃiti]
forest ranger	лісник (ч)	[lis'nik]
protection	охорона (ж)	[oho'rɔna]
to protect (~ nature)	охороняти	[ohoro'nʲati]
poacher	браконьєр (ч)	[brako'nʲɛr]
steel trap	пастка (ж)	['pastka]
to gather, to pick (vt)	збирати	[zbi'rati]
to lose one's way	заблукати	[zablu'kati]

205. Natural resources

natural resources	природні ресурси (мн)	[pri'rɔdni rɛ'sursi]
minerals	корисні копалини (мн)	['kɔrisni ko'palini]
deposits	поклади (мн)	['pɔkladi]
field (e.g. oilfield)	родовище (c)	[ro'dɔwiɕɛ]
to mine (extract)	добувати	[dobu'wati]
mining (extraction)	добування (c)	[dobu'wanʲa]
ore	руда (ж)	[ru'da]
mine (e.g. for coal)	копальня (ж)	[ko'palʲnʲa]
shaft (mine ~)	шахта (ж)	['ʃahta]
miner	шахтар (ч)	[ʃah'tar]
gas (natural ~)	газ (ч)	[haz]
gas pipeline	газопровід (ч)	[hazopro'wid]

oil (petroleum)	нафта (ж)	['nafta]
oil pipeline	нафтопровід (ч)	[nafto'prɔwid]
oil well	нафтова вишка (ж)	['naftowa 'wiʃka]
derrick (tower)	свердлова вежа (ж)	[swɛrd'lɔwa 'wɛʒa]
tanker	танкер (ч)	['tankɛr]

sand	пісок (ч)	[pi'sɔk]
limestone	вапняк (ч)	[wap'nʲak]
gravel	гравій (ч)	['ɦrawij]
peat	торф (ч)	[torf]
clay	глина (ж)	['ɦlina]
coal	вугілля (с)	[wu'ɦilʲa]

iron (ore)	залізо (с)	[za'lizo]
gold	золото (с)	['zɔloto]
silver	срібло (с)	['sriblo]
nickel	нікель (ч)	['nikɛlʲ]
copper	мідь (ж)	[midʲ]

zinc	цинк (ч)	['ʦink]
manganese	марганець (ч)	['marɦanɛts]
mercury	ртуть (ж)	[rtutʲ]
lead	свинець (ч)	[swi'nɛts]

mineral	мінерал (ч)	[minɛ'ral]
crystal	кристал (ч)	[kris'tal]
marble	мармур (ч)	['marmur]
uranium	уран (ч)	[u'ran]

The Earth. Part 2

206. Weather

weather	погода (ж)	[po'ɦɔda]
weather forecast	прогноз (ч) погоди (ж)	[proɦ'nɔz po'ɦɔdi]
temperature	температура (ж)	[tɛmpɛra'tura]
thermometer	термометр (ч)	[tɛr'mɔmɛtr]
barometer	барометр (ч)	[ba'rɔmɛtr]
humidity	вологість (ж)	[woloɦistʲ]
heat (extreme ~)	спека (ж)	['spɛka]
hot (torrid)	гарячий	[ɦa'rʲatʃij]
it's hot	спекотно	[spɛ'kɔtno]
it's warm	тепло	['tɛplo]
warm (moderately hot)	теплий	['tɛplij]
it's cold	холодно	['hɔlodno]
cold (adj)	холодний	[ho'lɔdnij]
sun	сонце (с)	['sɔnʦɛ]
to shine (vi)	світити	[swi'titi]
sunny (day)	сонячний	['sɔnʲatʃnij]
to come up (vi)	зійти	[zij'ti]
to set (vi)	сісти	['sisti]
cloud	хмара (ж)	['hmara]
cloudy (adj)	хмарний	['hmarnij]
rain cloud	хмара (ж)	['hmara]
somber (gloomy)	похмурний	[poh'murnij]
rain	дощ (ч)	[doɕ]
it's raining	йде дощ	[jdɛ doɕ]
rainy (~ day, weather)	дощовий	[doɕo'wij]
to drizzle (vi)	накрапати	[nakra'pati]
pouring rain	проливний дощ (ч)	[proliw'nij doɕ]
downpour	злива (ж)	['zliwa]
heavy (e.g. ~ rain)	сильний	['silʲnij]
puddle	калюжа (ж)	[ka'lʲuʒa]
to get wet (in rain)	мокнути	['mɔknuti]
fog (mist)	туман (ч)	[tu'man]
foggy	туманний	[tu'manij]
snow	сніг (ч)	[sniɦ]
it's snowing	йде сніг (ч)	[jdɛ sniɦ]

207. Severe weather. Natural disasters

thunderstorm	гроза (ж)	[ɦro'za]
lightning (~ strike)	блискавка (ж)	['bliskawka]
to flash (vi)	блискати	['bliskati]
thunder	грім (ч)	[ɦrim]
to thunder (vi)	гриміти	[ɦri'miti]
it's thundering	гримить грім	[ɦri'mitʲ ɦrim]
hail	град (ч)	[ɦrad]
it's hailing	йде град	[jdɛ ɦrad]
to flood (vt)	затопити	[zato'piti]
flood, inundation	повінь (ж)	['pɔwinʲ]
earthquake	землетрус (ч)	[zɛmlɛt'rus]
tremor, shoke	поштовх (ч)	['pɔʃtowh]
epicentre	епіцентр (ч)	[ɛpi'tsɛntr]
eruption	виверження (c)	['wiwɛrʒɛnʲa]
lava	лава (ж)	['lawa]
twister	смерч (ч)	[smɛrtʃ]
tornado	торнадо (ч)	[tor'nado]
typhoon	тайфун (ч)	[taj'fun]
hurricane	ураган (ч)	[uraɦan]
storm	буря (ж)	['burʲa]
tsunami	цунамі (c)	[tsu'nami]
cyclone	циклон (ч)	[tsik'lɔn]
bad weather	негода (ж)	[nɛ'ɦoda]
fire (accident)	пожежа (ж)	[po'ʒɛʒa]
disaster	катастрофа (ж)	[kata'strɔfa]
meteorite	метеорит (ч)	[mɛtɛo'rit]
avalanche	лавина (ж)	[la'wina]
snowslide	обвал (ч)	[ob'wal]
blizzard	заметіль (ж)	[zamɛ'tilʲ]
snowstorm	завірюха (ж)	[zawi'rʲuha]

208. Noises. Sounds

silence (quiet)	тиша (ж)	['tiʃa]
sound	звук (ч)	[zwuk]
noise	шум (ч)	[ʃum]
to make noise	шуміти	[ʃu'miti]
noisy (adj)	гучний	[ɦutʃ'nij]
loudly (to speak, etc.)	голосно	['ɦɔlosno]
loud (voice, etc.)	гучний	[ɦutʃ'nij]
constant (e.g., ~ noise)	постійний	[pos'tijnij]

cry, shout (n)	крик (ч)	[krik]
to cry, to shout (vi)	кричати	[kri'ʧati]
whisper	шепіт (ч)	['ʃɛpit]
to whisper (vi, vt)	шепотіти	[ʃɛpo'titi]
barking (dog's ~)	гавкіт (ч)	['ɦawkit]
to bark (vi)	гавкати	['ɦawkati]
groan (of pain, etc.)	стогін (ч)	['stɔɦin]
to groan (vi)	стогнати	[stɔɦ'nati]
cough	кашель (ч)	['kaʃɛlʲ]
to cough (vi)	кашляти	['kaʃlʲati]
whistle	свист (ч)	[swist]
to whistle (vi)	свистіти	[swis'titi]
knock (at the door)	стукіт (ч)	['stukit]
to knock (on the door)	стукати	['stukati]
to crack (vi)	тріщати	[tri'ɕati]
crack (cracking sound)	тріск (ч)	[trisk]
siren	сирена (ж)	[si'rɛna]
whistle (factory ~, etc.)	гудок (ч)	[ɦu'dɔk]
to whistle (ab. train)	гудіти	[ɦu'diti]
honk (car horn sound)	сигнал (ч)	[siɦ'nal]
to honk (vi)	сигналити	[siɦ'naliti]

209. Winter

winter (n)	зима (ж)	[zi'ma]
winter (as adj)	зимовий	[zi'mɔwij]
in winter	взимку	['wzimku]
snow	сніг (ч)	[sniɦ]
it's snowing	йде сніг (ч)	[jdɛ sniɦ]
snowfall	снігопад (ч)	[sniɦo'pad]
snowdrift	замет (ч)	[za'mɛt]
snowflake	сніжинка (ж)	[sni'ʒinka]
snowball	сніжка (ж)	['sniʒka]
snowman	сніговик (ч)	[sniɦo'wik]
icicle	бурулька (ж)	[bu'rulʲka]
December	грудень (ч)	['ɦrudɛnʲ]
January	січень (ч)	['sitʃɛnʲ]
February	лютий (ч)	['lʲutij]
frost (severe ~, freezing cold)	мороз (ч)	[mo'rɔz]
frosty (weather, air)	морозний	[mo'rɔznij]
below zero (adv)	нижче нуля	['niʒʧɛ nu'lʲa]
first frost	заморозки (мн)	['zamorozki]
hoarfrost	паморозь (ж)	['pamorozʲ]
cold (cold weather)	холод (ч)	['hɔlod]

it's cold	холодно	['hɔlodno]
fur coat	шуба (ж)	['ʃuba]
mittens	рукавиці (мн)	[ruka'witsi]

to fall ill	захворіти	[zahwo'riti]
cold (illness)	застуда (ж)	[za'studa]
to catch a cold	застудитися	[zastu'ditisʲa]

ice	крига (ж)	['kriħa]
black ice	ожеледиця (ж)	[oʒɛ'lɛditsʲa]
to freeze over (ab. river, etc.)	замерзнути	[za'mɛrznuti]
ice floe	крижина (ж)	[kri'ʒina]

skis	лижі (мн)	['liʒi]
skier	лижник (ч)	['liʒnik]
to ski (vi)	кататися на лижах	[ka'tatisʲa na 'liʒah]
to skate (vi)	кататися на ковзанах	[ka'tatisʲa na kowza'nah]

Fauna

210. Mammals. Predators

predator	хижак (ч)	[hiˈʒak]
tiger	тигр (ч)	[tiɦr]
lion	лев (ч)	[lɛw]
wolf	вовк (ч)	[wowk]
fox	лисиця (ж)	[liˈsitsʲa]
jaguar	ягуар (ч)	[jaɦuˈar]
leopard	леопард (ч)	[lɛoˈpard]
cheetah	гепард (ч)	[ɦɛˈpard]
black panther	пантера (ж)	[panˈtɛra]
puma	пума (ж)	[ˈpuma]
snow leopard	сніговий барс (ч)	[sniɦoˈwij bars]
lynx	рись (ж)	[risʲ]
coyote	койот (ч)	[koˈjot]
jackal	шакал (ч)	[ʃaˈkal]
hyena	гієна (ж)	[ɦiˈɛna]

211. Wild animals

animal	тварина (ж)	[twaˈrina]
beast (animal)	звір (ч)	[zwir]
squirrel	білка (ж)	[ˈbilka]
hedgehog	їжак (ч)	[jiˈʒak]
hare	заєць (ч)	[ˈzaɛts]
rabbit	кріль (ч)	[krilʲ]
badger	борсук (ч)	[borˈsuk]
raccoon	єнот (ч)	[ɛˈnot]
hamster	хом'як (ч)	[hoˈmʲʲak]
marmot	бабак (ч)	[baˈbak]
mole	кріт (ч)	[krit]
mouse	миша (ж)	[ˈmiʃa]
rat	щур (ч)	[ɕur]
bat	кажан (ч)	[kaˈʒan]
ermine	горностай (ч)	[ɦornoˈstaj]
sable	соболь (ч)	[ˈsobolʲ]
marten	куниця (ж)	[kuˈnitsʲa]
weasel	ласка (ж)	[ˈlaska]
mink	норка (ж)	[ˈnɔrka]

| beaver | бобер (ч) | [bo'bɛr] |
| otter | видра (ж) | ['widra] |

horse	кінь (ч)	[kinʲ]
moose	лось (ч)	[losʲ]
deer	олень (ч)	['ɔlɛnʲ]
camel	верблюд (ч)	[wɛr'blʲud]

bison	бізон (ч)	[bi'zɔn]
wisent	зубр (ч)	[zubr]
buffalo	буйвіл (ч)	['bujwil]

zebra	зебра (ж)	['zɛbra]
antelope	антилопа (ж)	[anti'lɔpa]
roe deer	косуля (ж)	[ko'sulʲa]
fallow deer	лань (ж)	[lanʲ]
chamois	сарна (ж)	['sarna]
wild boar	вепр (ч)	[wɛpr]

whale	кит (ч)	[kit]
seal	тюлень (ч)	[tʲu'lɛnʲ]
walrus	морж (ч)	[morʒ]
fur seal	котик (ч)	['kɔtik]
dolphin	дельфін (ч)	[dɛlʲ'fin]

bear	ведмідь (ч)	[wɛd'midʲ]
polar bear	білий ведмідь (ч)	['bilij wɛd'midʲ]
panda	панда (ж)	['panda]

monkey	мавпа (ж)	['mawpa]
chimpanzee	шимпанзе (ч)	[ʃimpan'zɛ]
orangutan	орангутанг (ч)	[oranɦu'tanɦ]
gorilla	горила (ж)	[ɦo'rila]
macaque	макака (ж)	[ma'kaka]
gibbon	гібон (ч)	[ɦi'bɔn]

elephant	слон (ч)	[slon]
rhinoceros	носоріг (ч)	[noso'riɦ]
giraffe	жирафа (ж)	[ʒirafa]
hippopotamus	бегемот (ч)	[bɛɦɛ'mɔt]

| kangaroo | кенгуру (ч) | [kɛnɦu'ru] |
| koala (bear) | коала (ч) | [ko'ala] |

mongoose	мангуст (ч)	[ma'nɦust]
chinchilla	шиншила (ж)	[ʃin'ʃila]
skunk	скунс (ч)	[skuns]
porcupine	дикобраз (ч)	[diko'braz]

212. Domestic animals

cat	кішка (ж)	['kiʃka]
tomcat	кіт (ч)	[kit]
horse	коняка (ж)	[ko'nʲaka]

| stallion (male horse) | жеребець (ч) | [ʒɛrɛˈbɛʦ] |
| mare | кобила (ж) | [koˈbila] |

cow	корова (ж)	[koˈrɔwa]
bull	бик (ч)	[bik]
ox	віл (ч)	[wil]

sheep (ewe)	вівця (ж)	[wiwˈʦʲa]
ram	баран (ч)	[baˈran]
goat	коза (ж)	[koˈza]
billy goat, he-goat	козел (ч)	[koˈzɛl]

| donkey | осел (ч) | [oˈsɛl] |
| mule | мул (ч) | [mul] |

pig	свиня (ж)	[swiˈnʲa]
piglet	порося (с)	[poroˈsʲa]
rabbit	кріль (ч)	[krilʲ]

| hen (chicken) | курка (ж) | [ˈkurka] |
| cock | півень (ч) | [ˈpiwɛnʲ] |

duck	качка (ж)	[ˈkaʧka]
drake	качур (ч)	[ˈkaʧur]
goose	гусак (ч)	[ɦuˈsak]

| tom turkey, gobbler | індик (ч) | [inˈdik] |
| turkey (hen) | індичка (ж) | [inˈdiʧka] |

domestic animals	домашні тварини (мн)	[doˈmaʃni twaˈrini]
tame (e.g. ~ hamster)	ручний	[rutʃˈnij]
to tame (vt)	приручати	[priruˈʧati]
to breed (vt)	вирощувати	[wiˈrɔɕuwati]

farm	ферма (ж)	[ˈfɛrma]
poultry	свійські птахи (мн)	[ˈswijsʲki ptaˈhi]
cattle	худоба (ж)	[ɦuˈdɔba]
herd (cattle)	стадо (с)	[ˈstado]

stable	конюшня (ж)	[koˈnʲuʃnʲa]
pigsty	свинарник (ч)	[swiˈnarnik]
cowshed	корівник (ч)	[koˈriwnik]
rabbit hutch	крільчатник (ч)	[krilʲˈʧatnik]
hen house	курник (ч)	[kurˈnik]

213. Dogs. Dog breeds

dog	собака (ч)	[soˈbaka]
sheepdog	вівчарка (ж)	[wiwˈʧarka]
poodle	пудель (ч)	[ˈpudɛlʲ]
dachshund	такса (ж)	[ˈtaksa]

| bulldog | бульдог (ч) | [bulʲˈdɔɦ] |
| boxer | боксер (ч) | [bokˈsɛr] |

mastiff	мастиф (ч)	[mas'tif]
Rottweiler	ротвейлер (ч)	[rot'wɛjlɛr]
Doberman	доберман (ч)	[dobɛr'man]

basset	басет (ч)	[ba'sɛt]
bobtail	бобтейл (ч)	[bob'tɛjl]
Dalmatian	далматинець (ч)	[dalma'tinɛts]
cocker spaniel	кокер-спанієль (ч)	['kɔkɛr spani'ɛlʲ]

| Newfoundland | ньюфаундленд (ч) | [njufaund'lɛnd] |
| Saint Bernard | сенбернар (ч) | [sɛnbɛr'nar] |

husky	хаскі (ч)	[haski]
Chow Chow	чау-чау (ч)	[tʃau tʃau]
spitz	шпіц (ч)	[ʃpits]
pug	мопс (ч)	[mops]

214. Sounds made by animals

barking (n)	гавкіт (ч)	['ɦawkit]
to bark (vi)	гавкати	['ɦawkati]
to miaow (vi)	нявкати	['nʲawkati]
to purr (vi)	муркотіти	[murko'titi]

to moo (vi)	мукати	['mukati]
to bellow (bull)	ревіти	[rɛ'witi]
to growl (vi)	ричати	[ri'tʃati]

howl (n)	виття (с)	[wit'tʲa]
to howl (vi)	вити	['witi]
to whine (vi)	скиглити	['skiɦliti]

to bleat (sheep)	бекати	['bɛkati]
to oink, to grunt (pig)	рохкати	['rɔhkati]
to squeal (vi)	вищати	[wi'ɕati]

to croak (vi)	кумкати	['kumkati]
to buzz (insect)	дзижчати	[dʑiʒ'tʃati]
to chirp (crickets, grasshopper)	стрекотати	[strɛko'tati]

215. Young animals

cub	дитинча (с)	[ditin'tʃa]
kitten	кошеня (с)	[koʃɛ'nʲa]
baby mouse	мишеня (с)	[miʃɛ'nʲa]
puppy	цуценя (с)	[tsutsɛ'nʲa]

leveret	зайченя (с)	[zajtʃɛ'nʲa]
baby rabbit	кроленя (с)	[krolɛ'nʲa]
wolf cub	вовченя (с)	[wowtʃɛ'nʲa]
fox cub	лисеня (с)	[lisɛ'nʲa]

bear cub	ведмежа (c)	[wɛdmɛ'ʒa]
lion cub	левеня (c)	[lɛwɛ'nʲa]
tiger cub	тигреня (c)	[tiɦrɛ'nʲa]
elephant calf	слоненя (c)	[slonɛ'nʲa]
piglet	порося (c)	[poro'sʲa]
calf (young cow, bull)	теля (c)	[tɛ'lʲa]
kid (young goat)	козеня (c)	[kozɛ'nʲa]
lamb	ягня (c)	[jaɦ'nʲa]
fawn (young deer)	оленя (c)	[olɛ'nʲa]
young camel	верблюденя (c)	[wɛrblʲudɛ'nʲa]
snakelet (baby snake)	змієня (c)	[zmiɛ'nʲa]
froglet (baby frog)	жабеня (c)	[ʒabɛ'nʲa]
baby bird	пташеня (c)	[ptaʃɛ'nʲa]
chick (of chicken)	курча (c)	[kur'ʧa]
duckling	каченя (c)	[kaʧɛ'nʲa]

216. Birds

bird	птах (ч)	[ptah]
pigeon	голуб (ч)	['ɦolub]
sparrow	горобець (ч)	[ɦoro'bɛʦ]
tit (great tit)	синиця (ж)	[si'niʦʲa]
magpie	сорока (ж)	[so'rɔka]
raven	ворон (ч)	['wɔron]
crow	ворона (ж)	[wo'rɔna]
jackdaw	галка (ж)	['ɦalka]
rook	грак (ч)	[ɦrak]
duck	качка (ж)	['kaʧka]
goose	гусак (ч)	[ɦu'sak]
pheasant	фазан (ч)	[fa'zan]
eagle	орел (ч)	[o'rɛl]
hawk	яструб (ч)	['ʲastrub]
falcon	сокіл (ч)	['sɔkil]
vulture	гриф (ч)	[ɦrif]
condor (Andean ~)	кондор (ч)	['kɔndor]
swan	лебідь (ч)	['lɛbidʲ]
crane	журавель (ч)	[ʒura'wɛlʲ]
stork	чорногуз (ч)	[ʧorno'ɦuz]
parrot	папуга (ч)	[pa'puɦa]
hummingbird	колібрі (ч)	[ko'libri]
peacock	пава (ж)	['pawa]
ostrich	страус (ч)	['straus]
heron	чапля (ж)	['ʧaplʲa]
flamingo	фламінго (c)	[fla'minɦo]
pelican	пелікан (ч)	[pɛli'kan]

| nightingale | соловей (ч) | [solo'wɛj] |
| swallow | ластівка (ж) | ['lastiwka] |

thrush	дрізд (ч)	[drizd]
song thrush	співучий дрізд (ч)	[spi'wutʃij 'drizd]
blackbird	чорний дрізд (ч)	['tʃɔrnij 'drizd]

swift	стриж (ч)	['striʒ]
lark	жайворонок (ч)	['ʒajworonok]
quail	перепел (ч)	['pɛrɛpɛl]

woodpecker	дятел (ч)	['dʲatɛl]
cuckoo	зозуля (ж)	[zo'zulʲa]
owl	сова (ж)	[so'wa]
eagle owl	пугач (ч)	[pu'ɦatʃ]
wood grouse	глухар (ч)	[ɦlu'har]
black grouse	тетерук (ч)	[tɛtɛ'ruk]
partridge	куріпка (ж)	[ku'ripka]

starling	шпак (ч)	[ʃpak]
canary	канарка (ж)	[ka'narka]
hazel grouse	рябчик (ч)	['rʲabtʃik]
chaffinch	зяблик (ч)	['zʲablik]
bullfinch	снігур (ч)	[sni'ɦur]

seagull	чайка (ж)	['tʃajka]
albatross	альбатрос (ч)	[alʲbat'rɔs]
penguin	пінгвін (ч)	[pinɦ'win]

217. Birds. Singing and sounds

to sing (vi)	співати	[spi'wati]
to call (animal, bird)	кричати	[kri'tʃati]
to crow (cock)	кукурікати	[kuku'rikati]
cock-a-doodle-doo	кукуріку	[kukuri'ku]

to cluck (hen)	кудкудакати	[kudku'dakati]
to caw (crow call)	каркати	['karkati]
to quack (duck call)	крякати	['krʲakati]
to cheep (vi)	пищати	[pi'ɕati]
to chirp, to twitter	цвірінькати	[ʦwi'rinʲkati]

218. Fish. Marine animals

bream	лящ (ч)	[lʲaɕ]
carp	короп (ч)	['kɔrop]
perch	окунь (ч)	['ɔkunʲ]
catfish	сом (ч)	[som]
pike	щука (ж)	['ɕuka]

| salmon | лосось (ч) | [lo'sɔsʲ] |
| sturgeon | осетер (ч) | [osɛ'tɛr] |

herring	оселедець (ч)	[osɛ'lɛdɛts]
Atlantic salmon	сьомга (ж)	['sʲomɦa]
mackerel	скумбрія (ж)	['skumbriʲa]
flatfish	камбала (ж)	[kamba'la]

zander, pike perch	судак (ч)	[su'dak]
cod	тріска (ж)	[tris'ka]
tuna	тунець (ч)	[tu'nɛts]
trout	форель (ж)	[fo'rɛlʲ]

eel	вугор (ч)	[wu'ɦor]
electric ray	електричний скат (ч)	[ɛlɛkt'ritʃnij skat]
moray eel	мурена (ж)	[mu'rɛna]
piranha	піранья (ж)	[pi'ranʲa]

shark	акула (ж)	[a'kula]
dolphin	дельфін (ч)	[dɛlʲ'fin]
whale	кит (ч)	[kit]

crab	краб (ч)	[krab]
jellyfish	медуза (ж)	[mɛ'duza]
octopus	восьминіг (ч)	[wosʲmi'niɦ]

starfish	морська зірка (ж)	[morsʲ'ka 'zirka]
sea urchin	морський їжак (ч)	[morsʲ'kij ji'ʒak]
seahorse	морський коник (ч)	[morsʲ'kij 'konik]

oyster	устриця (ж)	['ustritsʲa]
prawn	креветка (ж)	[krɛ'wɛtka]
lobster	омар (ч)	[o'mar]
spiny lobster	лангуст (ч)	[lan'ɦust]

219. Amphibians. Reptiles

| snake | змія (ж) | [zmiʲ'a] |
| venomous (snake) | отруйний | [ot'rujnij] |

viper	гадюка (ж)	[ɦa'dʲuka]
cobra	кобра (ж)	['kobra]
python	пітон (ч)	[pi'ton]
boa	удав (ч)	[u'daw]

grass snake	вуж (ч)	[wuʒ]
rattle snake	гримуча змія (ж)	[ɦri'mutʃa zmiʲ'a]
anaconda	анаконда (ж)	[ana'konda]

lizard	ящірка (ж)	['ʲaɕirka]
iguana	ігуана (ж)	[iɦu'ana]
monitor lizard	варан (ч)	[wa'ran]
salamander	саламандра (ж)	[sala'mandra]
chameleon	хамелеон (ч)	[ɦamɛlɛ'ɔn]
scorpion	скорпіон (ч)	[skorpi'ɔn]
turtle	черепаха (ж)	[tʃɛrɛ'paɦa]
frog	жабка (ж)	['ʒabka]

| toad | жаба (ж) | ['ʒaba] |
| crocodile | крокодил (ч) | [kroko'dil] |

220. Insects

insect	комаха (ж)	[ko'maha]
butterfly	метелик (ч)	[mɛ'tɛlik]
ant	мураха (ж)	[mu'raha]
fly	муха (ж)	['muha]
mosquito	комар (ч)	[ko'mar]
beetle	жук (ч)	[ʒuk]

wasp	оса (ж)	[o'sa]
bee	бджола (ж)	[bdʒo'la]
bumblebee	джміль (ч)	[dʒmilʲ]
gadfly (botfly)	овід (ч)	['ɔwid]

| spider | павук (ч) | [pa'wuk] |
| spider's web | павутиння (с) | [pawu'tinʲa] |

dragonfly	бабка (ж)	['babka]
grasshopper	коник (ч)	['kɔnik]
moth (night butterfly)	метелик (ч)	[mɛ'tɛlik]

cockroach	тарган (ч)	[tar'ɦan]
tick	кліщ (ч)	[kliɕ]
flea	блоха (ж)	['blɔha]
midge	мошка (ж)	['mɔʃka]

locust	сарана (ж)	[sara'na]
snail	равлик (ч)	['rawlik]
cricket	цвіркун (ч)	[tswir'kun]
firefly	світлячок (ч)	[switlʲa'tʃɔk]
ladybird	сонечко (с)	['sɔnɛtʃko]
cockchafer	хрущ (ч)	[hruɕ]

leech	п'явка (ж)	['pʲʲawka]
caterpillar	гусениця (ж)	['husɛnitsʲa]
earthworm	черв'як (ч)	[tʃɛr'wʲʲak]
larva	личинка (ж)	[li'tʃinka]

221. Animals. Body parts

beak	дзьоб (ч)	[dzʲob]
wings	крила (мн)	['krila]
foot (of the bird)	лапа (ж)	['lapa]
feathers (plumage)	пір'я (с)	['pirʲʲa]
feather	перо (с)	[pɛ'rɔ]
crest	чубчик (ч)	['tʃubtʃik]

| gills | зябра (мн) | ['zʲabra] |
| spawn | ікра (ж) | [ik'ra] |

larva	личинка (ж)	[liˈtʃinka]
fin	плавець (ч)	[plaˈwɛts]
scales (of fish, reptile)	луска (ж)	[lusˈka]

fang (canine)	ікло (с)	[ˈiklo]
paw (e.g. cat's ~)	лапа (ж)	[ˈlapa]
muzzle (snout)	морда (ж)	[ˈmɔrda]
mouth (cat's ~)	паща (ж)	[ˈpaɕa]
tail	хвіст (ч)	[hwist]
whiskers	вуса (мн)	[ˈwusa]

| hoof | копито (с) | [koˈpito] |
| horn | ріг (ч) | [riɦ] |

carapace	панцир (ч)	[ˈpantsir]
shell (mollusk ~)	мушля (ж)	[ˈmuʃlʲa]
eggshell	шкаралупа (ж)	[ʃkaraˈlupa]

| animal's hair (pelage) | шерсть (ж) | [ʃɛrstʲ] |
| pelt (hide) | шкура (ж) | [ˈʃkura] |

222. Actions of animals

| to fly (vi) | літати | [liˈtati] |
| to fly in circles | кружляти | [kruʒˈlʲati] |

| to fly away | полетіти | [polɛˈtiti] |
| to flap (~ the wings) | махати | [maˈhati] |

| to peck (vi) | клювати | [klʲuˈwati] |
| to sit on eggs | висиджувати яйця | [wiˈsidʒuwati ˈjajtsʲa] |

| to hatch out (vi) | вилуплюватися | [wiˈluplʲuwatisʲa] |
| to build a nest | мостити | [mosˈtiti] |

to slither, to crawl	повзати	[ˈpɔwzati]
to sting, to bite (insect)	жалити	[ˈʒaliti]
to bite (ab. animal)	кусати	[kuˈsati]

to sniff (vt)	нюхати	[ˈnʲuhati]
to bark (vi)	гавкати	[ˈɦawkati]
to hiss (snake)	шипіти	[ʃiˈpiti]

| to scare (vt) | лякати | [lʲaˈkati] |
| to attack (vt) | нападати | [napaˈdati] |

to gnaw (bone, etc.)	гризти	[ˈɦrizti]
to scratch (with claws)	дряпати	[ˈdrʲapati]
to hide (vi)	ховатися	[hoˈwatisʲa]

to play (kittens, etc.)	бавитись	[ˈbawitisʲ]
to hunt (vi, vt)	полювати	[polʲuˈwati]
to hibernate (vi)	бути в сплячці	[ˈbuti w splʲatʃtsi]
to go extinct	вимерти	[ˈwimɛrti]

223. Animals. Habitats

habitat	середовище (c) проживання	[sɛrɛ'dɔwiɕɛ prɔʒi'wanʲa]
migration	міграція (ж)	[miĥ'ratsiʲa]
mountain	гора (ж)	[ĥo'ra]
reef	риф (ч)	[rif]
cliff	скеля (ж)	['skɛlʲa]
forest	ліс (ч)	[lis]
jungle	джунглі (мн)	['dʒunĥli]
savanna	савана (ж)	[sa'wana]
tundra	тундра (ж)	['tundra]
steppe	степ (ч)	['stɛp]
desert	пустеля (ж)	[pus'tɛlʲa]
oasis	оаза (ж)	[o'aza]
sea	море (c)	['mɔrɛ]
lake	озеро (c)	['ɔzɛro]
ocean	океан (ч)	[okɛ'an]
swamp (marshland)	болото (c)	[bo'lɔto]
freshwater (adj)	прісноводний	[prisno'wɔdnij]
pond	став (ч)	['staw]
river	ріка (ж)	['rika]
den (bear's ~)	барліг (ч)	[bar'liĥ]
nest	гніздо (c)	[ĥniz'dɔ]
tree hollow	дупло (c)	[dup'lɔ]
burrow (animal hole)	нора (ж)	[no'ra]
anthill	мурашник (ч)	[muraʃ'nik]

224. Animal care

zoo	зоопарк (ч)	[zoo'park]
nature reserve	заповідник (ч)	[zapo'widnik]
breeder (cattery, kennel, etc.)	розплідник (ч)	[rozp'lidnik]
open-air cage	вольєра (ж)	[wo'lʲɛra]
cage	клітка (ж)	['klitka]
kennel	буда (ж)	['buda]
dovecot	голубник (ч)	[ĥolub'nik]
aquarium (fish tank)	акваріум (ч)	[ak'warium]
dolphinarium	дельфінарій (ч)	[dɛlʲfi'narij]
to breed (animals)	розводити	[roz'wɔditi]
brood, litter	потомство (c)	[po'tɔmstwo]
to tame (vt)	приручати	[priru'ʧati]
to train (animals)	дресирувати	[drɛsiru'wati]
feed (fodder, etc.)	корм (ч)	[korm]

to feed (vt)	годувати	[ɦodu'wati]
pet shop	зоомагазин (ч)	[zoomaɦa'zin]
muzzle (for dog)	намордник (ч)	[na'mɔrdnik]
collar (e.g., dog ~)	нашийник (ч)	[na'ʃijnik]
name (of an animal)	кличка (ж)	['kliʈʂka]
pedigree (dog's ~)	родовід (ч)	[rodo'wid]

225. Animals. Miscellaneous

pack (wolves)	зграя (ж)	[zɦ'raʲa]
flock (birds)	зграя (ж)	[zɦ'raʲa]
shoal, school (fish)	зграя (ж)	[zɦ'raʲa]
herd (horses)	табун (ч)	[ta'bun]
male (n)	самець (ч)	[sa'mɛʦ]
female (n)	самка (ж)	['samka]
hungry (adj)	голодний	[ɦo'lɔdnij]
wild (adj)	дикий	['dikij]
dangerous (adj)	небезпечний	[nɛbɛz'pɛʧnij]

226. Horses

horse	кінь (ч)	[kinʲ]
breed (race)	порода (ж)	[po'rɔda]
foal	лоша (с)	[lo'ʃa]
mare	кобила (ж)	[ko'bila]
mustang	мустанг (ч)	[mus'tanɦ]
pony	поні (ч)	['pɔni]
draught horse	ваговоз (ч)	[waɦo'wɔz]
mane	грива (ж)	['ɦriwa]
tail	хвіст (ч)	[hwist]
hoof	копито (с)	[ko'pito]
horseshoe	підкова (ж)	[pid'kɔwa]
to shoe (vt)	підкувати	[pidku'wati]
blacksmith	коваль (ч)	[ko'walʲ]
saddle	сідло (с)	[sid'lɔ]
stirrup	стремено (с)	[strɛ'mɛno]
bridle	вуздечка (ж)	[wuz'dɛʧka]
reins	віжки (мн)	[wiʒ'ki]
whip (for riding)	батіг (ч)	[ba'tiɦ]
rider	наїзник (ч)	[na'jiznik]
to saddle up (vt)	осідлати	[osid'lati]
to mount a horse	сісти в сідло	['sisti w sid'lɔ]
gallop	галоп (ч)	[ɦa'lɔp]
to gallop (vi)	скакати галопом	[ska'kati ɦa'lɔpom]

trot (n)	клус (ч)	[klus]
at a trot (adv)	клусом	['klusom]
racehorse	скаковий кінь (ч)	[skako'wij kinʲ]
horse racing	перегони (мн)	[pɛrɛ'ɦɔni]
stable	конюшня (ж)	[ko'nʲuʃnʲa]
to feed (vt)	годувати	[ɦodu'wati]
hay	сіно (с)	['sino]
to water (animals)	поїти	[po'jiti]
to wash (horse)	чистити	['ʧistiti]
horse-drawn cart	віз (ч)	[wiz]
to graze (vi)	пастися	['pastisʲa]
to neigh (vi)	іржати	[ir'ʒati]
to kick (to buck)	брикнути	[brik'nuti]

Flora

227. Trees

tree	**дерево** (с)	['dɛrɛwo]
deciduous (adj)	**модринове**	[mod'rinowɛ]
coniferous (adj)	**хвойне**	['hwɔjnɛ]
evergreen (adj)	**вічнозелене**	[witʃnozɛ'lɛnɛ]
apple tree	**яблуня** (ж)	['ʲablunʲa]
pear tree	**груша** (ж)	['hruʃa]
sweet cherry tree	**черешня** (ж)	[ʧɛ'rɛʃnʲa]
sour cherry tree	**вишня** (ж)	['wiʃnʲa]
plum tree	**слива** (ж)	['sliwa]
birch	**береза** (ж)	[bɛ'rɛza]
oak	**дуб** (ч)	[dub]
linden tree	**липа** (ж)	['lipa]
aspen	**осика** (ж)	[o'sika]
maple	**клен** (ч)	[klɛn]
spruce	**ялина** (ж)	[ja'lina]
pine	**сосна** (ж)	[sos'na]
larch	**модрина** (ж)	[mod'rina]
fir tree	**ялиця** (ж)	[ja'litsʲa]
cedar	**кедр** (ч)	[kɛdr]
poplar	**тополя** (ж)	[to'pɔlʲa]
rowan	**горобина** (ж)	[horo'bina]
willow	**верба** (ж)	[wɛr'ba]
alder	**вільха** (ж)	['wilʲha]
beech	**бук** (ч)	[buk]
elm	**в'яз** (ч)	[wʲʲaz]
ash (tree)	**ясен** (ч)	['ʲasɛn]
chestnut	**каштан** (ч)	[kaʃ'tan]
magnolia	**магнолія** (ж)	[mah'nɔliʲa]
palm tree	**пальма** (ж)	['palʲma]
cypress	**кипарис** (ч)	[kipa'ris]
mangrove	**мангрове дерево** (с)	['manhrowɛ 'dɛrɛwo]
baobab	**баобаб** (ч)	[bao'bab]
eucalyptus	**евкаліпт** (ч)	[ɛwka'lipt]
sequoia	**секвоя** (ж)	[sɛk'wɔʲa]

228. Shrubs

bush	**кущ** (ч)	[kuɕ]
shrub	**кущі** (мн)	[ku'ɕi]

| grapevine | виноград (ч) | [wino'ɦrad] |
| vineyard | виноградник (ч) | [wino'ɦradnik] |

raspberry bush	малина (ж)	[ma'lina]
redcurrant bush	порічки (мн)	[po'ritʃki]
gooseberry bush	аґрус (ч)	['agrus]

acacia	акація (ж)	[a'katsiʲa]
barberry	барбарис (ч)	[barba'ris]
jasmine	жасмин (ч)	[ʒas'min]

juniper	ялівець (ч)	[jali'wɛts]
rosebush	трояндовий кущ (ч)	[troʲandowij kuɕ]
dog rose	шипшина (ж)	[ʃip'ʃina]

229. Mushrooms

mushroom	гриб (ч)	[ɦrib]
edible mushroom	їстівний гриб (ч)	[jis'tiwnij ɦrib]
poisonous mushroom	отруйний гриб (ч)	[ot'rujnij ɦrib]
cap	шапка (ж)	['ʃapka]
stipe	ніжка (ж)	['niʒka]

cep, penny bun	білий гриб (ч)	['bilij 'ɦrib]
orange-cap boletus	підосичник (ч)	[pido'sitʃnik]
birch bolete	підберезник (ч)	[pidbɛ'rɛznik]
chanterelle	лисичка (ж)	[li'sitʃka]
russula	сироїжка (ж)	[siro'jiʒka]

morel	зморшок (ч)	['zmɔrʃok]
fly agaric	мухомор (ч)	[muho'mɔr]
death cap	поганка (ж)	[po'ɦanka]

230. Fruits. Berries

apple	яблуко (с)	['ʲabluko]
pear	груша (ж)	['ɦruʃa]
plum	слива (ж)	['sliwa]

strawberry (garden ~)	полуниця (ж)	[polu'nitsʲa]
sour cherry	вишня (ж)	['wiʃnʲa]
sweet cherry	черешня (ж)	[tʃɛ'rɛʃnʲa]
grape	виноград (ч)	[wino'ɦrad]

raspberry	малина (ж)	[ma'lina]
blackcurrant	чорна смородина (ж)	['tʃorna smo'rɔdina]
redcurrant	порічки (мн)	[po'ritʃki]
gooseberry	аґрус (ч)	['agrus]
cranberry	журавлина (ж)	[ʒuraw'lina]

| orange | апельсин (ч) | [apɛlʲ'sin] |
| tangerine | мандарин (ч) | [manda'rin] |

pineapple	ананас (ч)	[ana'nas]
banana	банан (ч)	[ba'nan]
date	фінік (ч)	['finik]
lemon	лимон (ч)	[li'mɔn]
apricot	абрикос (ч)	[abri'kɔs]
peach	персик (ч)	['pɛrsik]
kiwi	ківі (ч)	['kiwi]
grapefruit	грейпфрут (ч)	[ɦrɛjp'frut]
berry	ягода (ж)	['ʲaɦoda]
berries	ягоди (мн)	['ʲaɦodi]
cowberry	брусниця (ж)	[brus'nitsʲa]
wild strawberry	суниця (ж)	[su'nitsʲa]
bilberry	чорниця (ж)	[tʃor'nitsʲa]

231. Flowers. Plants

flower	квітка (ж)	['kwitka]
bouquet (of flowers)	букет (ч)	[bu'kɛt]
rose (flower)	троянда (ж)	[tro'ʲanda]
tulip	тюльпан (ч)	[tʲulʲ'pan]
carnation	гвоздика (ж)	[ɦwoz'dika]
gladiolus	гладіолус (ч)	[ɦladi'ɔlus]
cornflower	волошка (ж)	[wo'lɔʃka]
harebell	дзвіночок (ч)	[dzwi'nɔtʃok]
dandelion	кульбаба (ж)	[kulʲ'baba]
camomile	ромашка (ж)	[ro'maʃka]
aloe	алое (ч)	[a'lɔɛ]
cactus	кактус (ч)	['kaktus]
rubber plant, ficus	фікус (ч)	['fikus]
lily	лілея (ж)	[li'lɛʲa]
geranium	герань (ж)	[ɦɛ'ranʲ]
hyacinth	гіацинт (ч)	[ɦia'tsint]
mimosa	мімоза (ж)	[mi'mɔza]
narcissus	нарцис (ч)	[nar'tsis]
nasturtium	настурція (ж)	[nas'turtsiʲa]
orchid	орхідея (ж)	[orhi'dɛʲa]
peony	півонія (ж)	[pi'wɔniʲa]
violet	фіалка (ж)	[fi'alka]
pansy	братки (мн)	[brat'ki]
forget-me-not	незабудка (ж)	[nɛza'budka]
daisy	стокротки (мн)	[stok'rɔtki]
poppy	мак (ч)	[mak]
hemp	коноплі (мн)	[ko'nɔpli]
mint	м'ята (ж)	['mʲʲata]

| lily of the valley | конвалія (ж) | [kon'waliʲa] |
| snowdrop | пролісок (ч) | ['prɔlisok] |

nettle	кропива (ж)	[kropi'wa]
sorrel	щавель (ч)	[ɕa'wɛlʲ]
water lily	латаття (с)	[la'tattʲa]
fern	папороть (ж)	['paporotʲ]
lichen	лишайник (ч)	[li'ʃajnik]

conservatory (greenhouse)	оранжерея (ж)	[oranʒɛ'rɛʲa]
lawn	газон (ч)	[ɦa'zɔn]
flowerbed	клумба (ж)	['klumba]

plant	рослина (ж)	[ros'lina]
grass	трава (ж)	[tra'wa]
blade of grass	травинка (ж)	[tra'winka]

leaf	листок (ч)	[lis'tɔk]
petal	пелюстка (ж)	[pɛ'lʲustka]
stem	стебло (с)	[stɛb'lɔ]
tuber	бульба (ж)	['bulʲba]

| young plant (shoot) | паросток (ч) | ['parostok] |
| thorn | колючка (ч) | [ko'lʲutʃka] |

to blossom (vi)	цвісти	[tswis'ti]
to fade, to wither	в'янути	['wʲʲanuti]
smell (odour)	запах (ч)	['zapah]
to cut (flowers)	зрізати	['zrizati]
to pick (a flower)	зірвати	[zir'wati]

232. Cereals, grains

grain	зерно (с)	[zɛr'nɔ]
cereal crops	зернові рослини (мн)	[zɛrno'wi ros'lini]
ear (of barley, etc.)	колос (ч)	['kɔlos]

wheat	пшениця (ж)	[pʃɛ'nitsʲa]
rye	жито (с)	['ʒito]
oats	овес (ч)	[o'wɛs]

| millet | просо (с) | ['prɔso] |
| barley | ячмінь (ч) | [jatʃ'minʲ] |

maize	кукурудза (ж)	[kuku'rudza]
rice	рис (ч)	[ris]
buckwheat	гречка (ж)	['ɦrɛtʃka]

| pea plant | горох (ч) | [ɦo'rɔh] |
| kidney bean | квасоля (ж) | [kwa'sɔlʲa] |

soya	соя (ж)	['sɔʲa]
lentil	сочевиця (ж)	[sotʃɛ'witsʲa]
beans (pulse crops)	боби (мн)	[bo'bi]

233. Vegetables. Greens

vegetables	овочі (мн)	['ɔwotʃi]
greens	зелень (ж)	['zɛlɛnʲ]
tomato	помідор (ч)	[pomi'dɔr]
cucumber	огірок (ч)	[oɦi'rɔk]
carrot	морква (ж)	['mɔrkwa]
potato	картопля (ж)	[kar'tɔplʲa]
onion	цибуля (ж)	[tsi'bulʲa]
garlic	часник (ч)	[tʃas'nik]
cabbage	капуста (ж)	[ka'pusta]
cauliflower	кольорова капуста (ж)	[kolʲo'rɔwa ka'pusta]
Brussels sprouts	брюссельська капуста (ж)	[brʲu'sɛlʲsʲka ka'pusta]
beetroot	буряк (ч)	[bu'rʲak]
aubergine	баклажан (ч)	[bakla'ʒan]
marrow	кабачок (ч)	[kaba'tʃɔk]
pumpkin	гарбуз (ч)	[ɦar'buz]
turnip	ріпа (ж)	['ripa]
parsley	петрушка (ж)	[pɛt'ruʃka]
dill	кріп (ч)	[krip]
lettuce	салат (ч)	[sa'lat]
celery	селера (ж)	[sɛ'lɛra]
asparagus	спаржа (ж)	['sparʒa]
spinach	шпинат (ч)	[ʃpi'nat]
pea	горох (ч)	[ɦo'rɔh]
beans	боби (мн)	[bo'bi]
maize	кукурудза (ж)	[kuku'rudza]
kidney bean	квасоля (ж)	[kwa'sɔlʲa]
pepper	перець (ч)	['pɛrɛts]
radish	редька (ж)	['rɛdʲka]
artichoke	артишок (ч)	[arti'ʃɔk]

REGIONAL GEOGRAPHY

234. Western Europe

Europe	Європа (ж)	[ɛw'rɔpa]
European Union	Європейський Союз (ч)	[ɛwro'pɛjsʲkij soʲˈuz]
European (n)	європеєць (ч)	[ɛwro'pɛeʦ]
European (adj)	європейський	[ɛwro'pɛjsʲkij]

Austria	Австрія (ж)	['awstriʲa]
Austrian (masc.)	австрієць (ч)	[aw'striɛʦ]
Austrian (fem.)	австрійка (ж)	[aw'strijka]
Austrian (adj)	австрійський	[aw'strijsʲkij]

Great Britain	Великобританія (ж)	[wɛlikobri'taniʲa]
England	Англія (ж)	['anɦliʲa]
British (masc.)	англієць (ч)	[anɦ'liɛʦ]
British (fem.)	англійка (ж)	[anɦ'lijka]
English, British (adj)	англійський	[anɦ'lijsʲkij]

Belgium	Бельгія (ж)	['bɛlʲɦiʲa]
Belgian (masc.)	бельгієць (ч)	[bɛlʲˈɦiɛʦ]
Belgian (fem.)	бельгійка (ж)	[bɛlʲˈɦijka]
Belgian (adj)	бельгійський	[bɛlʲˈɦijsʲkij]

Germany	Німеччина (ж)	[ni'mɛʧina]
German (masc.)	німець (ч)	['nimɛʦ]
German (fem.)	німкеня (ж)	[nim'kɛnʲa]
German (adj)	німецький	[ni'mɛʦkij]

Netherlands	Нідерланди (ж)	[nidɛr'landi]
Holland	Голландія (ж)	[ɦo'landiʲa]
Dutch (masc.)	голландець (ч)	[ɦo'landɛʦ]
Dutch (fem.)	голландка (ж)	[ɦo'landka]
Dutch (adj)	голландський	[ɦo'landsʲkij]

Greece	Греція (ж)	['ɦrɛtsiʲa]
Greek (masc.)	грек (ч)	[ɦrɛk]
Greek (fem.)	грекиня (ж)	[ɦrɛ'kinʲa]
Greek (adj)	грецький	['ɦrɛʦkij]

Denmark	Данія (ж)	['daniʲa]
Dane (masc.)	данець (ч)	['danɛʦ]
Dane (fem.)	данка (ж)	['danka]
Danish (adj)	данський	['dansʲkij]

Ireland	Ірландія (ж)	[ir'landiʲa]
Irish (masc.)	ірландець (ч)	[ir'landɛʦ]
Irish (fem.)	ірландка (ж)	[ir'landka]
Irish (adj)	ірландський	[ir'landsʲkij]

Iceland	**Ісландія** (ж)	[is'landi/a]
Icelander (masc.)	**ісландець** (ч)	[is'landɛts]
Icelander (fem.)	**ісландка** (ж)	[is'landka]
Icelandic (adj)	**ісландський**	[is'lands/kij]

Spain	**Іспанія** (ж)	[ispani/a]
Spaniard (masc.)	**іспанець** (ч)	[ispanɛts]
Spaniard (fem.)	**іспанка** (ж)	[ispanka]
Spanish (adj)	**іспанський**	[ispans/kij]

Italy	**Італія** (ж)	[i'tali/a]
Italian (masc.)	**італієць** (ч)	[ita'liɛts]
Italian (fem.)	**італійка** (ж)	[ita'lijka]
Italian (adj)	**італійський**	[ita'lijs/kij]

Cyprus	**Кіпр** (ж)	[kipr]
Cypriot (masc.)	**кіпріот** (ч)	[kipri'ɔt]
Cypriot (fem.)	**кіпріотка** (ж)	[kipri'ɔtka]
Cypriot (adj)	**кіпрський**	['kiprs/kij]

Malta	**Мальта** (ж)	['mal/ta]
Maltese (masc.)	**мальтієць** (ч)	[mal/'tiɛts]
Maltese (fem.)	**мальтійка** (ж)	[mal/'tijka]
Maltese (adj)	**мальтійський**	[mal/'tijs/kij]

Norway	**Норвегія** (ж)	[nor'wɛɦi/a]
Norwegian (masc.)	**норвежець** (ч)	[nor'wɛʒɛts]
Norwegian (fem.)	**норвежка** (ж)	[nor'wɛʒka]
Norwegian (adj)	**норвезький**	[nor'wɛz/kij]

Portugal	**Португалія** (ж)	[portu'ɦali/a]
Portuguese (masc.)	**португалець** (ч)	[portu'ɦalɛts]
Portuguese (fem.)	**португалка** (ж)	[portu'ɦalka]
Portuguese (adj)	**португальський**	[portu'ɦal/s/kij]

Finland	**Фінляндія** (ж)	[fin'l/andi/a]
Finn (masc.)	**фін** (ч)	[fin]
Finn (fem.)	**фінка** (ж)	['finka]
Finnish (adj)	**фінський**	['fins/kij]

France	**Франція** (ж)	['frantsi/a]
French (masc.)	**француз** (ч)	[fran'tsuz]
French (fem.)	**французка** (ж)	[fran'tsuzka]
French (adj)	**французький**	[fran'tsuz/kij]

Sweden	**Швеція** (ж)	['ʃwɛtsi/a]
Swede (masc.)	**швед** (ч)	[ʃwɛd]
Swede (fem.)	**шведка** (ж)	['ʃwɛdka]
Swedish (adj)	**шведський**	['ʃwɛds/kij]

Switzerland	**Швейцарія** (ж)	[ʃwɛj'tsari/a]
Swiss (masc.)	**швейцарець** (ч)	[ʃwɛj'tsarɛts]
Swiss (fem.)	**швейцарка** (ж)	[ʃwɛj'tsarka]
Swiss (adj)	**швейцарський**	[ʃwɛj'tsars/kij]
Scotland	**Шотландія** (ж)	[ʃot'landi/a]
Scottish (masc.)	**шотландець** (ч)	[ʃot'landɛts]

| Scottish (fem.) | шотландка (ж) | [ʃot'landka] |
| Scottish (adj) | шотландський | [ʃot'landsʲkij] |

Vatican City	Ватикан (ч)	[wati'kan]
Liechtenstein	Ліхтенштейн (ч)	[lihtɛn'ʃtɛjn]
Luxembourg	Люксембург (ч)	[lʲuksɛm'burɦ]
Monaco	Монако (с)	[mo'nako]

235. Central and Eastern Europe

Albania	Албанія (ж)	[al'baniʲa]
Albanian (masc.)	албанець (ч)	[al'banɛts]
Albanian (fem.)	албанка (ж)	[al'banka]
Albanian (adj)	албанський	[al'bansʲkij]

Bulgaria	Болгарія (ж)	[bol'ɦariʲa]
Bulgarian (masc.)	болгарин (ч)	[bol'ɦarin]
Bulgarian (fem.)	болгарка (ж)	[bol'ɦarka]
Bulgarian (adj)	болгарський	[bol'ɦarsʲkij]

Hungary	Угорщина (ж)	[u'ɦorçina]
Hungarian (masc.)	угорець (ч)	[u'ɦorɛts]
Hungarian (fem.)	угорка (ж)	[u'ɦorka]
Hungarian (adj)	угорський	[u'ɦorsʲkij]

Latvia	Латвія (ж)	['latwiʲa]
Latvian (masc.)	латвієць (ч)	[lat'wiɛts]
Latvian (fem.)	латвійка (ж)	[lat'wijka]
Latvian (adj)	латиський	[la'tisʲkij]

Lithuania	Литва (ж)	[lit'wa]
Lithuanian (masc.)	литовець (ч)	[li'towɛts]
Lithuanian (fem.)	литовка (ж)	[li'towka]
Lithuanian (adj)	литовський	[li'towsʲkij]

Poland	Польща (ж)	['polʲça]
Pole (masc.)	поляк (ч)	[po'lʲak]
Pole (fem.)	полька (ж)	['polʲka]
Polish (adj)	польський	['polʲsʲkij]

Romania	Румунія (ж)	[ru'muniʲa]
Romanian (masc.)	румун (ч)	[ru'mun]
Romanian (fem.)	румунка (ж)	[ru'munka]
Romanian (adj)	румунський	[ru'munsʲkij]

Serbia	Сербія (ж)	['sɛrbiʲa]
Serbian (masc.)	серб (ч)	[sɛrb]
Serbian (fem.)	сербка (ж)	['sɛrbka]
Serbian (adj)	сербський	['sɛrbsʲkij]

Slovakia	Словаччина (ж)	[slo'watʃina]
Slovak (masc.)	словак (ч)	[slo'wak]
Slovak (fem.)	словачка (ж)	[slo'watʃka]
Slovak (adj)	словацький	[slo'watskij]

Croatia	**Хорватія** (ж)	[hor'watiˈa]
Croatian (masc.)	**хорват** (ч)	[hor'wat]
Croatian (fem.)	**хорватка** (ж)	[hor'watka]
Croatian (adj)	**хорватський**	[hor'watsˈkij]

Czech Republic	**Чехія** (ж)	['ʧɛhiˈa]
Czech (masc.)	**чех** (ч)	[ʧɛh]
Czech (fem.)	**чешка** (ж)	['ʧɛʃka]
Czech (adj)	**чеський**	['ʧɛsˈkij]

Estonia	**Естонія** (ж)	[ɛs'toniˈa]
Estonian (masc.)	**естонець** (ч)	[ɛs'tonɛts]
Estonian (fem.)	**естонка** (ж)	[ɛs'tonka]
Estonian (adj)	**естонський**	[ɛs'tonsˈkij]

Bosnia and Herzegovina	**Боснія і Герцеговина** (ж)	['bosniˈa i ɦɛrtsɛɦo'wina]
North Macedonia	**Македонія** (ж)	[makɛ'doniˈa]
Slovenia	**Словенія** (ж)	[slo'wɛniˈa]
Montenegro	**Чорногорія** (ж)	[ʧorno'ɦoriˈa]

236. Former USSR countries

Azerbaijan	**Азербайджан** (ч)	[azɛrbaj'dʒan]
Azerbaijani (masc.)	**азербайджанець** (ч)	[azɛrbaj'dʒanɛts]
Azerbaijani (fem.)	**азербайджанка** (ж)	[azɛrbaj'dʒanka]
Azerbaijani, Azeri (adj)	**азербайджанський**	[azɛrbaj'dʒansˈkij]

Armenia	**Вірменія** (ж)	[wir'mɛniˈa]
Armenian (masc.)	**вірменин** (ч)	[wirmɛ'nin]
Armenian (fem.)	**вірменка** (ж)	[wir'mɛnka]
Armenian (adj)	**вірменський**	[wir'mɛnsˈkij]

Belarus	**Білорусь** (ж)	[bilo'rusˈ]
Belarusian (masc.)	**білорус** (ч)	[bilo'rus]
Belarusian (fem.)	**білоруска** (ж)	[bilo'ruska]
Belarusian (adj)	**білоруський**	[bilo'rusˈkij]

Georgia	**Грузія** (ж)	['ɦruziˈa]
Georgian (masc.)	**грузин** (ч)	[ɦru'zin]
Georgian (fem.)	**грузинка** (ж)	[ɦru'zinka]
Georgian (adj)	**грузинський**	[ɦru'zinsˈkij]

Kazakhstan	**Казахстан** (ч)	[kazah'stan]
Kazakh (masc.)	**казах** (ч)	[ka'zah]
Kazakh (fem.)	**казашка** (ж)	[ka'zaʃka]
Kazakh (adj)	**казахський**	[ka'zahsˈkij]

Kirghizia	**Киргизстан** (ч)	[kirɦiz'stan]
Kirghiz (masc.)	**киргиз** (ч)	[kir'ɦiz]
Kirghiz (fem.)	**киргизка** (ж)	[kir'ɦizka]
Kirghiz (adj)	**киргизький**	[kir'ɦizˈkij]

Moldova, Moldavia	**Молдова** (ж)	[mol'dowa]
Moldavian (masc.)	**молдованин** (ч)	[moldo'wanin]

| Moldavian (fem.) | молдаванка (ж) | [molda'wanka] |
| Moldavian (adj) | молдавський | [mol'dawsʲkij] |

Russia	Росія (ж)	[ro'siʲa]
Russian (masc.)	росіянин (ч)	[rosiʲanin]
Russian (fem.)	росіянка (ж)	[rosiʲanka]
Russian (adj)	російський	[ro'sijskij]

Tajikistan	Таджикистан (ч)	[tadʒiki'stan]
Tajik (masc.)	таджик (ч)	[ta'dʒik]
Tajik (fem.)	таджичка (ж)	[ta'dʒitʃka]
Tajik (adj)	таджицький	[ta'dʒitskij]

Turkmenistan	Туркменістан (ч)	[turkmɛni'stan]
Turkmen (masc.)	туркмен (ч)	[turk'mɛn]
Turkmen (fem.)	туркменка (ж)	[turk'mɛnka]
Turkmenian (adj)	туркменський	[turk'mɛnsʲkij]

Uzbekistan	Узбекистан (ч)	[uzbɛki'stan]
Uzbek (masc.)	узбек (ч)	[uz'bɛk]
Uzbek (fem.)	узбечка (ж)	[uz'bɛtʃka]
Uzbek (adj)	узбецький	[uz'bɛtskij]

Ukraine	Україна (ж)	[ukra'jina]
Ukrainian (masc.)	українець (ч)	[ukra'jinɛts]
Ukrainian (fem.)	українка (ж)	[ukra'jinka]
Ukrainian (adj)	український	[ukra'jinsʲkij]

237. Asia

| Asia | Азія (ж) | ['aziʲa] |
| Asian (adj) | азіатський | [azi'atsʲkij] |

Vietnam	В'єтнам (ч)	[wʲɛt'nam]
Vietnamese (masc.)	в'єтнамець (ч)	[wʲɛt'namɛts]
Vietnamese (fem.)	в'єтнамка (ж)	[wʲɛt'namka]
Vietnamese (adj)	в'єтнамський	[wʲɛt'namsʲkij]

India	Індія (ж)	['indiʲa]
Indian (masc.)	індієць (ч)	[in'diɛts]
Indian (fem.)	індійка (ж)	[in'dijka]
Indian (adj)	індійський	[in'dijsʲkij]

Israel	Ізраїль (ч)	[iz'rajilʲ]
Israeli (masc.)	ізраїльтянин (ч)	[izrajilʲ'tʲanin]
Israeli (fem.)	ізраїльтянка (ж)	[izrajilʲ'tʲanka]
Israeli (adj)	ізраїльський	[iz'rajilʲsʲkij]

Jew (n)	єврей (ч)	[ɛw'rɛj]
Jewess (n)	єврейка (ж)	[ɛw'rɛjka]
Jewish (adj)	єврейський	[ɛw'rɛjsʲkij]

| China | Китай (ч) | [ki'taj] |
| Chinese (masc.) | китаєць (ч) | [ki'taɛts] |

| Chinese (fem.) | китаянка (ж) | [kita'¹anka] |
| Chinese (adj) | китайський | [ki'tajsʲkij] |

Korean (masc.)	кореєць (ч)	[ko'rɛets]
Korean (fem.)	кореянка (ж)	[korɛ'¹anka]
Korean (adj)	корейський	[ko'rɛjsʲkij]

Lebanon	Ліван (ч)	[li'wan]
Lebanese (masc.)	ліванець (ч)	[li'wanɛts]
Lebanese (fem.)	ліванка (ж)	[li'wanka]
Lebanese (adj)	ліванський	[li'wansʲkij]

Mongolia	Монголія (ж)	[mon'hɔliʲa]
Mongolian (masc.)	монгол (ч)	[mon'hɔl]
Mongolian (fem.)	монголка (ж)	[mon'hɔlka]
Mongolian (adj)	монгольський	[mon'hɔlʲsʲkij]

Malaysia	Малайзія (ж)	[ma'lajziʲa]
Malaysian (masc.)	малаєць (ч)	[ma'laɛts]
Malaysian (fem.)	малайка (ж)	[ma'lajka]
Malaysian (adj)	малайський	[ma'lajsʲkij]

Pakistan	Пакистан (ч)	[paki'stan]
Pakistani (masc.)	пакистанець (ч)	[paki'stanɛts]
Pakistani (fem.)	пакистанка (ж)	[paki'stanka]
Pakistani (adj)	пакистанський	[paki'stansʲkij]

Saudi Arabia	Саудівська Аравія (ж)	[sa'udiwsʲka a'rawiʲa]
Arab (masc.)	араб (ч)	[a'rab]
Arab (fem.)	арабка (ж)	[a'rabka]
Arabic, Arabian (adj)	арабський	[a'rabsʲkij]

Thailand	Таїланд (ч)	[taji'land]
Thai (masc.)	таєць (ч)	['taɛts]
Thai (fem.)	тайка (ж)	['tajka]
Thai (adj)	тайський	['tajsʲkij]

Taiwan	Тайвань (ч)	[taj'wanʲ]
Taiwanese (masc.)	тайванець (ч)	[taj'wanɛts]
Taiwanese (fem.)	тайванка (ж)	[taj'wanka]
Taiwanese (adj)	тайванський	[tajwansʲkij]

Turkey	Туреччина (ж)	[tu'rɛtʃina]
Turk (masc.)	турок (ч)	['turok]
Turk (fem.)	туркеня (ж)	[tur'kɛnʲa]
Turkish (adj)	турецький	[tu'rɛtskij]

Japan	Японія (ж)	[ja'pɔniʲa]
Japanese (masc.)	японець (ч)	[ja'pɔnɛts]
Japanese (fem.)	японка (ж)	[ja'pɔnka]
Japanese (adj)	японський	[ja'pɔnsʲkij]

Afghanistan	Афганістан (ч)	[afhani'stan]
Bangladesh	Бангладеш (ч)	[banhla'dɛʃ]
Indonesia	Індонезія (ж)	[indo'nɛziʲa]
Jordan	Йорданія (ж)	['ʲor'daniʲa]

Iraq	Ірак (ч)	[i'rak]
Iran	Іран (ч)	[i'ran]
Cambodia	Камбоджа (ж)	[kam'bɔdʒa]
Kuwait	Кувейт (ч)	[ku'wɛjt]

Laos	Лаос (ч)	[la'ɔs]
Myanmar	М'янма (ж)	['mʲanma]
Nepal	Непал (ч)	[nɛ'pal]
United Arab Emirates	Об'єднані Арабські емірати (мн)	[o'bʲɛdnani a'rabsʲki ɛmi'rati]

Syria	Сирія (ж)	['siriʲa]
Palestine	Палестинська автономія (ж)	[palɛ'stinsʲka awto'nɔmiʲa]
South Korea	Південна Корея (ж)	[piw'dɛna ko'rɛʲa]
North Korea	Північна Корея (ж)	[piw'nitʃna ko'rɛʲa]

238. North America

United States of America	Сполучені Штати Америки (мн)	[spo'lutʃɛni 'ʃtati a'mɛriki]
American (masc.)	американець (ч)	[amɛri'kanɛts]
American (fem.)	американка (ж)	[amɛri'kanka]
American (adj)	американський	[amɛri'kansʲkij]

Canada	Канада (ж)	[ka'nada]
Canadian (masc.)	канадець (ч)	[ka'nadɛts]
Canadian (fem.)	канадка (ж)	[ka'nadka]
Canadian (adj)	канадський	[ka'nadsʲkij]

Mexico	Мексика (ж)	['mɛksika]
Mexican (masc.)	мексиканець (ч)	[mɛksi'kanɛts]
Mexican (fem.)	мексиканка (ж)	[mɛksi'kanka]
Mexican (adj)	мексиканський	[mɛksi'kansʲkij]

239. Central and South America

Argentina	Аргентина (ж)	[arɦɛn'tina]
Argentinian (masc.)	аргентинець (ч)	[arɦɛn'tinɛts]
Argentinian (fem.)	аргентинка (ж)	[arɦɛn'tinka]
Argentinian (adj)	аргентинський	[arɦɛn'tinsʲkij]

Brazil	Бразилія (ж)	[bra'ziliʲa]
Brazilian (masc.)	бразилець (ч)	[bra'zilɛts]
Brazilian (fem.)	бразилійка (ж)	[brazi'lijka]
Brazilian (adj)	бразильський	[bra'zilʲsʲkij]

Colombia	Колумбія (ж)	[ko'lumbiʲa]
Colombian (masc.)	колумбієць (ч)	[kolum'biɛts]
Colombian (fem.)	колумбійка (ж)	[kolum'bijka]
Colombian (adj)	колумбійський	[kolum'bijsʲkij]
Cuba	Куба (ж)	['kuba]

Cuban (masc.)	кубинець (ч)	[ku'binɛts]
Cuban (fem.)	кубинка (ж)	[ku'binka]
Cuban (adj)	кубинський	[ku'binsʲkij]

Chile	Чилі (ж)	['ʧili]
Chilean (masc.)	чилієць (ч)	[ʧi'liɛts]
Chilean (fem.)	чилійка (ж)	[ʧi'lijka]
Chilean (adj)	чилійський	[ʧi'lijsʲkij]

Bolivia	Болівія (ж)	[bo'liwiʲa]
Venezuela	Венесуела (ж)	[wɛnɛsu'ɛla]
Paraguay	Парагвай (ч)	[parah'waj]
Peru	Перу (ж)	[pɛ'ru]

Suriname	Суринам (ч)	[suri'nam]
Uruguay	Уругвай (ч)	[uruh'waj]
Ecuador	Еквадор (ч)	[ɛkwa'dɔr]

The Bahamas	Багамські острови (мн)	[ba'hamsʲki ostro'wi]
Haiti	Гаїті (ч)	[ha'jiti]
Dominican Republic	Домініканська республіка (ж)	[domini'kansʲka rɛs'publika]
Panama	Панама (ж)	[pa'nama]
Jamaica	Ямайка (ж)	[ja'majka]

240. Africa

Egypt	Єгипет (ч)	[ɛ'hipɛt]
Egyptian (masc.)	єгиптянин (ч)	[ɛhip'tʲanin]
Egyptian (fem.)	єгиптянка (ж)	[ɛhip'tʲanka]
Egyptian (adj)	єгипетський	[ɛ'hipɛtsʲkij]

Morocco	Марокко (с)	[ma'rɔkko]
Moroccan (masc.)	марокканець (ч)	[maro'kanɛts]
Moroccan (fem.)	марокканка (ж)	[maro'kanka]
Moroccan (adj)	марокканський	[maro'kansʲkij]

Tunisia	Туніс (ч)	[tu'nis]
Tunisian (masc.)	тунісець (ч)	[tu'nisɛts]
Tunisian (fem.)	туніска (ж)	[tu'niska]
Tunisian (adj)	туніський	[tu'nisʲkij]

Ghana	Гана (ж)	['hana]
Zanzibar	Занзібар (ч)	[zanzi'bar]
Kenya	Кенія (ж)	['kɛniʲa]
Libya	Лівія (ж)	['liwiʲa]
Madagascar	Мадагаскар (ч)	[madaha'skar]

Namibia	Намібія (ж)	[na'mibiʲa]
Senegal	Сенегал (ч)	[sɛnɛ'hal]
Tanzania	Танзанія (ж)	[tan'zaniʲa]
South Africa	Південно-Африканська Республіка (ж)	[piw'dɛno afri'kansʲka rɛs'publika]
African (masc.)	африканець (ч)	[afri'kanɛts]

| African (fem.) | африканка (ж) | [afri'kanka] |
| African (adj) | африканський | [afri'kansʲkij] |

241. Australia. Oceania

Australia	Австралія (ж)	[aw'straliʲa]
Australian (masc.)	австралієць (ч)	[awstra'liɛʦ]
Australian (fem.)	австралійка (ж)	[awstra'lijka]
Australian (adj)	австралійський	[awstra'lijsʲkij]

New Zealand	Нова Зеландія (ж)	[no'wa zɛ'landiʲa]
New Zealander (masc.)	новозеландець (ч)	[nowozɛ'landɛʦ]
New Zealander (fem.)	новозеландка (ж)	[nowozɛ'landka]
New Zealand (as adj)	новозеландський	[nowozɛ'landsʲkij]

| Tasmania | Тасманія (ж) | [tas'maniʲa] |
| French Polynesia | Французька Полінезія (ж) | [fran'ʦuzʲka poli'nɛziʲa] |

242. Cities

Amsterdam	Амстердам (ч)	[amstɛr'dam]
Ankara	Анкара (ж)	[anka'ra]
Athens	Афіни (с)	[a'fini]
Baghdad	Багдад (ч)	[baɦ'dad]
Bangkok	Бангкок (ч)	[banɦ'kɔk]
Barcelona	Барселона (ж)	[barsɛ'lɔna]

Beijing	Пекін (ч)	[pɛ'kin]
Beirut	Бейрут (ч)	['bɛjrut]
Berlin	Берлін (ч)	[bɛr'lin]
Mumbai (Bombay)	Бомбей (ч)	[bom'bɛj]
Bonn	Бонн (ч)	[bon]

Bordeaux	Бордо (с)	[bor'dɔ]
Bratislava	Братислава (ж)	[brati'slawa]
Brussels	Брюссель (ч)	[brʲu'sɛlʲ]
Bucharest	Бухарест (ч)	[buha'rɛst]
Budapest	Будапешт (ч)	[buda'pɛʃt]

Cairo	Каїр (ч)	[ka'jir]
Kolkata (Calcutta)	Калькутта (ж)	[kalʲ'kutta]
Chicago	Чикаго (с)	[ʧi'kaɦo]
Copenhagen	Копенгаген (ч)	[kopɛ'nɦaɦɛn]

Dar-es-Salaam	Дар ес Салам (ч)	[dar ɛs sa'lam]
Delhi	Делі (с)	['dɛli]
Dubai	Дубаї (с)	[du'baji]
Dublin	Дублін (ч)	['dublin]
Düsseldorf	Дюссельдорф (ч)	[dʲusɛlʲ'dorf]

| Florence | Флоренція (ж) | [flo'rɛnʦiʲa] |
| Frankfurt | Франкфурт (ч) | ['frankfurt] |

Geneva	Женева (ж)	[ʒɛˈnɛwa]
The Hague	Гаага (ж)	[haˈaɦa]
Hamburg	Гамбург (ч)	[ˈɦamburɦ]
Hanoi	Ханой (ч)	[haˈnɔj]
Havana	Гавана (ж)	[ɦaˈwana]
Helsinki	Гельсінкі (с)	[ˈɦɛlʲsinki]
Hiroshima	Хіросіма (ж)	[hiroˈsima]
Hong Kong	Гонконг (ч)	[ɦonˈkɔnɦ]

Istanbul	Стамбул (ч)	[stamˈbul]
Jerusalem	Єрусалим (ч)	[ɛrusaˈlim]
Kyiv	Київ (ч)	[kiˈjiw]
Kuala Lumpur	Куала-Лумпур (ч)	[kuˈala lumˈpur]
Lisbon	Лісабон (ч)	[lisaˈbɔn]
London	Лондон (ч)	[ˈlɔndon]
Los Angeles	Лос-Анджелес (ч)	[los ˈandʒɛlɛs]
Lyons	Ліон (ч)	[liˈɔn]

Madrid	Мадрид (ч)	[madˈrid]
Marseille	Марсель (ч)	[marˈsɛlʲ]
Mexico City	Мехіко (с)	[ˈmɛhiko]
Miami	Маямі (с)	[maˈʲami]
Montreal	Монреаль (ч)	[monrɛˈalʲ]
Moscow	Москва (ж)	[moskˈwa]
Munich	Мюнхен (ч)	[ˈmʲunhɛn]

Nairobi	Найробі (с)	[najˈrɔbi]
Naples	Неаполь (ч)	[nɛˈapolʲ]
New York	Нью-Йорк (ч)	[nju ˈjork]
Nice	Ніцца (ж)	[ˈniʦa]

| Oslo | Осло (с) | [ˈɔslo] |
| Ottawa | Оттава (ж) | [otˈtawa] |

| Paris | Париж (ч) | [paˈriʒ] |
| Prague | Прага (ж) | [ˈpraɦa] |

| Rio de Janeiro | Ріо-де-Жанейро (с) | [ˈrio dɛ ʒaˈnɛjro] |
| Rome | Рим (ч) | [rim] |

Saint Petersburg	Санкт-Петербург (ч)	[sankt pɛtɛrˈburɦ]
Seoul	Сеул (ч)	[sɛˈul]
Shanghai	Шанхай (ч)	[ʃanˈhaj]
Singapore	Сінгапур (ч)	[sinɦaˈpur]

| Stockholm | Стокгольм (ч) | [stokˈɦɔlʲm] |
| Sydney | Сідней (ч) | [ˈsidnɛj] |

Taipei	Тайбей (ч)	[tajˈbɛj]
Tokyo	Токіо (с)	[ˈtɔkio]
Toronto	Торонто (с)	[toˈrɔnto]

Venice	Венеція (ж)	[wɛˈnɛʦiʲa]
Vienna	Відень (ч)	[ˈwidɛnʲ]
Warsaw	Варшава (ж)	[warˈʃawa]
Washington	Вашингтон (ч)	[waʃinɦˈtɔn]

243. Politics. Government. Part 1

politics	політика (ж)	[po'litika]
political (adj)	політичний	[poli'titʃnij]
politician	політик (ч)	[po'litik]

state (country)	держава (ж)	[dɛr'ʒawa]
citizen	громадянин (ч)	[ɦromadʲa'nin]
citizenship	громадянство (с)	[ɦroma'dʲanstwo]

| national emblem | національний герб (ч) | [natsio'nalʲnij 'ɦɛrb] |
| national anthem | державний гімн (ч) | [dɛr'ʒawnij ɦimn] |

government	уряд (ч)	['urʲad]
head of state	керівник (ч) країни	[kɛriw'nik kra'jini]
parliament	парламент (ч)	[par'lamɛnt]
party	партія (ж)	['partiʲa]

| capitalism | капіталізм (ч) | [kapita'lizm] |
| capitalist (adj) | капіталістичний | [kapitalis'titʃnij] |

| socialism | соціалізм (ч) | [sotsia'lizm] |
| socialist (adj) | соціалістичний | [sotsialis'titʃnij] |

communism	комунізм (ч)	[komu'nizm]
communist (adj)	комуністичний	[komunis'titʃnij]
communist (n)	комуніст (ч)	[komu'nist]

democracy	демократія (ж)	[dɛmok'ratiʲa]
democrat	демократ (ч)	[dɛmok'rat]
democratic (adj)	демократичний	[dɛmokra'titʃnij]
Democratic party	демократична партія (ж)	[dɛmokra'titʃna 'partiʲa]

| liberal (n) | ліберал (ч) | [libɛ'ral] |
| Liberal (adj) | ліберальний | [libɛ'ralʲnij] |

| conservative (n) | консерватор (ч) | [konsɛr'wator] |
| conservative (adj) | консервативний | [konsɛrwa'tiwnij] |

republic (n)	республіка (ж)	[rɛs'publika]
republican (n)	республіканець (ч)	[rɛspubli'kanɛts]
Republican party	республіканська партія (ж)	[rɛspubli'kansʲka 'partiʲa]

elections	вибори (мн)	['wibori]
to elect (vt)	обирати	[obiʲrati]
elector, voter	виборець (ч)	['wiborɛts]
election campaign	виборча компанія (ж)	['wibortʃa kom'paniʲa]

voting (n)	голосування (с)	[ɦolosu'wanʲa]
to vote (vi)	голосувати	[ɦolosu'wati]
suffrage, right to vote	право (с) голосу (ч)	['prawo 'ɦolosu]

candidate	кандидат (ч)	[kandi'dat]
to run for (~ President)	балотуватися	[balotu'watisʲa]
campaign	кампанія (ж)	[kam'paniʲa]

| opposition (as adj) | опозиційний | [opozi'tsijnij] |
| opposition (n) | опозиція (ж) | [opo'zitsiᵢa] |

visit	візит (ч)	[wi'zit]
official visit	офіційний візит (ч)	[ofi'tsijnij wi'zit]
international (adj)	міжнародний	[miʒna'rɔdnij]

| negotiations | переговори (мн) | [pɛrɛɦo'wɔri] |
| to negotiate (vi) | вести переговори | ['wɛsti pɛrɛɦo'wɔri] |

244. Politics. Government. Part 2

society	суспільство (с)	[sus'pilᵢstwo]
constitution	конституція (ж)	[konsti'tutsiᵢa]
power (political control)	влада (ж)	['wlada]
corruption	корупція (ж)	[ko'ruptsiᵢa]

| law (justice) | закон (ч) | [za'kɔn] |
| legal (legitimate) | законний | [za'kɔnij] |

| justice (fairness) | справедливість (ж) | [sprawɛd'liwistᵢ] |
| just (fair) | справедливий | [sprawɛd'liwij] |

committee	комітет (ч)	[komi'tɛt]
bill (draft law)	законопроект (ч)	[zakonopro'ɛkt]
budget	бюджет (ч)	[bᵢu'dʒɛt]
policy	політика (ж)	[po'litika]
reform	реформа (ж)	[rɛ'fɔrma]
radical (adj)	радикальний	[radi'kalᵢnij]

power (strength, force)	сила (ж)	['sila]
powerful (adj)	сильний	['silᵢnij]
supporter	прибічник (ч)	[pri'bitʃnik]
influence	вплив (ч)	[wpliw]

regime (e.g. military ~)	режим (ч)	[rɛ'ʒim]
conflict	конфлікт (ч)	[kon'flikt]
conspiracy (plot)	змова (ж)	['zmɔwa]
provocation	провокація (ж)	[prowo'katsiᵢa]

to overthrow (regime, etc.)	скинути	['skinuti]
overthrow (of a government)	скинення (с)	['skinɛnᵢa]
revolution	революція (ж)	[rɛwo'lᵢutsiᵢa]

| coup d'état | переворот (ч) | [pɛrɛwo'rɔt] |
| military coup | військовий переворот (ч) | [wijsᵢ'kɔwij pɛrɛwo'rɔt] |

crisis	криза (ж)	['kriza]
economic recession	економічний спад (ч)	[ɛkono'mitʃnij spad]
demonstrator (protester)	демонстрант (ч)	[dɛmon'strant]
demonstration	демонстрація (ж)	[dɛmon'stratsiᵢa]
martial law	воєнний стан (ч)	[wo'ɛnij stan]
military base	військова база (ж)	[wijsᵢ'kɔwa 'baza]
stability	стабільність (ж)	[sta'bilᵢnistᵢ]

stable (adj)	стабільний	[sta'bilʲnij]
exploitation	експлуатація (ж)	[ɛksplua'tatsiʲa]
to exploit (workers)	експлуатувати	[ɛkspluatu'wati]

racism	расизм (ч)	[ra'sizm]
racist	расист (ч)	[ra'sist]
fascism	фашизм (ч)	[fa'ʃizm]
fascist	фашист (ч)	[fa'ʃist]

245. Countries. Miscellaneous

foreigner	іноземець (ч)	[ino'zɛmɛts]
foreign (adj)	іноземний	[ino'zɛmnij]
abroad (in a foreign country)	за кордоном	[za kor'dɔnom]

emigrant	емігрант (ч)	[ɛmiɦ'rant]
emigration	еміграція (ж)	[ɛmiɦ'ratsiʲa]
to emigrate (vi)	емігрувати	[ɛmiɦru'wati]

the West	Захід (ч)	['zahid]
the East	Схід (ч)	[shid]
the Far East	Далекий Схід (ч)	[da'lɛkij shid]

civilization	цивілізація (ж)	[tsiwili'zatsiʲa]
humanity (mankind)	людство (с)	['lʲudstwo]
the world (earth)	світ (ч)	[swit]
peace	мир (ч)	[mir]
worldwide (adj)	світовий	[swito'wij]

homeland	батьківщина (ж)	[batʲkiw'ɕina]
people (population)	народ (ч)	[na'rɔd]
population	населення (с)	[na'sɛlɛnʲa]
people (a lot of ~)	люди (мн)	['lʲudi]
nation (people)	нація (ж)	['natsiʲa]
generation	покоління (с)	[poko'linʲa]

territory (area)	територія (ж)	[tɛri'tɔriʲa]
region	регіон (ч)	[rɛɦi'ɔn]
state (part of a country)	штат (ч)	[ʃtat]

tradition	традиція (ч)	[tra'ditsiʲa]
custom (tradition)	звичай (ч)	['zwitʃaj]
ecology	екологія (ж)	[ɛko'lɔɦiʲa]

Indian (Native American)	індіанець (ч)	[indi'anɛts]
Gypsy (masc.)	циган (ч)	[tsi'ɦan]
Gypsy (fem.)	циганка (ж)	[tsi'ɦanka]
Gypsy (adj)	циганський	[tsi'ɦansʲkij]

empire	імперія (ж)	[im'pɛriʲa]
colony	колонія (ж)	[ko'lɔniʲa]
slavery	рабство (с)	['rabstwo]
invasion	навала (ж)	[na'wala]
famine	голодомор (ч)	[ɦolodo'mɔr]

246. Major religious groups. Confessions

| religion | релігія (ж) | [rɛ'lihiʲa] |
| religious (adj) | релігійний | [rɛli'hijnij] |

faith, belief	віра (ж)	['wira]
to believe (in God)	вірити	['wiriti]
believer	віруючий	['wiruʲutʃij]

| atheism | атеїзм (ч) | [atɛ'jizm] |
| atheist | атеїст (ч) | [atɛ'jist] |

Christianity	християнство (с)	[hristiʲ'anstwo]
Christian (n)	християнин (ч)	[hristiʲ'anin]
Christian (adj)	християнський	[hristiʲ'ansʲkij]

Catholicism	Католицизм (ч)	[katoli'tsizm]
Catholic (n)	католик (ч)	[ka'tɔlik]
Catholic (adj)	католицький	[kato'litskij]

Protestantism	Протестантство (с)	[protɛs'tantstwo]
Protestant Church	Протестантська церква (ж)	[protɛs'tantsʲka 'tsɛrkwa]
Protestant (n)	протестант (ч)	[protɛs'tant]

Orthodoxy	Православ'я (с)	[prawo'slawʲʲa]
Orthodox Church	Православна церква (ж)	[prawos'lawna 'tsɛrkwa]
Orthodox (n)	православний	[prawos'lawnij]

Presbyterianism	Пресвітеріанство (с)	[prɛswitɛri'anstwo]
Presbyterian Church	Пресвітеріанська церква (ж)	[prɛswitɛri'ansʲka 'tsɛrkwa]
Presbyterian (n)	пресвітеріанин (ч)	[prɛswitɛri'anin]

| Lutheranism | Лютеранська церква (ж) | [lʲutɛ'ransʲka 'tsɛrkwa] |
| Lutheran (n) | лютеранин (ч) | [lʲutɛ'ranin] |

| Baptist Church | Баптизм (ч) | [bap'tizm] |
| Baptist (n) | баптист (ч) | [bap'tist] |

| Anglican Church | Англіканська церква (ж) | [anhli'kansʲka 'tsɛrkwa] |
| Anglican (n) | англіканин (ч) | [anhli'kanin] |

| Mormonism | Мормонство (с) | [mor'mɔnstwo] |
| Mormon (n) | мормон (ч) | [mor'mɔn] |

| Judaism | Іудаїзм (ч) | [iuda'jizm] |
| Jew (n) | іудей (ч) | [iu'dɛj] |

| Buddhism | Буддизм (ч) | [bud'dizm] |
| Buddhist (n) | буддист (ч) | [bud'dist] |

Hinduism	Індуїзм (ч)	[indu'jizm]
Hindu (n)	індуїст (ч)	[indu'jist]
Islam	Іслам (ч)	[is'lam]
Muslim (n)	мусульманин (ч)	[musulʲ'manin]

Muslim (adj)	мусульманський	[musulʲˈmansʲkij]
Shiah Islam	Шиїзм (ч)	[ʃiˈjizm]
Shiite (n)	шиїт (ч)	[ʃiˈjit]

| Sunni Islam | Сунізм (ч) | [suˈnizm] |
| Sunnite (n) | суніт (ч) | [suˈnit] |

247. Religions. Priests

| priest | священик (ч) | [swʲaˈɕɛnik] |
| the Pope | Папа Римський | [ˈpapa ˈrimsʲkij] |

monk, friar	чернець (ч)	[ʧɛrˈnɛʦ]
nun	черниця (ж)	[ʧɛrˈniʦʲa]
pastor	пастор (ч)	[ˈpastor]

abbot	абат (ч)	[aˈbat]
vicar (parish priest)	вікарій (ч)	[wiˈkarij]
bishop	єпископ (ч)	[ɛˈpiskop]
cardinal	кардинал (ч)	[kardiˈnal]

preacher	проповідник (ч)	[propoˈwidnik]
preaching	проповідь (ч)	[ˈprɔpowidʲ]
parishioners	парафіяни (мн)	[parafiˈʲani]

| believer | віруючий (ч) | [ˈwiruʲutʃij] |
| atheist | атеїст (ч) | [atɛˈjist] |

248. Faith. Christianity. Islam

| Adam | Адам (ч) | [aˈdam] |
| Eve | Єва (ж) | [ˈɛwa] |

God	Бог (ч)	[boɦ]
the Lord	Господь (ч)	[ɦosˈpɔdʲ]
the Almighty	Всесильний (ч)	[wsɛˈsilʲnij]

sin	гріх (ч)	[ɦrih]
to sin (vi)	грішити	[ɦriˈʃiti]
sinner (masc.)	грішник (ч)	[ˈɦriʃnik]
sinner (fem.)	грішниця (ж)	[ˈɦriʃniʦʲa]

| hell | пекло (с) | [ˈpɛklo] |
| paradise | рай (ч) | [raj] |

| Jesus | Ісус (ч) | [iˈsus] |
| Jesus Christ | Ісус Христос (ч) | [iˈsus hrisˈtɔs] |

the Holy Spirit	Святий Дух (ч)	[swʲaˈtij duh]
the Saviour	Спаситель (ч)	[spaˈsitɛlʲ]
the Virgin Mary	Богородиця (ж)	[boɦoˈrɔdiʦʲa]
the Devil	диявол (ч)	[diˈʲawol]

devil's (adj)	**диявольський**	[di'ǀawolǀsǀkij]
Satan	**Сатана** (ч)	[sata'na]
satanic (adj)	**сатанинський**	[sata'ninsǀkij]
angel	**ангел** (ч)	['anɦɛl]
guardian angel	**ангел-охоронець** (ч)	['anɦɛl oɦo'rɔnɛts]
angelic (adj)	**ангельський**	['anɦɛlǀsǀkij]
apostle	**апостол** (ч)	[a'pɔstol]
archangel	**архангел** (ч)	[ar'ɦanɦɛl]
the Antichrist	**антихрист** (ч)	[an'tihrist]
Church	**церква** (ж)	['tsɛrkwa]
Bible	**Біблія** (ж)	['bibliǀa]
biblical (adj)	**біблійний**	[bib'lijnij]
Old Testament	**Старий Завіт** (ч)	[sta'rij za'wit]
New Testament	**Новий Завіт** (ч)	[no'wij za'wit]
Gospel	**Євангеліє** (с)	[ɛ'wanɦɛliɛ]
Holy Scripture	**Священне Писання** (с)	[swǀa'ɕɛnɛ pi'sanǀa]
Heaven	**Небо** (с)	['nɛbo]
Commandment	**заповідь** (ж)	['zapowidǀ]
prophet	**пророк** (ч)	[pro'rɔk]
prophecy	**пророцтво** (с)	[pro'rɔtstwo]
Allah	**Аллах** (ч)	[a'lah]
Mohammed	**Магомет** (ч)	[maɦo'mɛt]
the Koran	**Коран** (ч)	[ko'ran]
mosque	**мечеть** (ж)	[mɛ'tʃɛtǀ]
mullah	**мула** (ч)	[mu'la]
prayer	**молитва** (ж)	[mo'litwa]
to pray (vi, vt)	**молитися**	[mo'litisǀa]
pilgrimage	**паломництво** (с)	[pa'lɔmnitstwo]
pilgrim	**паломник** (ч)	[pa'lɔmnik]
Mecca	**Мекка** (ж)	['mɛkka]
church	**церква** (ж)	['tsɛrkwa]
temple	**храм** (ч)	[hram]
cathedral	**собор** (ч)	[so'bɔr]
Gothic (adj)	**готичний**	[ɦo'titʃnij]
synagogue	**синагога** (ж)	[sina'ɦɔɦa]
mosque	**мечеть** (ж)	[mɛ'tʃɛtǀ]
chapel	**каплиця** (ж)	[kap'litsǀa]
abbey	**абатство** (с)	[a'batstwo]
convent	**монастир** (ч)	[monas'tir]
monastery	**монастир** (ч)	[monas'tir]
bell (church ~s)	**дзвін** (ч)	[dzwin]
bell tower	**дзвіниця** (ж)	[dzwi'nitsǀa]
to ring (ab. bells)	**дзвонити**	[dzwo'niti]
cross	**хрест** (ч)	[hrɛst]
cupola (roof)	**купол** (ч)	['kupol]

icon	ікона (ж)	[i'kɔna]
soul	душа (ж)	[du'ʃa]
fate (destiny)	доля (ж)	['dɔlʲa]
evil (n)	зло (с)	[zlo]
good (n)	добро (с)	[dob'rɔ]
vampire	вампір (ч)	[wam'pir]
witch (evil ~)	відьма (ж)	['widʲma]
demon	демон (ч)	['dɛmon]
spirit	дух (ч)	[duh]
redemption (giving us ~)	спокута (ж)	[spo'kuta]
to redeem (vt)	спокутувати	[spo'kutuwati]
church service	меса (ж)	['mɛsa]
to say mass	служити	[slu'ʒiti]
confession	сповідь (ж)	['spɔwidʲ]
to confess (vi)	сповідатися	[spowi'datisʲa]
saint (n)	святий (ч)	[swʲa'tij]
sacred (holy)	священний	[swʲa'ɕɛnij]
holy water	свята вода (ж)	[swʲa'ta wo'da]
ritual (n)	ритуал (ч)	[ritu'al]
ritual (adj)	ритуальний	[ritu'alʲnij]
sacrifice	жертвування (с)	['ʒɛrtwuwanʲa]
superstition	забобони (мн)	[zabo'bɔni]
superstitious (adj)	забобонний	[zabo'bɔnij]
afterlife	загробне життя (с)	[zaɦ'rɔbnɛ ʒit'tʲa]
eternal life	вічне життя (с)	['witʃnɛ ʒit'tʲa]

MISCELLANEOUS

249. Various useful words

background (green ~)	**фон** (ч)	[fon]
balance (of the situation)	**баланс** (ч)	[ba'lans]
barrier (obstacle)	**перешкода** (ж)	[pɛrɛʃ'kɔda]
base (basis)	**база** (ж)	['baza]
beginning	**початок** (ч)	[po'tʃatok]
category	**категорія** (ж)	[katɛ'ɦɔriʲa]
cause (reason)	**причина** (ж)	[pri'tʃina]
choice	**вибір** (ч)	['wibir]
coincidence	**збіг** (ч)	[zbiɦ]
comfortable (~ chair)	**зручний**	[zrutʃ'nij]
comparison	**порівняння** (с)	[poriw'nʲanʲa]
compensation	**компенсація** (ж)	[kompɛn'satsiʲa]
degree (extent, amount)	**ступінь** (ч)	['stupinʲ]
development	**розвиток** (ч)	['rɔzwitok]
difference	**різниця** (ж)	[riz'nitsʲa]
effect (e.g. of drugs)	**ефект** (ч)	[ɛ'fɛkt]
effort (exertion)	**зусилля** (с)	[zu'silʲa]
element	**елемент** (ч)	[ɛlɛ'mɛnt]
end (finish)	**закінчення** (с)	[za'kintʃɛnʲa]
example (illustration)	**приклад** (ч)	['priklad]
fact	**факт** (ч)	[fakt]
frequent (adj)	**приватний**	[pri'watnij]
growth (development)	**зростання** (с)	[zros'tanʲa]
help	**допомога** (ж)	[dopo'mɔɦa]
ideal	**ідеал** (ч)	[idɛ'al]
kind (sort, type)	**вид** (ч)	[wid]
labyrinth	**лабіринт** (ч)	[labi'rint]
mistake, error	**помилка** (ж)	[po'milka]
moment	**момент** (ч)	[mo'mɛnt]
object (thing)	**об'єкт** (ч)	[o'bʲɛkt]
obstacle	**перешкода** (ж)	[pɛrɛʃ'kɔda]
original (original copy)	**оригінал** (ч)	[oriɦi'nal]
part (~ of sth)	**частина** (ж)	[tʃas'tina]
particle, small part	**частка** (ж)	['tʃastka]
pause (break)	**пауза** (ж)	['pauza]
position	**позиція** (ж)	[po'zitsiʲa]
principle	**принцип** (ч)	['printsip]
problem	**проблема** (ж)	[prob'lɛma]
process	**процес** (ч)	[pro'tsɛs]

progress	прогрес (ч)	[proh'rɛs]
property (quality)	властивість (ж)	[wlas'tiwistʲ]
reaction	реакція (ж)	[rɛ'aktsiʲa]
risk	ризик (ч)	['rizik]

secret	таємниця (ж)	[taɛm'nitsʲa]
series	серія (ж)	['sɛriʲa]
shape (outer form)	форма (ж)	['forma]
situation	ситуація (ж)	[situ'atsiʲa]
solution	рішення (с)	['riʃɛnʲa]

standard (adj)	стандартний	[stan'dartnij]
standard (level of quality)	стандарт (ч)	[stan'dart]
stop (pause)	перерва (ж)	[pɛ'rɛrwa]
style	стиль (ч)	[stilʲ]

system	система (ж)	[sis'tɛma]
table (chart)	таблиця (ж)	[tab'litsʲa]
tempo, rate	темп (ч)	[tɛmp]
term (word, expression)	термін (ч)	['tɛrmin]
thing (object, item)	річ (ж)	[riʧ]

truth (e.g. moment of ~)	істина (ж)	['istina]
turn (please wait your ~)	черга (ж)	['ʧɛrɦa]
type (sort, kind)	тип (ч)	[tip]
urgent (adj)	терміновий	[tɛrmi'nɔwij]
urgently	терміново	[tɛrmi'nɔwo]

utility (usefulness)	користь (ж)	['kɔristʲ]
variant (alternative)	варіант (ч)	[wari'ant]
way (means, method)	спосіб (ч)	['spɔsib]
zone	зона (ж)	['zɔna]

250. Modifiers. Adjectives. Part 1

additional (adj)	додатковий	[dodat'kɔwij]
ancient (~ civilization)	давній	['dawnij]
artificial (adj)	штучний	['ʃtuʧnij]
back, rear (adj)	задній	['zadnij]
bad (adj)	поганий	[po'ɦanij]

beautiful (~ palace)	гарний	['ɦarnij]
beautiful (person)	гарний	['ɦarnij]
big (in size)	великий	[wɛ'likij]
bitter (taste)	гіркий	[hir'kij]
blind (sightless)	сліпий	[sli'pij]

calm, quiet (adj)	спокійний	[spo'kijnij]
careless (negligent)	недбалий	[nɛd'balij]
caring (~ father)	турботливий	[tur'bɔtliwij]
central (adj)	центральний	[tsɛn'tralʲnij]

| cheap (low-priced) | дешевий | [dɛ'ʃɛwij] |
| cheerful (adj) | веселий | [wɛ'sɛlij] |

children's (adj)	дитячий	[dɪ't'atʃij]
civil (~ law)	громадянський	[ɦromaˈd'ansʲkij]
clandestine (secret)	підпільний	[pidˈpilʲnij]
clean (free from dirt)	чистий	['tʃistij]
clear (explanation, etc.)	зрозумілий	[zrozuˈmilij]
clever (intelligent)	розумний	[roˈzumnij]
close (near in space)	близький	[blizʲˈkij]
closed (adj)	закритий	[zaˈkritij]
cloudless (sky)	безхмарний	[bɛzˈhmarnij]
cold (drink, weather)	холодний	[hoˈlɔdnij]
compatible (adj)	сумісний	[suˈmisnij]
contented (satisfied)	задоволений	[zadoˈwolɛnij]
continuous (uninterrupted)	безперервний	[bɛzpɛˈrɛrwnij]
cool (weather)	прохолодний	[prohoˈlɔdnij]
dangerous (adj)	небезпечний	[nɛbɛzˈpɛtʃnij]
dark (room)	темний	['tɛmnij]
dead (not alive)	мертвий	['mɛrtwij]
dense (fog, smoke)	щільний	['ɕilʲnij]
destitute (extremely poor)	жебрак (ч)	[ʒɛbˈrak]
difficult (decision)	важкий	[waʒˈkij]
difficult (problem, task)	складний	[skladˈnij]
dim, faint (light)	тьмяний	[tʲˈmʲanij]
dirty (not clean)	брудний	[brudˈnij]
distant (in space)	далекий	[daˈlɛkij]
dry (clothes, etc.)	сухий	[suˈhij]
easy (not difficult)	легкий	[lɛɦˈkij]
empty (glass, room)	пустий	[pusˈtij]
even (e.g. ~ surface)	рівний	['riwnij]
exact (amount)	точний	['tɔtʃnij]
excellent (adj)	добрий	['dɔbrij]
excessive (adj)	надмірний	[nadˈmirnij]
expensive (adj)	дорогий	[doroˈɦij]
exterior (adj)	зовнішній	['zɔwniʃnij]
far (the ~ East)	далекий	[daˈlɛkij]
fast (quick)	швидкий	[ʃwidˈkij]
fatty (food)	жирний	['ʒirnij]
fertile (land, soil)	родючий	[roˈd'utʃij]
flat (~ panel display)	плаский	['plaskij]
foreign (adj)	іноземний	[inoˈzɛmnij]
fragile (china, glass)	крихкий	[krihˈkij]
free (at no cost)	безкоштовний	[bɛzkoʃˈtɔwnij]
free (unrestricted)	вільний	['wilʲnij]
fresh (~ water)	прісний	['prisnij]
fresh (e.g. ~ bread)	свіжий	['swiʒij]
frozen (food)	заморожений	[zamoˈrɔʒɛnij]
full (completely filled)	повний	['pɔwnij]
gloomy (house, forecast)	похмурий	[pohˈmurij]

good (book, etc.)	хороший	[ho'rɔʃij]
good, kind (kindhearted)	добрий	['dɔbrij]
grateful (adj)	вдячний	['wdʲatʃnij]

happy (adj)	щасливий	[ɕas'liwij]
hard (not soft)	твердий	[twɛr'dij]
heavy (in weight)	важкий	[waʒ'kij]
hostile (adj)	ворожий	[wo'rɔʒij]
hot (adj)	гарячий	[ɦa'rʲatʃij]

huge (adj)	величезний	[wɛli'tʃɛznij]
humid (adj)	вологий	[wo'lɔɦij]
hungry (adj)	голодний	[ɦo'lɔdnij]
ill (sick, unwell)	хворий	['hwɔrij]
immobile (adj)	нерухомий	[nɛru'hɔmij]

important (adj)	важливий	[waʒ'liwij]
impossible (adj)	неможливий	[nɛmoʒ'liwij]
incomprehensible	незрозумілий	[nɛzrozu'milij]
indispensable (adj)	необхідний	[nɛob'hidnij]
inexperienced (adj)	недосвідчений	[nɛdos'widtʃɛnij]

insignificant (adj)	незначний	[nɛznatʃ'nij]
interior (adj)	внутрішній	['wnutriʃnij]
joint (~ decision)	спільний	['spilʲnij]
last (e.g. ~ week)	минулий	[mi'nulij]

last (final)	останній	[os'tanij]
left (e.g. ~ side)	лівий	['liwij]
legal (legitimate)	законний	[za'kɔnij]
light (in weight)	легкий	[lɛɦ'kij]
light (pale color)	світлий	['switlij]

limited (adj)	обмежений	[ob'mɛʒɛnij]
liquid (fluid)	рідкий	[rid'kij]
long (e.g. ~ hair)	довгий	['dɔwɦij]
loud (voice, etc.)	гучний	[ɦutʃ'nij]
low (voice)	тихий	['tihij]

251. Modifiers. Adjectives. Part 2

main (principal)	головний	[ɦolow'nij]
matt, matte	матовий	['matowij]
meticulous (job)	охайний	[o'hajnij]
mysterious (adj)	загадковий	[zaɦad'kɔwij]
narrow (street, etc.)	вузький	[wuzʲ'kij]

native (~ country)	рідний	['ridnij]
nearby (adj)	ближній	['bliʒnij]
needed (necessary)	потрібний	[pot'ribnij]
negative (~ response)	негативний	[nɛɦa'tiwnij]

| neighbouring (adj) | сусідній | [su'sidnij] |
| nervous (adj) | нервовий | [nɛr'wɔwij] |

new (adj)	новий	[no'wij]
next (e.g. ~ week)	наступний	[na'stupnij]
nice (agreeable)	милий	['mɨlij]
pleasant (voice)	приємний	[pri'ɛmnij]
normal (adj)	нормальний	[nor'malʲnij]
not big (adj)	невеликий	[nɛwɛ'likij]
not difficult (adj)	неважкий	[nɛwaʒ'kij]
obligatory (adj)	обов'язковий	[obowʲaz'kɔwij]
old (house)	старий	[sta'rij]
open (adj)	відкритий	[wid'kritij]
opposite (adj)	протилежний	[proti'lɛʒnij]
ordinary (usual)	звичайний	[zwi'tʃajnij]
original (unusual)	оригінальний	[oriɦi'nalʲnij]
past (recent)	минулий	[mɨ'nulij]
permanent (adj)	постійний	[pos'tijnij]
personal (adj)	персональний	[pɛrso'nalʲnij]
polite (adj)	ввічливий	['wwitʃliwij]
poor (not rich)	бідний	['bidnij]
possible (adj)	можливий	[moʒ'liwij]
present (current)	справжній	['sprawʒnij]
principal (main)	основний	[osnow'nij]
private (~ jet)	особистий	[oso'bistij]
probable (adj)	імовірний	[imo'wirnij]
prolonged (e.g. ~ applause)	тривалий	[tri'walij]
public (open to all)	громадський	[ɦro'madsʲkij]
punctual (person)	пунктуальний	[punktu'alʲnij]
quiet (tranquil)	тихий	['tihij]
rare (adj)	рідкісний	['ridkisnij]
raw (uncooked)	сирий	[si'rij]
right (not left)	правий	['prawij]
right, correct (adj)	вірний	['wirnij]
ripe (fruit)	дозрілий	[do'zrilij]
risky (adj)	ризикований	[rizi'kɔwanij]
sad (~ look)	сумний	[sum'nij]
sad (depressing)	сумний	[sum'nij]
safe (not dangerous)	безпечний	[bɛz'pɛtʃnij]
salty (food)	солоний	[so'lɔnij]
satisfied (customer)	задоволений	[zado'wɔlɛnij]
second hand (adj)	уживаний	[u'ʒiwanij]
shallow (water)	мілкий	[mil'kij]
sharp (blade, etc.)	гострий	['ɦɔstrij]
short (in length)	короткий	[ko'rɔtkij]
short, short-lived (adj)	короткочасний	[korotko'tʃasnij]
short-sighted (adj)	короткозорий	[korotko'zɔrij]
significant (notable)	значний	[znatʃ'nij]
similar (adj)	схожий	['sxɔʒij]

simple (easy)	простий	[pros'tij]
skinny	худий	[hu'dij]
smooth (surface)	гладкий	['ɦladkij]
soft (~ toys)	м'який	[mʲɑ'kij]
solid (~ wall)	міцний	[mits'nij]
sour (flavour, taste)	кислий	['kislij]
spacious (house, etc.)	просторий	[pros'tɔrij]
special (adj)	спеціальний	[spɛtsi'alʲnij]
straight (line, road)	прямий	[prʲa'mij]
strong (person)	сильний	['silʲnij]
stupid (foolish)	дурний	[dur'nij]
suitable (e.g. ~ for drinking)	придатний	[pri'datnij]
sunny (day)	сонячний	['sɔnʲatʃnij]
superb, perfect (adj)	чудовий	[tʃu'dɔwij]
swarthy (dark-skinned)	смаглявий	[smaɦ'lʲawij]
sweet (sugary)	солодкий	[so'lɔdkij]
tanned (adj)	засмаглий	[zas'maɦlij]
tasty (delicious)	смачний	[smatʃ'nij]
tender (affectionate)	ніжний	['niʒnij]
the highest (adj)	вищий	['wiɕij]
the most important	найважливіший	[najwaʒli'wiʃij]
the nearest	найближчий	[naj'bliʒtʃij]
the same, equal (adj)	однаковий	[od'nakowij]
thick (e.g. ~ fog)	густий	[ɦus'tij]
thick (wall, slice)	товстий	[tows'tij]
thin (person)	худий	[hu'dij]
tired (exhausted)	втомлений	['wtɔmlɛnij]
tiring (adj)	утомливий	[u'tɔmliwij]
transparent (adj)	прозорий	[pro'zɔrij]
unclear (adj)	неясний	[nɛ'ʲasnij]
unique (exceptional)	унікальний	[uni'kalʲnij]
warm (moderately hot)	теплий	['tɛplij]
wet (e.g. ~ clothes)	мокрий	['mɔkrij]
whole (entire, complete)	цілий	[tsi'lij]
wide (e.g. ~ road)	широкий	[ʃi'rɔkij]
young (adj)	молодий	[molo'dij]

MAIN 500 VERBS

252. Verbs A-C

to accompany (vt)	супроводжувати	[supro'wɔdʒuwati]
to accuse (vt)	звинувачувати	[zwinu'watʃuwati]
to acknowledge (admit)	визнавати	[wizna'wati]
to act (take action)	діяти	['diˈati]
to add (supplement)	додавати	[doda'wati]
to address (speak to)	звертатися	[zwɛr'tatisˈa]
to admire (vi)	захоплюватися	[za'hɔplˈuwatisˈa]
to advertise (vt)	рекламувати	[rɛklamu'wati]
to advise (vt)	радити	['raditi]
to affirm (assert)	стверджувати	['stwɛrdʒuwati]
to agree (say yes)	погоджуватися	[po'hɔdʒuwatisˈa]
to aim (to point a weapon)	цілитися	['ʦilitisˈa]
to allow (sb to do sth)	дозволяти	[dozwo'lˈati]
to amputate (vt)	ампутувати	[amputu'wati]
to answer (vi, vt)	відповідати	[widpowi'dati]
to apologize (vi)	вибачатися	[wiba'tʃatisˈa]
to appear (come into view)	з'являтися	[zˈaw'lˈatisˈa]
to applaud (vi, vt)	аплодувати	[aplodu'wati]
to appoint (assign)	призначати	[prizna'tʃati]
to approach (come closer)	підходити	[pid'hɔditi]
to arrive (ab. train)	прибувати	[pribu'wati]
to ask (~ sb to do sth)	просити	[pro'siti]
to aspire to …	прагнути	['prahnuti]
to assist (help)	асистувати	[asistu'wati]
to attack (mil.)	атакувати	[ataku'wati]
to attain (objectives)	досягати	[dosˈa'hati]
to avenge (get revenge)	мстити	['mstiti]
to avoid (danger, task)	уникати	[uni'kati]
to award (give a medal to)	нагородити	[naho'rɔditi]
to battle (vi)	битися	['bitisˈa]
to be (vi)	бути	['buti]
to be a cause of …	бути причиною	['buti pri'tʃinoˈu]
to be afraid	боятися	[bo'ˈatisˈa]
to be angry (with …)	гніватися	['hniwatisˈa]
to be at war	воювати	[woˈu'wati]
to be based (on …)	базуватися	[bazu'watisˈa]
to be bored	нудьгувати	[nudˈhu'wati]

to be convinced	переконуватися	[pɛrɛ'kɔnuwatisʲa]
to be enough	вистачати	[wista'ʧati]
to be envious	заздрити	['zazdriti]
to be indignant	обурюватися	[o'burʲuwatisʲa]
to be interested in ...	цікавитися	[ʦi'kawitisʲa]

to be lost in thought	замислитися	[za'mislitisʲa]
to be lying (~ on the table)	лежати	[lɛ'ʒati]
to be needed	бути потрібним	['buti po'tribnim]
to be perplexed (puzzled)	не розуміти	[nɛ rozu'miti]

to be preserved	зберігатися	[zbɛri'ɦatisʲa]
to be required	бути необхідним	['buti nɛob'hidnim]
to be surprised	дивуватись	[diwu'watisʲ]
to be worried	хвилюватися	[hwilʲu'watisʲa]

to beat (to hit)	бити	['biti]
to become (e.g. ~ old)	ставати	[sta'wati]
to behave (vi)	поводитися	[po'wɔditisʲa]
to believe (think)	вірити	['wiriti]

to belong to ...	належати	[na'lɛʒati]
to berth (moor)	причалювати	[pri'ʧalʲuwati]
to blind (other drivers)	осліплювати	[os'liplʲuwati]
to blow (wind)	дути	['duti]

to blush (vi)	червоніти	[ʧɛrwo'niti]
to boast (vi)	хвастатися	['hwastatisʲa]
to borrow (money)	позичати	[pozi'ʧati]
to break (branch, toy, etc.)	ламати	[la'mati]

to breathe (vi)	дихати	['dihati]
to bring (sth)	привозити	[pri'wɔziti]
to burn (paper, logs)	палити	[pa'liti]
to buy (purchase)	купляти	[kup'lʲati]

to call (~ for help)	кликати	['klikati]
to call (yell for sb)	покликати	[pok'likati]
to calm down (vt)	заспокоювати	[zaspo'kɔʲuwati]
can (v aux)	могти	[moɦ'ti]

to cancel (call off)	скасувати	[skasu'wati]
to cast off (of a boat or ship)	відчалювати	[wid'ʧalʲuwati]
to catch (e.g. ~ a ball)	ловити	[lo'witi]
to change (~ one's opinion)	поміняти	[pomi'nʲati]
to change (exchange)	міняти	[mi'nʲati]

to charm (vt)	зачаровувати	[zatʃa'rɔwuwati]
to choose (select)	вибирати	[wibiʲrati]
to chop off (with an axe)	відрубати	[widru'bati]
to clean (e.g. kettle from scale)	очищати	[otʃiʲɕati]

to clean (shoes, etc.)	чистити	['ʧistiti]
to clean up (tidy)	прибирати	[pribiʲrati]
to close (vt)	закривати	[zakriʲwati]

to comb one's hair	причісувати	[pri'tʃisuwati]
to come down (the stairs)	спускатися	[spus'katisʲa]
to come out (book)	вийти	['wijti]
to compare (vt)	зрівнювати	['zriwnʲuwati]
to compensate (vt)	компенсувати	[kompɛnsu'wati]

to compete (vi)	конкурувати	[konkuru'wati]
to compile (~ a list)	складати	[skla'dati]
to complain (vi, vt)	скаржитися	['skarʒitisʲa]
to complicate (vt)	ускладнювати	[us'kladnʲuwati]

to compose (music, etc.)	створити	[stwo'riti]
to compromise (reputation)	компрометувати	[komprometu'wati]
to concentrate (vi)	концентруватися	[kontsentru'watisʲa]
to confess (criminal)	признаватися	[prizna'watisʲa]

to confuse (mix up)	помилятися	[pomi'lʲatisʲa]
to congratulate (vt)	вітати	[wi'tati]
to consult (doctor, expert)	консультуватися з ...	[konsulʲtu'watisʲa z]
to continue (~ to do sth)	продовжувати	[pro'dɔwʒuwati]

to control (vt)	контролювати	[kontrolʲu'wati]
to convince (vt)	переконувати	[pɛrɛ'kɔnuwati]
to cooperate (vi)	співробітничати	[spiwro'bitnitʃati]
to coordinate (vt)	координувати	[koordinu'wati]

to correct (an error)	виправляти	[wipraw'lʲati]
to cost (vt)	коштувати	['kɔʃtuwati]
to count (money, etc.)	лічити	[li'tʃiti]
to count on ...	розраховувати на ...	[rozra'hɔwuwati na]

to crack (ceiling, wall)	тріскатися	['triskatisʲa]
to create (vt)	створити	[stwo'riti]
to crush, to squash (~ a bug)	розчавити	[roz'tʃawiti]
to cry (weep)	плакати	['plakati]
to cut off (with a knife)	відрізати	[widri'zati]

253. Verbs D-G

to dare (~ to do sth)	насмілюватися	[na'smilʲuwatisʲa]
to date from ...	датуватися	[datu'watisʲa]
to deceive (vi, vt)	обманювати	[ob'manʲuwati]
to decide (~ to do sth)	вирішувати	[wi'riʃuwati]

to decorate (tree, street)	прикрашати	[prikra'ʃati]
to dedicate (book, etc.)	присвячувати	[pris'wʲatʃuwati]
to defend (a country, etc.)	захищати	[zahi'çati]
to defend oneself	захищатись	[zahi'çatisʲ]

to demand (request firmly)	вимагати	[wima'ɦati]
to denounce (vt)	доносити	[do'nɔsiti]
to deny (vt)	заперечувати	[zapɛ'rɛtʃuwati]
to depend on ...	залежати	[za'lɛʒati]
to deprive (vt)	позбавляти	[pozbaw'lʲati]

to deserve (vt)	заслуговувати	[zaslu'ɦɔwuwati]
to design (machine, etc.)	проектувати	[prɔɛktu'wati]
to desire (want, wish)	бажати	[ba'ʒati]
to despise (vt)	зневажати	[znɛwa'ʒati]

to destroy (documents, etc.)	знищувати	['zniɕuwati]
to differ (from sth)	відрізнятися	[widriz'nʲatisʲa]
to dig (tunnel, etc.)	рити	['riti]
to direct (point the way)	направляти	[napraw'lʲati]

to disappear (vi)	зникнути	['zniknuti]
to discover (new land, etc.)	відкривати	[widkri'wati]
to discuss (vt)	обговорювати	[obɦo'wɔrʲuwati]
to distribute (leaflets, etc.)	поширювати	[po'ʃirʲuwati]

to disturb (vt)	заважати	[zawa'ʒati]
to dive (vi)	пірнати	[pir'nati]
to divide (math)	ділити	[di'liti]
to do (vt)	робити	[ro'biti]

to do the laundry	прати	['prati]
to double (increase)	подвоювати	[pod'wɔʲuwati]
to doubt (have doubts)	сумніватися	[sumni'watisʲa]
to draw a conclusion	робити висновок	[ro'biti 'wisnowok]

to dream (daydream)	мріяти	['mriʲati]
to dream (in sleep)	бачити сни	['batʃiti sni]
to drink (vi, vt)	пити	['piti]
to drive a car	вести машину	['wɛsti ma'ʃinu]
to drive away (scare away)	прогнати	[proɦ'nati]

to drop (let fall)	упускати	[upus'kati]
to drown (ab. person)	тонути	[to'nuti]
to dry (clothes, hair)	сушити	[su'ʃiti]
to eat (vi, vt)	їсти	['jisti]

to eavesdrop (vi)	підслухати	[pid'sluhati]
to emit (diffuse - odor, etc.)	наповнювати запахом	[na'pownʲuwati 'zapahom]
to enjoy oneself	веселитися	[wɛsɛ'litisʲa]
to enter (on the list)	уписувати	[u'pisuwati]

to enter (room, house, etc.)	увійти	[uwij'ti]
to entertain (amuse)	розважати	[rozwa'ʒati]
to equip (fit out)	обладнати	[oblad'nati]
to examine (proposal)	розглянути	[rozɦ'lʲanuti]

to exchange (sth)	обмінюватися	[ob'minʲuwatisʲa]
to excuse (forgive)	вибачати	[wiba'tʃati]
to exist (vi)	існувати	[isnu'wati]
to expect (anticipate)	очікувати	[o'tʃikuwati]

to expect (foresee)	передбачити	[pɛrɛd'batʃiti]
to expel (from school, etc.)	виключати	[wiklʲu'tʃati]
to explain (vt)	пояснювати	[po'ʲasnʲuwati]
to express (vt)	виразити	['wiraziti]
to extinguish (a fire)	тушити	[tu'ʃiti]

to fall in love (with …)	закохатися	[zako'hatisⁱa]
to fancy (vt)	подобатися	[po'dobatisⁱa]
to feed (provide food)	годувати	[ɦodu'wati]
to fight (against the enemy)	боротися	[bo'rɔtisⁱa]
to fight (vi)	битися	['bitisⁱa]
to fill (glass, bottle)	наповнювати	[na'pɔwnⁱuwati]
to find (~ lost items)	знаходити	[zna'ɦɔditi]
to finish (vt)	закінчувати	[za'kintʃuwati]
to fish (angle)	ловити рибу	[lo'witi 'ribu]
to fit (ab. dress, etc.)	пасувати	[pasu'wati]
to flatter (vt)	лестити	['lɛstiti]
to fly (bird, plane)	літати	[li'tati]
to follow … (come after)	іти слідом	[i'ti 'slidom]
to forbid (vt)	забороняти	[zaboro'nⁱati]
to force (compel)	примушувати	[pri'muʃuwati]
to forget (vi, vt)	забувати	[zabu'wati]
to forgive (pardon)	прощати	[pro'çati]
to form (constitute)	складати	[skla'dati]
to get dirty (vi)	забруднитися	[zabrud'nitisⁱa]
to get infected (with …)	заразитися	[zara'zitisⁱa]
to get irritated	дратуватися	[dratu'watisⁱa]
to get married	одружуватися	[od'ruʒuwatisⁱa]
to get rid of …	позбавлятися	[pozbaw'lⁱatisⁱa]
to get tired	втомлюватися	['wtɔmlⁱuwatisⁱa]
to get up (arise from bed)	підводитися	[pid'wɔditisⁱa]
to give (vt)	давати	[da'wati]
to give a bath (to bath)	купати	[ku'pati]
to give a hug, to hug (vt)	обіймати	[obij'mati]
to give in (yield to)	поступатися	[postu'patisⁱa]
to glimpse (vt)	побачити	[po'batʃiti]
to go (by car, etc.)	їхати	['jihati]
to go (on foot)	йти	[jti]
to go for a swim	купатися	[ku'patisⁱa]
to go out (for dinner, etc.)	вийти	['wijti]
to go to bed (go to sleep)	лягати спати	[lⁱa'ɦati 'spati]
to greet (vt)	вітати	[wi'tati]
to grow (plants)	вирощувати	[wi'rɔçuwati]
to guarantee (vt)	гарантувати	[ɦarantu'wati]
to guess (the answer)	відгадати	[widɦa'dati]

254. Verbs H-M

to hand out (distribute)	роздати	[roz'dati]
to hang (curtains, etc.)	вішати	['wiʃati]
to have (vt)	мати	['mati]

| to have a bath | митися | ['mitis'a] |
| to have a try | спробувати | ['sprobuwati] |

to have breakfast	снідати	['snidati]
to have dinner	вечеряти	[we'tʃɛr'ati]
to have lunch	обідати	[o'bidati]
to head (group, etc.)	очолювати	[o'tʃol'uwati]
to hear (vt)	чути	['tʃuti]

to heat (vt)	нагрівати	[nahri'wati]
to help (vt)	допомагати	[dopoma'hati]
to hide (vt)	ховати	[ho'wati]
to hire (e.g. ~ a boat)	наймати	[naj'mati]
to hire (staff)	наймати	[naj'mati]

to hope (vi, vt)	сподіватися	[spodi'watis'a]
to hunt (for food, sport)	полювати	[pol'u'wati]
to hurry (vi)	поспішати	[pospi'ʃati]
to imagine (to picture)	уявляти собі	[ujaw'l'ati so'bi]
to imitate (vt)	імітувати	[imitu'wati]

to implore (vt)	благати	[bla'hati]
to import (vt)	імпортувати	[importu'wati]
to increase (vi)	збільшуватися	['zbil'ʃuwatis'a]
to increase (vt)	збільшувати	['zbil'ʃuwati]
to infect (vt)	заражати	[zara'ʒati]

to influence (vt)	впливати	[wpli'wati]
to inform (e.g. ~ the police about …)	повідомляти	[powidom'l'ati]
to inform (vt)	інформувати	[informu'wati]
to inherit (vt)	успадкувати	[uspadku'wati]
to inquire (about …)	довідуватись	[do'widuwatis']

to insert (put in)	вставляти	[wstaw'l'ati]
to insinuate (imply)	натякати	[nat'a'kati]
to insist (vi, vt)	наполягати	[napol'a'hati]
to inspire (vt)	надихати	[ujaw'l'ati]
to instruct (teach)	інструктувати	[instruktu'wati]

to insult (offend)	ображати	[obra'ʒati]
to interest (vt)	цікавити	[tsi'kawiti]
to intervene (vi)	втручатися	[wtru'tʃatis'a]
to introduce (sb to sb)	знайомити	[zna'jomiti]

to invent (machine, etc.)	винаходити	[wina'hoditi]
to invite (vt)	запрошувати	[za'proʃuwati]
to iron (clothes)	прасувати	[prasu'wati]
to irritate (annoy)	дратувати	[dratu'wati]
to isolate (vt)	ізолювати	[izol'u'wati]

to join (political party, etc.)	приєднуватися	[pri'ɛdnuwatis'a]
to joke (be kidding)	жартувати	[ʒartu'wati]
to keep (old letters, etc.)	зберігати	[zbɛri'hati]
to keep silent, to hush	мовчати	[mow'tʃati]
to kill (vt)	убивати	[ubi'wati]

to knock (on the door)	стукати	['stukati]
to know (sb)	знати	['znati]
to know (sth)	знати	['znati]
to laugh (vi)	сміятися	[smiˈⁱatisⁱa]
to launch (start up)	запускати	[zapuˈskati]

to leave (~ for Mexico)	їхати	['jihati]
to leave (forget sth)	залишати	[zaliˈʃati]
to leave (spouse)	покидати	[pokiˈdati]
to liberate (city, etc.)	звільняти	[zwilⁱ'nⁱati]
to lie (~ on the floor)	лежати	[lɛˈʒati]

to lie (tell untruth)	брехати	[brɛˈhati]
to light (campfire, etc.)	запалити	[zapaˈliti]
to light up (illuminate)	освітлювати	[os'witlⁱuwati]
to limit (vt)	обмежувати	[ob'mɛʒuwati]

to listen (vi)	слухати	['sluhati]
to live (~ in France)	проживати	[proʒiˈwati]
to live (exist)	існувати	[isnuˈwati]
to load (gun)	заряджати	[zarⁱaˈdʒati]
to load (vehicle, etc.)	вантажити	[wanˈtaʒiti]

to look (I'm just ~ing)	дивитися	[diˈwitisⁱa]
to look for … (search)	шукати	[ʃuˈkati]
to look like (resemble)	бути схожим	['buti 'shɔʒim]

to lose (umbrella, etc.)	губити	[huˈbiti]
to love (e.g. ~ dancing)	любити	[lⁱuˈbiti]

to love (sb)	кохати	[koˈhati]
to lower (blind, head)	опускати	[opusˈkati]
to make (~ dinner)	готувати	[hotuˈwati]

to make a mistake	помилятися	[pomiˈlⁱatisⁱa]
to make angry	гнівити	[hniˈwiti]

to make easier	полегшити	[po'lɛhʃiti]
to make multiple copies	розмножити	[rozm'nɔʒiti]
to make the acquaintance	знайомитися	[zna'jɔmitisⁱa]

to make use (of …)	користуватися	[koristu'watisⁱa]
to manage, to run	керувати	[kɛruˈwati]

to mark (make a mark)	зазначити	[zaz'natʃiti]
to mean (signify)	значити	['znatʃiti]
to memorize (vt)	запам'ятати	[zapamʲaˈtati]

to mention (talk about)	згадувати	['zhaduwati]
to miss (school, etc.)	пропускати	[propusˈkati]

to mix (combine, blend)	змішувати	['zmiʃuwati]
to mock (make fun of)	насміхатися	[nasmiˈhatisⁱa]
to move (to shift)	пересувати	[pɛrɛsuˈwati]
to multiply (math)	множити	['mnɔʒiti]
must (v aux)	бути винним	['buti 'winim]

255. Verbs N-R

to name, to call (vt)	називати	[nazi'wati]
to negotiate (vi)	вести переговори	['wɛsti pɛrɛho'wɔri]
to note (write down)	позначити	[poz'natʃiti]
to notice (see)	помічати	[pomi'tʃati]
to obey (vi, vt)	підкорятися	[pidko'rʲatisʲa]
to object (vi, vt)	заперечувати	[zapɛ'rɛtʃuwati]
to observe (see)	спостерігати	[spostɛri'hati]
to offend (vt)	ображати	[obra'ʒati]
to omit (word, phrase)	пропускати	[propus'kati]
to open (vt)	відчинити	[widtʃi'niti]
to order (in restaurant)	замовляти	[zamow'lʲati]
to order (mil.)	наказувати	[na'kazuwati]
to organize (concert, party)	організовувати	[orhani'zowuwati]
to overestimate (vt)	переоцінювати	[pɛrɛo'tsinʲuwati]
to own (possess)	володіти	[wolo'diti]
to participate (vi)	брати участь	['brati 'utʃastʲ]
to pass through (by car, etc.)	минути	[mi'nuti]
to pay (vi, vt)	платити	[pla'titi]
to peep, to spy on	підглядати	[pidhlʲa'dati]
to penetrate (vt)	проникати	[proni'kati]
to permit (vt)	дозволяти	[dozwo'lʲati]
to pick (flowers)	рвати	['rwati]
to place (put, set)	розташовувати	[rozta'ʃowuwati]
to plan (~ to do sth)	планувати	[planu'wati]
to play (actor)	грати	['hrati]
to play (children)	грати	['hrati]
to point (~ the way)	указати	[uka'zati]
to pour (liquid)	наливати	[nali'wati]
to pray (vi, vt)	молитися	[mo'litisʲa]
to prefer (vt)	воліти	[wo'liti]
to prepare (~ a plan)	підготувати	[pidhotu'wati]
to present (sb to sb)	рекомендувати	[rɛkomɛndu'wati]
to preserve (peace, life)	зберігати	[zbɛri'hati]
to prevail (vt)	переважати	[pɛrɛwa'ʒati]
to progress (move forward)	просуватися	[prosu'watisʲa]
to promise (vt)	обіцяти	[obi'tsʲati]
to pronounce (vt)	вимовляти	[wimow'lʲati]
to propose (vt)	пропонувати	[proponu'wati]
to protect (e.g. ~ nature)	охороняти	[ohoro'nʲati]
to protest (vi)	протестувати	[protɛstu'wati]
to prove (vt)	доводити	[do'wɔditi]
to provoke (vt)	провокувати	[prowoku'wati]
to pull (~ the rope)	тягти	[tʲah'ti]
to punish (vt)	покарати	[poka'rati]

to push (~ the door)	штовхати	[ʃtow'hati]
to put away (vt)	сховати	[sho'wati]
to put in order	привести до ладу	[pri'wɛsti do 'ladu]
to put, to place	класти	['klasti]
to quote (cite)	цитувати	[tsitu'wati]
to reach (arrive at)	досягати	[dosʲa'hati]
to read (vi, vt)	читати	[tʃi'tati]
to realize (a dream)	здійснювати	['zdijsnʲuwati]
to recognize (identify sb)	узнавати	[uzna'wati]
to recommend (vt)	рекомендувати	[rɛkomɛndu'wati]
to recover (~ from flu)	видужувати	[wi'duʒuwati]
to redo (do again)	переробляти	[pɛrɛrob'lʲati]
to reduce (speed, etc.)	зменшувати	['zmɛnʃuwati]
to refuse (~ sb)	відмовляти	[widmow'lʲati]
to regret (be sorry)	жалкувати	[ʒalku'wati]
to reinforce (vt)	зміцнювати	['zmitsnʲuwati]
to remember (Do you ~ me?)	пам'ятати	[pamʲa'tati]
to remember (I can't ~ her name)	згадувати	['zɦaduwati]
to remind of …	нагадувати	[na'ɦaduwati]
to remove (~ a stain)	виводити	[wi'wɔditi]
to remove (~ an obstacle)	усувати	[usu'wati]
to rent (sth from sb)	наймати	[naj'mati]
to repair (mend)	ремонтувати	[rɛmontu'wati]
to repeat (say again)	повторювати	[pow'torʲuwati]
to report (make a report)	доповідати	[dopowi'dati]
to reproach (vt)	докоряти	[doko'rʲati]
to reserve, to book	бронювати	[bronʲu'wati]
to restrain (hold back)	утримувати	[ut'rimuwati]
to return (come back)	повертатися	[powɛr'tatisʲa]
to risk, to take a risk	ризикувати	[riziku'wati]
to rub out (erase)	стерти	['stɛrti]
to run (move fast)	бігти	['biɦti]
to rush (hurry sb)	квапити	['kwapiti]

256. Verbs S-W

to satisfy (please)	задовольняти	[zadowolʲ'nʲati]
to save (rescue)	рятувати	[rʲatu'wati]
to say (~ thank you)	сказати	[ska'zati]
to scold (vt)	лаяти	['laʲati]
to scratch (with claws)	дряпати	['drʲapati]
to select (to pick)	вибрати	['wibrati]
to sell (goods)	продавати	[proda'wati]
to send (a letter)	відправляти	[widpraw'lʲati]
to send back (vt)	відправити назад	[wid'prawiti na'zad]

to sense (~ danger)	почувати	[potʃu'wati]
to sentence (vt)	присуджувати	[pri'sudʒuwati]
to serve (in restaurant)	обслуговувати	[obslu'howuwati]

to settle (a conflict)	залагоджувати	[zala'hodʒuwati]
to shake (vt)	трясти	[trʲas'ti]
to shave (vi)	голитися	[ɦo'litisʲa]
to shine (gleam)	блищати	[bliˈɕati]

to shiver (with cold)	тремтіти	[trɛm'titi]
to shoot (vi)	стріляти	[stri'lʲati]
to shout (vi)	кричати	[kri'tʃati]
to show (to display)	показувати	[po'kazuwati]

to shudder (vi)	здригатися	[zdri'ɦatisʲa]
to sigh (vi)	зітхнути	[zith'nuti]
to sign (document)	підписувати	[pid'pisuwati]
to signify (mean)	означати	[ozna'tʃati]

to simplify (vt)	спрощувати	['sproɕuwati]
to sin (vi)	грішити	[ɦri'ʃiti]
to sit (be sitting)	сидіти	[si'diti]
to sit down (vi)	сісти	['sisti]

to smell (emit an odor)	пахнути	['pahnuti]
to smell (inhale the odor)	нюхати	['nʲuhati]
to smile (vi)	посміхатися	[posmi'hatisʲa]
to snap (vi, ab. rope)	розірватися	[rozir'watisʲa]

to solve (problem)	розв'язувати	[roz'wʲazuwati]
to sow (seed, crop)	сіяти	['siʲati]
to spill (liquid)	проливати	[proli'wati]

to spit (vi)	плювати	[plʲu'wati]
to stand (toothache, cold)	терпіти	[tɛr'piti]
to start (begin)	починати	[potʃi'nati]
to steal (money, etc.)	красти	['krasti]

to stop (for pause, etc.)	зупинятися	[zupi'nʲatisʲa]
to stop (please ~ calling me)	припиняти	[pripi'nʲati]
to stop talking	замовчати	[zamow'tʃati]
to stroke (caress)	гладити	['ɦladiti]

to study (vt)	вивчати	[wiw'tʃati]
to suffer (feel pain)	страждати	[straʒ'dati]
to support (cause, idea)	підтримати	[pid'trimati]
to suppose (assume)	припускати	[pripus'kati]

to surface (ab. submarine)	спливати	[spli'wati]
to surprise (amaze)	дивувати	[diwu'wati]
to suspect (vt)	підозрювати	[pi'dozrʲuwati]
to swim (vi)	плавати	['plawati]
to take (get hold of)	брати	['brati]
to take a rest	відпочивати	[widpotʃi'wati]
to take away (e.g. about waiter)	відносити	[wid'nɔsiti]

to take off (aeroplane)	злітати	[zli'tati]
to take off (painting, curtains, etc.)	знімати	[zni'mati]
to take pictures	фотографувати	[fotoɦrafu'wati]
to talk to …	розмовляти з …	[rozmow'lʲati z]
to teach (give lessons)	навчати	[naw'tʃati]
to tear off, to rip off (vt)	відірвати	[widir'wati]
to tell (story, joke)	розповідати	[rozpowi'dati]
to thank (vt)	дякувати	['dʲakuwati]
to think (believe)	вважати	[wva'ʒati]
to think (vi, vt)	думати	['dumati]
to threaten (vt)	погрожувати	[poɦ'rɔʒuwati]
to throw (stone, etc.)	кидати	[ki'dati]
to tie to …	прив'язувати	[pri'wʲazuwati]
to tie up (prisoner)	зв'язувати	['zwʲazuwati]
to tire (make tired)	стомлювати	['stɔmlʲuwati]
to touch (one's arm, etc.)	торкатися	[tor'katisʲa]
to tower (over …)	підноситися	[pid'nɔsitisʲa]
to train (animals)	дресирувати	[drɛsiru'wati]
to train (sb)	тренувати	[trɛnu'wati]
to train (vi)	тренуватися	[trɛnu'watisʲa]
to transform (vt)	трансформувати	[transformu'wati]
to translate (vt)	перекладати	[pɛrɛkla'dati]
to treat (illness)	лікувати	[liku'wati]
to trust (vt)	довіряти	[dowi'rʲati]
to try (attempt)	намагатися	[nama'ɦatisʲa]
to turn (e.g., ~ left)	повертати	[powɛr'tati]
to turn away (vi)	відвертатися	[widwɛr'tatisʲa]
to turn off (the light)	гасити	[ɦa'siti]
to turn on (computer, etc.)	вмикати	[wmi'kati]
to turn over (stone, etc.)	перевернути	[pɛrɛwɛr'nuti]
to underestimate (vt)	недооцінювати	[nɛdoo'tsinʲuwati]
to underline (vt)	підкреслити	[pid'krɛsliti]
to understand (vt)	розуміти	[rozu'miti]
to undertake (vt)	здійснювати	['zdijsnʲuwati]
to unite (vt)	об'єднувати	[o'bʲɛdnuwati]
to untie (vt)	відв'язувати	[wid'wʲazuwati]
to use (phrase, word)	уживати	[uʒi'wati]
to vaccinate (vt)	робити щеплення	[ro'biti 'ɕɛplɛnʲa]
to vote (vi)	голосувати	[ɦolosu'wati]
to wait (vt)	чекати	[tʃɛ'kati]
to wake (sb)	будити	[bu'diti]
to want (wish, desire)	хотіти	[ho'titi]
to warn (of a danger)	попереджувати	[popɛ'rɛdʒuwati]
to wash (clean)	мити	['miti]
to water (plants)	поливати	[poli'wati]

to wave (the hand)	махати	[ma'hati]
to weigh (have weight)	важити	['waʒiti]
to work (vi)	працювати	[pratsʲu'wati]
to worry (make anxious)	хвилювати	[hwilʲu'wati]
to worry (vi)	хвилюватися	[hwilʲu'watisʲa]
to wrap (parcel, etc.)	загортати	[zahor'tati]
to wrestle (sport)	боротися	[bo'rɔtisʲa]
to write (vt)	писати	[pi'sati]
to write down	записувати	[za'pisuwati]

Printed in Great Britain
by Amazon

83474775R00140